PERSONAL REMINISCENCES

BY

CHORLEY, PLANCHÉ, AND YOUNG

BRIC-A-BRAC SERIES.

I.

PERSONAL REMINISCENCES BY CHORLEY, PLANCHÉ, AND YOUN

II.

ANECDOTE BIOGRAPHIES OF THACKERAY AND DICKENS.

III.

PROSPER MÉRIMÉE'S LETTERS TO AN INCOGNITA; WI
RECOLLECTIONS BY LAMARTINE AND GEORGE SAND.

IV.

PERSONAL REMINISCENCES BY BARHAM, HARNESS, AND HO
DER.

V.

THE GREVILLE MEMOIRS.

VI.

PERSONAL REMINISCENCES BY MOORE AND JERDAN.

VII.

PERSONAL REMINISCENCES BY CORNELIA KNIGHT AND THOM
RAIKES.

VIII.

PERSONAL REMINISCENCES BY MICHAEL KELLY, JOHN O'KEEFF
AND JOHN TAYLOR.

IX.

PERSONAL RECOLLECTIONS OF LAMB, HAZLITT, AND OTHE

X.

PERSONAL REMINISCENCES BY CONSTABLE AND GILLIES

Each 1 vol. sq. 12mo. Per vol. $1.50.

Sent, post-paid, on receipt of price by the Publishers.

Bric-a-Brac Series

PERSONAL REMINISCENCES

BY

CHORLEY, PLANCHÉ, AND YOUNG

EDITED BY

RICHARD HENRY STODDARD

NEW YORK
SCRIBNER, ARMSTRONG, AND COMPANY
1876

RIVERSIDE, CAMBRIDGE:
STEREOTYPED AND PRINTED BY
H. O. HOUGHTON AND COMPANY.

CONTENTS.

YOUNG.

PREFACE.

HE Literature of Personal Reminiscence is more extensive than its casual readers might suppose, and is of a more entertaining character, it seems to me, than any other kind of Literature. The historian, the novelist, the dramatist, depict men and women, but generally at the expense of some truth which escapes them, or which they conceal. They are like portrait painters who place their sitters in the most striking attitudes, and under the most favorable light. They profess to paint likenesses, and the most skillful do, perhaps, but they paint something more, and something less. There is a restraint in art which is not in nature: the inner life that lurks in the curve of a lip, that flashes out suddenly from the eye, that is perceived in the carriage of the body, — these elude the artist. Could he come upon his sitter unawares, they might be caught and transferred to his canvas. This is the reason why so many portraits are disappointing, and the reason why so many biographies are disappointing; for what is true of Art is true of Literature. There is that in men and women which eludes the literary artists who essay to paint them elaborately, but which is sometimes caught by others, who are mere sketchers, as these artists would have us believe, but who,

nevertheless, have the knack of hitting off a likeness. They seem to come upon character unawares,

"And snatch a grace beyond the reach of art."

From the latest of these sketchers, if they must be considered such, I have selected three, who are represented in this volume, — Chorley, Planché, and Young. The reasons that led me to select these writers in preference to others that might be named, and to associate them together here, are, that they were contemporaries (Chorley and Planché may almost be said to be neighbors); that each knew the friends of the others, and recorded in some instances the impressions they made upon him; and that they introduce us to the intellectual life of the same period. It is one in which we are all interested, being the most brilliant as regards its Literature, of any since

"The spacious times of great Elizabeth,"

and coming so near our own that we are stirred as by personal emotion at the mention of its illustrious names. As the reader will soon find himself among them, he may like to know something about the gentlemen who are to usher him into their presence.

Henry Fothergill Chorley was born on the 15th of December, 1808, at Blackley Hurst, near Billinge, in Lancashire. His father and mother were nominally members of the Society of Friends, though neither ever wore the dress of that body, nor conformed to its ascetic discipline and testimonies. The Chorleys were an old family belonging to the gentry of Lancashire, and in old times were of credit and substance. Two of its members were beheaded at Preston, in Lancashire, in chastisement for their having gone out with the Stuarts in 1715, and their landed property was then confiscated. From that time, the principal branch of the family, to which Henry belonged, gradually decayed. They had not the art of making or keeping money ; and Henry's father dying in his eighth year, John Rutter of Liverpool, his mother's half brother, stood betwixt the family and want.

Chorley differed in nothing from ordinary children, except, perhaps, in his early fondness for music, which he probably inherited from his mother, who had a sweet but unformed voice, and a piano-forte, upon which she played but indifferently. He could not remember when or where he began to associate the printed symbols with the popular sounds of music, but before he could put his hand on the piano he could read the notes somehow, and could represent to himself somehow that which they signified. The Chorleys moved to Liverpool in 1819, and Henry and his brothers were placed at the school of the Royal Institution, where little actually was taught, save Latin and Greek ; an odd training for boys among which ninety out of the hundred were to make their way in commercial life. By some favor he was admitted a year or two before he ought to have been: and no favor did it prove, so far as happiness was concerned, for being the smallest, most nervous creature in the place, inexpert at any game, and shabbily dressed, and being also credited with some quickness, he was a good deal plagued and rudely treated by the elder boys ; not so much disliked as cruelly teased, and in great difficulties as to the finding a playmate or a comrade. Years after, he used to wake up from a sort of nightmare dream that he was going to school, and had not his exercise ready. He learned Greek with greater relish than Latin, his favorite authors being Herodotus, and Euripides, whose "Hecuba" he translated from beginning to end for his own pleasure.

There was a music-shop which the Chorley children used to pass on their way to school, and Henry got into the good graces of the people who kept it, and as the daughter of the house had been trained as a mistress of the piano, he was sometimes allowed to hear her play. His desire was to be a musician, and he felt in after life that if his elders had understood him, and had apprenticed him to a musician, he might have done England an artist's service. But it was not to be. He was taken from school at an early age, and assigned to a clerkship in the office of Messrs. Cropper, Benson, & Co., a prosperous firm of American merchants in Liverpool. How long he remained with them does not appear, but the occupation not being to his liking, he was transferred to a seat in the office of a Sicilian wine house. Commercial life was distasteful to him, and by way of compensation for enduring it, he embraced every opportunity to indulge his love of music, and to cultivate his taste for literature. He wrote a series of sketches of characters and manners, drawn from his observation of Liverpool life, besides tales, lyrics, and hymns, a dramatic poem of which Stradella was the hero, and musical criticisms, which were probably of some value. A few of these productions appeared in the "Winter Wreath" and the "Sacred Offering," and other annuals, to which his mother and sister, and his two brothers, were contributors. He went to London in his twenty-second year, and was taken by Archdeacon Wrangham to breakfast at the house of Mr. Basil Montagu. He is described as being at this time a romantic, enthusiastic youth, with plain features, and red hair: his manners were gentlemanly, but marked by a nervous timidity, which he retained to the last, and a touch of Quaker quaintness, which greatly interested Mr. Montagu, who was much attached to the sect.

Music was his ruling passion, to which was soon to be added musical criticism. He heard his brother and a friend speaking with delight of certain musical criticisms of the German humorist, Hoffman, and as he had no knowledge of German, he asked this friend to translate for him two chapters from the "Phantasienstücke," which roused his enthusiasm. "That is what *I* can do," he said, "and what I *will* do." It was not long before an opportunity was offered him. Among the contributors to the London "Athenæum" was Miss Maria Jewsbury, afterwards Mrs. Fletcher, who mentioned Chorley to the editor, Mr. Charles Wentworth Dilke, as one who might be of service to the paper; and in September, 1830, Mr. Dilke asked him to write an account of the ceremonies that were to inaugurate the new railway between Liverpool and Manchester. He complied, but with many misgivings: he said he should be most happy to contribute light articles in prose and verse, and if the editor should at any time like to have musical papers, he would give him his best efforts, as he loved the art dearly, and had spent much time in its cultivation. He forwarded to the "Athenæum" several lyrics and musical criticisms, which were duly inserted, and which determined his future career. Finally, in September, 1833, he applied to Mr. Dilke for admission on the staff of his paper, and was accepted on what would now seem very hard terms — the sum of £50 for six months' service. He was to live in the neighborhood of Mr. Dilke, and was to render him any and every assistance that he might suggest. He accepted without hesitation, went to London, and until within a few years of his death, was attached to the "Athenæum."

There have been editors whose lives have been eventful, but Chorley was not one of them. He began as a drudge, he ended as an authority. Industrious he certainly was, and in many directions. He had hardly set foot in London, before he put to press "Sketches of a Seaport Town," — the sketches in question being those that he had written in Liverpool. His profession brought him in contact with the literary celebrities of the day, — Proctor, Hood, Atherstone, G. P. R. James, and Thackeray, who was then only Michael Angelo Titmarsh, — and stimulated his literary ambition. The following is a list of his writings: "Conti the Discarded, with other Tales and Fancies in Music" (1835), "Memorials of the Life of Mrs. Hemans" (1836), "The Authors of England" (1838), "The Lion, a Tale of the Coteries" (1839), "Music and Manners in France and North Germany" (1841), "Pomfret, or Public Opinion and Private Judgment" (1845), "Old Love and New Fortune" (1850), "The Lovelock" (1854), "The Duchess Eleanour" (1854), "Fairy Gold for Young and Old" (1857), "Roccabella" (1859), and "The Prodigy, a Tale of Music," 1866. Of the first, fourth, sixth, eleventh, and last of these works, which were in a certain sense novels, it is enough to say that they were not successful. Browning, however, expressed a high opinion of "Pomfret," and Dickens and Hawthorne were charmed with "Roccabella." "Old Love and New Fortune," a five act play in blank verse, was produced at the Surry Theatre, and was a thorough success. "The Lovelock," a fantastic sort of morality, interspersed with lyrics, was played without success, to the no great disappointment of Chorley, who wrote to the editor of the "Athenæum" the next morning, to promise a review upon which he was working, "in proof that though *damned*, I am not dead." "The Duchess Eleanour" was moderately successful, but for one night only. Besides these works, and his musical and art criticisms and reviews in the "Athenæum," he wrote for the "British Foreign," and the "New Quarterly" Reviews, "Bentley's Miscellany," "The People's Journal," and "Jerrold's Magazine"; and he edited the second series of Miss Mitford's letters. It was as a musical critic, rather than as an author, that Chorley was best known, and in this special walk of literature, for he made it one, he was without a rival in England. He was known to the whole musical profession, by whom he was held in great esteem, as a thoroughly capable and impartial critic, and he enjoyed the friendship of Mendelssohn, and other European composers. He was an authority on music while he was connected with the "Athenæum," which was taken by many for his articles alone.

Chorley resided for upwards of twenty years in Eaton Place West, and nearly all that was distinguished in Art, Science, and Literature, was constantly to be met at his house. In the later years of his life he removed to Belgravia, were he perpetrated a grim joke at his own expense. The house which he took was a small one, and the agent who showed him over it on the completion of his purchase made an apology for the narrowness of the staircase. "Never mind," said Chorley, "I shall require a very narrow coffin." "I have sold a great many leases of houses, sir." said the man, astonished, "but I never heard a gentleman make such an observation before." Chorley died on the 16th of February, 1872, in the sixty-fourth year of his age.

James Robinson Planché was born in London, on the 27th of February, 1796. His parents, who were cousins, were the children of French refugees. His father was employed when a young man in the house of Vulliamy & Co., watchmakers to his youthful majesty George the Third, who took a great fancy to him, and often talked to him in the most familiar manner. One day, going to St. James's with the king's watch, he remarked to the page that the ribbon was rather dirty. The king heard him, and coming to the door said, in the sharp, quick way which was habitual to him, "What's that, Planché? What's that?" The young watchmaker repeated his observation, and suggested a new ribbon. "New ribbon, Planché! What for? Can't it be washed? Can't it be washed?" Planché's mother died before he was nine, while he was at boarding-school, unlearning French, which he spoke with great fluency. He worried himself home before he was fourteen, and the question was what to do with him. He had a playmate in an attorney's office, and wished to be an attorney. He was fond of drawing, and desired, therefore, to be an artist. His father, who had known what it was to be almost a beggar, but who had obtained a competency by his own industry and honesty, declared that he should have a trade or profession. Planché said that he would be an artist, and was sent to study geometry and perspective under a French landscape painter of some ability, who died before he could be of any great service to him. His art life ended, the capricious lad took to scribbling, and, in the hope of one day publishing his own works, determined to be a bookseller. He was apprenticed to one, and during the time that he remained with him developed a propensity common to young men, the belief that he was an actor, and as his father died in his twentieth year, he was able to carry it into practice. He turned amateur, and at various private theatres murdered sundry great personages to his entire satisfaction, in company with other juvenile aspirants, who afterwards rose to eminence on the stage. Finding nothing in Shakespeare or Sheridan worthy of his abilities, he resolved to write a play himself. It was a burlesque, after the manner of "Bombastes Furioso," and was entitled "Amoroso, King of Little Britain." It was handed round among his brother amateurs, by one of whom it was shown to Mr. Harley of the Theatre Royal, Drury Lane, and that establishment being at the moment in a state of starvation, this humble morsel was snapped at. "Amoroso" was produced on the 21st of April, 1818, and sustained by the acting and singing of Harley, Knight, Oxberry, Mrs. Orger, and Mrs. Bland, it made a hit. It put no money in Planché's pocket, but it decided his vocation. He was a dramatist from that day forth. He lived, moved, and had his being in the theatre. He went home to dine, and reluctantly to sleep. We read of the fecundity of Lope de Vega, but I question whether that prolific writer ever turned off more plays from his "prentice han'" than did Planché, from his twenty-second to his thirty-seventh year, when he had put upon the stage, of one description and another, seventy-six plays! He early learned one secret of success, and he practiced it, not as since became the fashion with the craft, but in an honorable manner. This secret was the translation of French plays, which, when notable, he was generally the first English dramatist to witness, and to put upon the English stage. He did not pass them off as his own, but gave their authors the credit that their invention deserved. One of his earliest translations, "The Vampire," was produced at the Lyceum, and Planché vainly endeavored to induce the manager to let him change the scene of the play from Scotland, where the French dramatist had recklessly placed it, but where the Vampire superstition did not exist, to some place where it did. The manager had set his heart on Scotch music and dresses, and the play was produced with them, and had a long run. The time came when Planché had his own way in matters like this. It commenced at Covent Garden Theatre with the revival of "King John," which was produced under his direction, with strict historical accuracy. He was assisted by the advice of Francis Douce, the well known antiquary, and Sir Samuel Meyrick, the greatest authority in England on ancient arms and armor. The revival was a great success, surprising the actors, who had no faith in historical accuracy.

The life of Planché was marked by no event of importance, unless his marriage in 1821 may be considered one. It was crowded with literary work, and good work, too, but not of a kind that lives as Literature. It was written for the day, and for whatever theatre Planché was connected with, and embraced the whole range of the acting English drama, to which he added upwards of two hundred plays. I question whether Planché himself could make out a complete list of his dramatic works, and I am certain if he did that it would not interest us much now. Those by which he was best known at the height of his popularity, are as follows: "Success, or a Hit if you Like it," "The Merchant's Wedding," "Charles the Twelfth," "The Brigand," "Olympic Revels," "The Romance of a Day," "The Legion of Honor," "A Friend at Court," "The Army of the North," The Love Charm," "Olympic Devils," "His First Campaign," "The Student of Jena," "Gustavus the Third," "Secret Service," "The

Red Mask," "Court Favor," "The Two Figaros," "Blue Beard," "Faint Heart never won Fair Lady," "The Follies of a Night," "Fortunio," "Graciosa and Percinet," "The Golden Fleece," "The Pride of the Market," "The Loan of a Lover," "The Yellow Dwarf," "King Charming," and "The King of the Peacocks." Old play-goers will recall many of these, for a successful play by Planché was sure to be produced wherever the English language was spoken. They were good plays, his best, well constructed and full of interest, and the characters were clearly individualized. They contrasted strongly with the plays that are most in vogue now, in that the morals were sound, and the manners good, which is but another way of saying that they were written by a gentleman.

The antiquarian studies of Planché, which he cultivated assiduously in the midst of his dramatic writings, introduced him to other audiences than those which witnessed his plays, and placed his name among scholars in this department of letters. His first antiquarian work, "The History of British Costume," brought him to the notice of the leading English painters of the time, Haydon, Maclise, Etty, Prout, Uwins, the Landseers, Cattermole, and others, who sought his advice, and profited by his knowledge. He contributed, Mr. Allibone informs us, the Costume for Knight's "Pictorial Shakespeare," the Costume and Furniture in the chapters on Manners and Customs in the "Pictorial History of England;" and edited, with Critical and Explanatory Notes, editions of Strutt's "Regal and Ecclesiastical Antiquities of England," and "The Dresses and Habits of the People of England," and "An Introduction to Heraldry," by Hugh Clark. He also wrote "Regal Records; Coronation of Queens," "Souvenirs of the Bal Costumé," and "The Pursuivant of Arms, or

Heraldry Founded upon Facts." Nor did he confine himself to works of an antiquarian character, his first literary effort being a volume entitled, "Lays and Legends of the Rhine." It was followed by "The Descent of the Danube from Ratisbon to Vienna," "Shere Afkun. a Legend of Hindoostan," and translations of the fairy-tales of the Countess d'Aulnoy and Charles Perrault. In 1851 he was appointed Rouge Croix Pursuivant, and in 1866 was promoted to the office of Somerset Herald, which he now holds.

Julian Charles Young was born at Manchester, on the 7th of July, 1806. His father, Charles Mayne Young, was the son of an eminent surgeon, whose brutality to his family drove his wife and children into separating from him, and induced Charles to go upon the stage, in order to maintain his mother. He made his *début* in Liverpool, in 1798, as Mr. Green, in the character of Douglas, and meeting with great success he resumed his own name the next year, and played the leading parts in Manchester, Liverpool, Glasgow, and Edinburgh, and at length in London, where for years he divided the honors with his great master John Kemble, and that fiery meteor, Edmund Kean. He was a disciple of the Kemble school of acting, and, if contemporary criticism may be trusted, its ablest and most intelligent one. He excelled both in tragedy and comedy, his list of characters embracing such parts as Don Felix, Osmond, Rolla, Penruddock, Petruchio, and The Stranger, as well as Hamlet, King John, and Romeo. Hamlet was his favorite part, and he selected it when he took leave of the stage, which he adorned for over thirty years, at the age of fifty-three, — a prosperous gentleman, in the full maturity of his powers and fame. He died on the 28th of June, 1856, at the age of seventy-nine, and just fifty years after the death of his young wife.

She was an Italian lady, and of noble blood, being a descendant of the Grimanis, and as good as she was beautiful. The death of her father left her mother and brothers, and a younger sister, in poverty, and, like Young, she determined to better their fortunes by going upon the stage, and in spite of all remonstrances from her titled friends, did so, appearing at Bath in the "Grecian Daughter," in 1802 or 1803. She was so triumphant in this play, that in 1804, she obtained a London engagement, and made her *début* in Juliet, which was received with great applause. In the autumn of the same year she was engaged to fill all the first parts at the Liverpool Theatre. It was there that she met a handsome young tragedian of twenty-seven, who loved her at first sight, and whose Romeo, we may suppose, was as fervid as her Juliet. Charles Mayne Young and Julia Grimani were married on the 9th of March, 1805. Mrs. Young died on the 17th of July, 1806, of puerperal fever, ten days after the birth of her son, Julian Charles. The motherless child was consigned to the care of a daughter of a captain in the Royal Navy, by whom he was tenderly cared for until he was six years old. He was then sent to Clapham, where Dr. Charles Richardson, the lexicographer, had a school, and where he remained nine years, Charles James Mathews, a son of the comedian, being one of his school-fellows, and John Mitchell Kemble, a son of Charles Kemble, another. When he was fifteen, he was considered too old to remain longer at a private school to advantage, so his father wrote to Walter Scott, by whom he was highly esteemed, and inquired if the youth of Julian would disqualify him for admission to the University of St

Andrew's. Scott thought not, and suggested that father and son should come and stay a few days at Abbotsford. They did so, and in due time Julian was transplanted to St. Andrew's, where he was his own master, doing whatever he would, and attending what lectures he pleased He remained at St. Andrew's three years, having a vacation of five months in each year, which he spent in England. When he was nineteen his heart was set on taking Holy Orders, and as it was necessary for him to go through a preliminary course of three years at one of the universities, his father was at a loss to know at what college to enter him. While he was puzzling over the matter, he met the Duke of York, who asked how his boy was getting on, and on being told that he was thinking of sending him to Oxford, answered, "Oh, send him to Christ Church, by all means." "I am afraid, sir, it is too aristocratic a place for my son: he might be led into expenses I could ill afford, and into society above his class." "Pooh, pooh," replied the Duke, "you leave it to me." It was left to him. He turned his horse's head, and followed by his groom, rode to see Lord Liverpool about it. His lordship said it was no easy matter for any one — be his rank what it might — to get admittance into Christ Church, but if any one could serve his *protégé*, it was Peel. Peel was not able to do so, for just then rooms at Christ Church were not to be had for love, or interest, or money. Rooms were, however, secured for Julian at Worcester College, Oxford, whither he repaired in 1825, and where he remained until he took his degree of B. A. He then went to London to read, under a private tutor, for Holy Orders, and returned to keep his Master's term. He was ordained priest by the Bishop of Chichester in the summer of 1830, and in the autumn of that year was appointed chaplain of the Palace, Hampton Court. In the spring of 1832, he married Elizabeth Ann Georgiana Willis, of Freshwater House, and Atherfield, Isle of Wight. Lord Brougham offered him the living of Barton near Market Keeping, in Lincolnshire, which he accepted. At a later period he was made rector of Ilmington. He died last year, after forty-three years' service in his holy office, a shrewd, observant, kind-hearted, genial English gentleman.

This is all that the reader need know about Young, Planché, and Chorley, who will shortly speak for themselves, and the men and women they knew. For the present volume, it is enough to say that it is selected from their writings; the portion devoted to Young from "A Memoir of Charles Mayne Young, Tragedian, with Extracts from his Son's Journal, by Charles Young, A. M., Rector of Ilmington" (London, 1871); the portion devoted to Planché, from "The Recollections and Reflections of J. R. Planché (Somerset Herald), A Professional Biography" (London, 1872); and the portion devoted to Chorley, from "Henry Fothergill Chorley: Autobiography, Memoir, and Letters. Compiled by Henry G. Hewlett" (London, 1873). The two last named, which are in two volumes each, are so heavily padded that one has to read 624 pages of Planché's writing, and 682 pages of the writing of Chorley and Hewlett, in order to glean the best of their reminiscences. I believe I have them here, as well as the best of Young's, which for point and spirit excel theirs, I think. Of this, however, and of other matters pertaining to these worthies, the reader will judge for himself.

R. H. S.

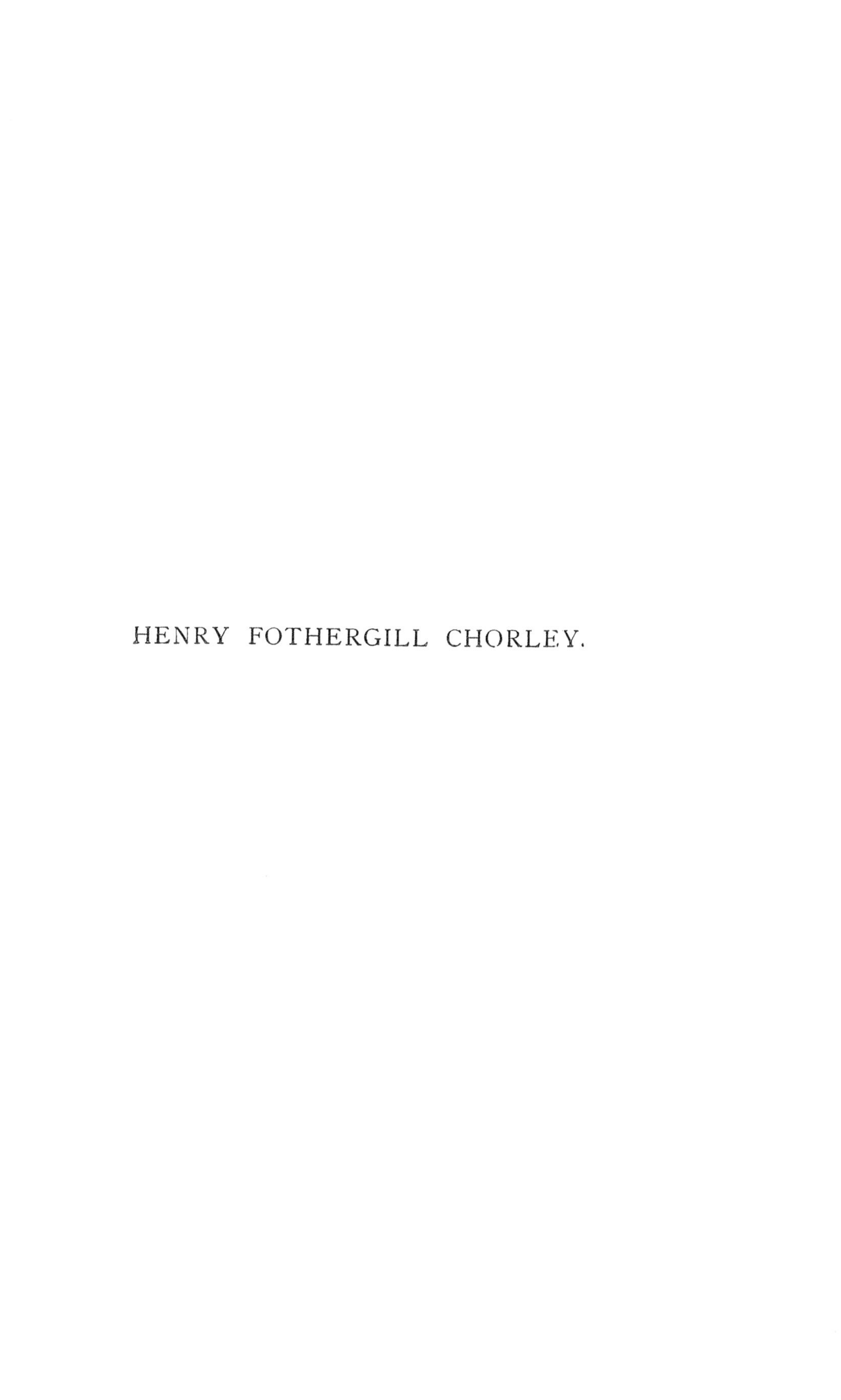

HENRY FOTHERGILL CHORLEY.

HENRY FOTHERGILL CHORLEY.

THE ATHENÆUM.

N 1834 the "Athenæum" was largely supported, in point of contributions, by many of Mr. Dilke's former comrades in "The London Magazine." Charles Lamb gave the journal some of his last and not least racy fragments. Hood, too, when he could be prevailed on to cast off the habits of procrastination which had so disturbing an effect on his fortunes, lent a hand from time to time; and some of his whimsical criticisms are not even to be surpassed by the best comicalities in his "Whims and Oddities." It must be an increasing object of regret to all who love that which is original or powerful in imaginative prose and verse, that Hood gave such small time and labor to the public. Though he used to profess that he could not control his demon, as an excuse for his indolence, a time always arrived when it became a matter of life and death, of daily and nightly toil, to hurry through the work, long contracted and largely paid for in advance. For years this amounted to nothing beyond the small annual volume of comic and grotesque fancies.

Then, too, the "Athenæum" was from time to time enriched by Barry Cornwall's gem-like and musical verses, and by the brilliant, yet not always refined, criticisms of Hood's brother-in-law and partner in the "Odes and Addresses to Great People," John Hamilton Reynolds.[1] On another man of yet greater

[1] Few, save perhaps surviving members of the Garrick Club, will be found who recollect the name of this writer. Yet it was brought before the world by no meaner

power and peculiarity, who belonged to the same set, abused as cockney by the immaculate Tory critics of Edinburgh, I must dwell more in detail: this was George Darley, one of the most original human beings whom I have ever known, and who cannot be forgotten by any of the few who had the opportunity, which chance gave me, of studying so gifted, yet so eccentric, a man near at hand.

George Darley.

Many years ago, when Miss Paton, the singer, was in her prime — dividing honors as a first-class English singer with Miss Stephens — she used to make one of her great effects in a ballad "I've been roaming," set to ballad music by Horn — one of those delicious and refined English tune composers to whom the time present offers no equivalent. The words, odd, fantastic, and full of suggestion, were by Darley, from a curious pastoral, "Sylvia, or the May Queen," a sort of half fairy, half-sylvan masque, almost as charming, and quite as little intelligible, as a certain tale, "Phantasmion," published some years ago, and attributed to the gifted Sara Coleridge, which, possibly, ten persons besides myself have read.

At the time when my connection with the "Athenæum" began, this strange reserved being, who conceived himself largely shut out from companionship with his brother poets by a terrible impediment of speech, was wandering in Italy, and sending home to the journal in question a series of letters on Art, written in a forced and affected style, but pregnant with research, unborrowed speculation, excellent touches by which the nature of a work and of its maker are characterized. The taste in composition, the general severity of the judgments pronounced, might be questioned; but no one could read them without being stirred to compare and to think. In particular,

a judge than Lord Byron, who praised his "Safie;" and there is hardly an anthology devoted to verse of this century which does not include that deliciously musical lyric —

"Go where the water glideth gently ever,"

than which our Laureate himself has produced nothing more melodious.

he laid stress on the elder painters, whose day had not yet come for England, on Giotto, on Perugino, on Francesco Francia, and on Lionardo da Vinci. To myself, as to a then untravelled man, the value of these letters was great indeed.

Talfourd's "Ion."

On the return of Darley to London, he took up in the "Athenæum" the position of dramatic reviewer — not critic to the hour — in the most truculent and uncompromising fashion conceivable. When Talfourd's "Ion" was published, it appeared to myself (as it still appears) to be the most noble, highly finished, and picturesque modern classical tragedy existing on the English stage. It was not its large private distribution, not merely the great reputation of its author, but the vital, pathetic excellence of the drama, and the rich poetry of the diction, which, on the night of the production of the play at Covent Garden, filled that great theatre with an audience the like of which, in point of distinction, I have never seen in any English theatre. There were the flower of our poets, the best of our lawyers, artists of every world and every quality. There was a poor actor of some enterprise and promise, Mr. Cathcart, who, in the fullness of zeal and expectation, absolutely walked up to London from Brighton, to be present at the first performance.

The success of this was superb, and established its author once for all among the real dramatists of England. And yet it was a success under disadvantages. With all his passion and poetry of execution, and subtlety of conception, no magic could make Mr. Macready thoroughly acceptable as the young hero. The part was afterwards again and again tried by actresses in male attire — always a disappointing, when it is not a repulsive expedient. One could not escape from the tones and attitudes of Werner, and Virginius, and Macbeth. "Ion" has yet to be seen. Nor did the charming "Clemanthe" of Miss Ellen Tree group well with the hero. The other persons of the play were either weakly or boisterously presented. There had been no particular pains bestowed on scenery or appointments. But of the entire, unquestionable triumph of the tragedy, there could not be an instant's doubt on the part of any unprejudiced spectator. I have rarely been so warmed, so moved in any theatre.

T. N. Talfourd.

I had met the author at Lady Blessington's; and she--in no respect more generously constant to her friends till the very last than in trying to serve younger artists and men of letters in whom she fancied promise—presented me to the orator and the dramatist of that one great play—it may be (for this I cannot say), as a writer in connection with a rising journal. I have since thought that such *must* have been the case, without false thought or purpose on her part, but in her wish to set me out to the best advantage. As matters turned out, her genuine regard and desire to present me resulted in no good influence on my fortunes, literary or critical, but absolutely the reverse.

An ill chance for me threw the critic's task, as regarded the "Athenæum," into the hands of Darley—hands never more vigorous than when they were using the axe and scalpel. That the grace of propriety was utterly wanting to him, his own dramas, "Thomas à Becket" and "Athelstan" attest.

I was only known to Mr. Talfourd as one who wrote in the "Athenæum," and having in person expressed to him what I thought and felt in regard to the play, it was necessary for me at once, with the utmost earnestness, to write to him on the appearance of the criticism against which I had privately protested, but in vain, with the strongest possible disclaimer of its unjust and uncouth severity, and an equally strong assertion of my own utter powerlessness to interfere in suppression or mitigation. My letter, I fear, was not believed to be sincere. It was said that, had I been in earnest, I could easily have attested my sincerity, by entire withdrawal from a publication so wicked and malignant—a stringent suggestion, truly! But few have admitted the right of private judgment so grudgingly as the most advanced Liberals; few have been so despotic in their partisanship. The damage done me by that article was inconceivable. Not only did it cost me the good understanding of the poet himself, but, for years, I was set up as a mark to be decried by all the *coterie* round him.

CHORLEY ABUSED.

Whenever I attempted any appearance in print, I had such a phrase as this sent to me in a newspaper-cutting (lest I should fail to see it): the writer spoke of "the Chorleys and *chawbacons* of literature." Not merely were such coarse personalities sent to me, but they were righteously forwarded to my family at Liverpool, some of whom they succeeded in troubling greatly. I can truly say that they only disturbed me inasmuch as they placed hard material obstacles in the way of my maintaining myself as a literary man.

Some of the specimens of abuse with which I was favored were diverting, rather than offensive, by their utter vulgarity. I kept by me, for some years, a collection of such flowers of rhetoric, the most exquisite of which was a letter written in very black ink, beginning,

"You *Worm!!!*"

That this prevailing and explicable antipathy was a serious injury to me, whenever I attempted appearance before the public, is beyond doubt. To some degree one may live it down; but there are many who to the last of an author's career will revert to it, and their judgments be influenced accordingly, in obedience to the popular adage that "where there is smoke there must be fire."

I cannot call to mind a writer more largely neglected, sneered at, and grudgingly analyzed than myself. I can truly say, however, that seriously as this most unnatural treatment was a hinderance, whether to the securing that ease of spirit which ought to accompany composition, or in maintaining a modest position as regards gain without an incessant and anxious struggle, I have suffered all my life singularly little from bitterness under severe criticism on what I have written. I do not remember, in this relation between myself and my fellow men, to have ever felt resentment, still less a desire to retaliate. I deserve no credit for this patience or indifference, as may be. It was, in great part, a case of temperament; in small part, of resolution to go on without looking to the right or left, or listening to the "black stones" of the Arabian tale, which mocked and tried to affright the pilgrim as he struggled up the steep hill; nor should I have stated the case, save for the assistance of those who may come after me. Let them count the cost of the struggle before they begin; and once having begun, keep their minds as clear as they can of comparison and irritation.

Who would not sicken at times of literature, literary men, and literary things when such sweetmeats as the following come by post — this with a third edition of a Preface to "Satan" Montgomery's "Luther," which had been sharply handled in the "Athenæum," but had never even been seen by H. F. C.?

"Be sure your sin will find you out! One who is well acquainted with Mr. Chorley's infamous trade of defamation and envy against his betters, in the 'Athenæum,' commends the inclosed to his conscience. If not yet too indurated, it will suggest moral justice to a mean and malignant trader in literature!"

MISS LANDON.

At the time when I joined the "Athenæum," its vigor and value to the world of letters were not acknowledged as they have since been. The "Literary Gazette," conducted by Mr. Jerdan, who was the puppet of certain booksellers, and dispensed praise or blame at their bidding, and it may be feared "for a consideration," was in the ascendancy; and its conductors and writers spared no pains to attack, to vilipend, and to injure, so far as they could, any one who had to do with a rising journal so merciless in its exposure of a false and demoralizing system.

It would not be easy to sum up the iniquities of criticism (the word is not too strong), perpetrated at the instance of publisher's, by a young writer and a woman, who was in the grasp of Mr. Jerdan, and who gilt or blackened all writers of the time, as he ordained. When I came to London to join the "Athenæum," she was "flinging about fire" as a journalist in sport, according to the approved fashion of her school, and not a small quantity of the fire fell on the head of one who belonged to "the opposition" camp, like myself. It is hard to conceive any one, by flimsiness and by flippancy, made more distasteful to those who did not know her, than was Miss Landon.

For years, the amount of gibing sarcasm and imputation to which I was exposed, was largely swelled by this poor woman's commanded spite. That it did not make me seriously unhappy was probably an affair of temperament; those who would have been pained by it were, happily, beyond reach of hearing. But that these things most assuredly had a bad influence on my power as a worker, I do not entertain the slightest doubt. Perhaps it is only the lingering vanity of an elderly man which I mistake for conviction.

In spite of the miserably low standard of her literary morality, Miss Landon (for a while put forward as Mrs. Hemans's rival) was meant for better things. She was incomplete, but she was worthy of being completed; she was ignorant, but she was quick, and capable of receiving culture, had she been allowed a chance. If she was unrefined, it was because she had fallen into the hands of a coarse set of men — the Tories of a provincial capital — such as then made a noise and a flare in the "Noctes Ambrosianæ" of "Blackwood's Magazine," second-hand followers of Lockhart and Professor Wilson and Theodore Hook; the most noisy and most reprehensible of whom — and yet one of the cleverest — was Dr. Maginn. Not merely did they, at a very early period of the girl's career, succeed in bringing her name into a coarse repute, from which it never wholly extricated itself, but, by the ridiculous exaggeration of such natural gifts as she possessed (no doubt accompanied by immediate gain), flattered her into the idea that small further cultivation was required by one who could rank with a Baillie, a Tighe, a Hemans — if not their superior, at least their equal. Further, she was not fortunate in her home position, called on to labor incessantly for the support of those around her. All this resulted in what may be called a *bravado* in her intercourse with the public, which excited immense distaste among those who were not of the *coterie* to which she belonged.

As years went on, the ephemeral success of Miss Landon's verses subsided: and, indeed, she had rendered herself next to incapable of anything like a sustained effort, though some of her smaller lyrics were more earnest and more real in their sentiment and sweetness than her earlier love-tales and ditties had been. There was amendment, too, in her versification. She attempted drama, in the tragedy, I think, of "Castruccio Castrucani," but without the smallest success. She wrote a volume of sacred verse, which was sentimental rather than serious. She took Annuals in hand, but the result was the same, and it must have been felt so by herself. At last she began to write imaginative prose; and the coterie who supported her blew the trumpet before her first novel, "Romance and Reality," as no one would do nowadays were a new Dickens, or a new Bulwer on the threshold. But she held out bravely; wearing out life and health and hope, as all who work on ground which is not solid *must* do; bravely holding up those who looked to her for position and subsistence in life, and keeping up before such of the friends she retained, and such of the society as she mixed in sparingly, those hectic, hysterical high-spirits, which are even more depressing to meet than any melancholy. There was a certain audacious brightness in her talk; but it was only false glitter, not real brilliancy; it was smart, not sound.

The truth of Miss Landon's story and her situation had for some time oozed out; it was felt that her literary reputation had been exaggerated; that her social position was, so to say, not the pleasantest in the world. Those who had, in some measure, compromised her, were in no case to assist her; those who had stood aside had become aware of the deep and real struggle and sorrow which had darkened her whole life, from its youth upwards, and the many, many pleas for forbearance implied in such knowledge.

There came a time for the recognition of these. A relative of hers was proposed to fill an office, in the giving away of which literary men had some words to say. And he was unimpeachably eligible. He had rested on her support. It was right that her devotion to her own family should not be allowed to drag her down; that her literary industry should be recognized — especially now, when it was failing of its reward. It was felt among some of us, that, in this matter, there was a claim to be upheld. I had to see her on the subject. It was, for both of us, an awkward visit. She received me with an air of astonishment and bravado, talking with a rapid and unrefined frivolity, the tone and taste of which were most distasteful, and the flow difficult to interrupt. When, at last, I was allowed to explain my errand, the change was instant and painful. She burst into a flood of hysterical tears. "Oh!" she cried, "you don't know the ill-natured things I have written about you!" From that time I saw her occasionally, and am satisfied of the sincerity of her feelings. Then, I came to perceive how much of what was good and real in her nature had been strangled and poisoned by the self-interested thoughtlessness of those who should have shielded her. Some growing conviction of this it was, I have always thought, which drove her into a desire for escape, and this into her marriage. It seemed next to impossible that the husband she chose could have anything in common with her. Her melancholy death (curiously foreshadowed in her "Ethel Churchill"), painfully sudden as it was, may have delivered her from heart-ache and weariness to come. But her ill-fortune pursued her after the catastrophe at Cape Coast Castle, caused by her mistake of one medicine for another. It would be worse than fruitless to rake up the scandals to which this gave rise, and which had their usual complement of malicious listeners. "Very sorrowful," says the author, "is the life of a woman;" but of all the lives of literary women which I have studied, that of L. E. L. seems to me the most sorrowful.

The Chevalier Neukomm.

Of all the men of talent whom I have ever known, he was the most deliberate in turning to account every gift, every talent, every creature-comfort to be procured from others; withal, shrewd, pleasant, universally educated beyond the generality of the musical composers of his period. A man who had been largely "knocked about," and had been hardened by the process into the habit or duty of knocking about any one whom he could fascinate into believing in him. Never was any man more adroit in catering for his own comforts — in administering vicarious benevolence. Once having gained entrance into a house, he remained there, with a possession of self-possession the like of which I have never seen. There was no possibility of dislodging him, save at his own deliberate will and pleasure. He would have hours and usages regulated in conformity with his own tastes; and these were more regulated by individual whimsy than universal convenience. He must dine at one peculiar hour — at no other. Having embraced homœopathy to its fullest extent, he would have his own dinner expressly made and provided. The light must be regulated to suit his eyes — the temperature to fit his endurance. But, as rarely fails to be the case in this world of shy or sycophantic persons, he compelled obedience to his decrees; and, on the strength of a slender musical talent, a smooth diplomatic manner, and some small insight into other worlds than his own, he maintained a place, in its lesser sphere, as astounding and autocratic as that of the great Samuel Johnson, when he ruled the household of the Thrales with a rod of iron. Neukomm had no artistic vigor or skill to insure a lasting popularity for his music. It has passed and gone into the limbo of oblivion. Yet, for some five years, he held a first place in England, and was in honored request at every great provincial music-meeting. He was at Manchester; at Derby, where, I think, his oratorio "Mount Sinai" was produced; most prominent at Birmingham, for which he wrote his unsuccessful "David" — for a while called "The King of Birmingham." I question whether a note of his music lives in any man's recollection, unless it be "The Sea," to the spirited and stirring words of Barry Cornwall.

This song made at once a striking mark on the public ear and heart. The spirited setting bore out the spirited words; and the spirited singing and saying of both by Mr. Henry Phillips had no small share in the brilliant success. I can only call to mind another modern sea song — Bishop's "O Firm as Oak," which in the least holds its place by the side of Neukomm's in right of merit. Neither are sung for the moment. Both may return. The Chevalier was as cunning in his generation as his poet was the reverse. On the strength of this success and his partner's simplicity, the musician beguiled the poet to write some half-hundred lyrics for music, the larger number of which are already among the classics of English song, in grace and melody recalling the best of our old dramatists, and surprisingly little touched by conceit. Will it be believed, that for such admirable service the noble-hearted poet was never even offered the slightest share in gains, which would have had no existence save for his suggesting genius, by the miserable Chevalier? It only dawned on him that his share of the songs must have some value, when the publishers, without hint or solicitation, in acknowledgment of the success, sent a slight present of jewelry to a member of his family. It is sadly true that too many musicians have shown a like disregard of the laws of *meum* and *tuum* in regard to the verse they have set. The case, in every one's interest, cannot be too plainly stated; but a more flagrant illustration does not exist than the dealings of Neukomm with the author of "Mirandola."

Herr Moscheles.

Enough of a distasteful subject. My own gains from the notice of the Chevalier were of a different quality — gains beyond the desert of an obscure rhymster trying to struggle into print. It was on one of those hurried visits to London, without the excitement of which, the hated drudgery of mercantile life among uncongenial spirits would have become intolerable, that M. Neukomm introduced me to one of the happiest musical households and family circles I have ever known — that of Moscheles. This was only a few years after his marriage. Our good understanding remained unbroken till the last hour of his life. All that he had of what was genial in his nature, and agreeable in his life I was permitted to enjoy. In his house were to be met the best celebrities of literature and art. The standard of general cultivation, morals, and manners among musicians has risen largely during the last five-and-thirty years ; but there has been, I repeat, no ground such as that house offered, where the best of the best and the newest of the new met on such perfect terms of ease and equality. I have good reason to speak of it with most grateful remembrance.

I have never known a man in whom two entirely distinct natures — those of excessive caution and equal liberality — were so intimately combined. The caution in money matters, the liberality in time, counsel, interest given without stint or envy to all contemporary or rising artists. I detected no trace of jealousy in his nature ; on the other hand, a curiosity to make acquaintance with all that was new or promising, and as much liberality of judgment as was consistent with a closeness of character, which intensified his nationality.

N. P. Willis.

In the autumn of 1834, while travelling in Italy, Mr. N. P. Willis had met with a gentleman well acquainted with my elder brother. This gentleman had given a letter for my brother to Mr. Willis, who gathered introductions to persons of every degree of fortune or of every circle more solicitously than any one whom I have ever seen. Mr. Willis, meeting me by chance at a friend's house, naturally enough mistook me for the person to whom Mr. ——'s letter was addressed, and I was as naturally glad to make an agreeable acquaintance. And agreeable I found Mr. Willis, and kindly in his way, though flimsy in his acquirements and flashy in his manners — a thorough literary getter-on, but a better-natured one than many I have since known. At that time of my life, it seemed a necessity for me to have some one to talk over my schemes with, and to show my attempts to. He, too, seemed to have the same fancy, though it was an unequal bargain, since he wrote much less, because far more carefully than I. In short, it was an intimacy that could not, under any circumstances, have lasted long, but which, while it did last, was pleasant to both.

There was something very agreeable and fascinating in his manner — a sort of gentle flattery that made you feel as if he had become peculiarly interested in you. I have been always too prone to attach myself to any one who would let me, so took him up at once on his own showing. Then he was a literary man of my own age, and about my own means, with as much less of thought as he had more of cleverness. And I believe, for a time, he did like me in his way; gave me good advice about dress, manners, etc., — a little too magnificently I *now* think — and certainly was of use to me in making me modulate my voice. We passed a part of every day together; dreamed dreams, and schemed schemes, and canvassed our tailors' bills, etc. He read to me his "Melanie" in progress, and, which was better, listened while I read to him. With great diffidence I sent through him a *chanson* to my Lady Blessington, who was then his great patroness and friend; and this he gave her with many kind words. It was "Love at Sea;" on which she expressed a wish to see me.

[Chorley's acquaintance with Willis appears to have closed with the latter's departure for Scotland, full of the intention (as he professed himself) of marrying a Scotch lady with red hair, who (according to his usual story) had fallen in love with him. But he had fancied that Lady Blessington had already been smitten! As he had a box full of locks of hair, trophies of his continental Don Giovannism, perhaps he was excusable.]

Lady Blessington.

Lady Blessington was then gathering about her a circle of

the younger literary men of London, in addition to the older and more distinguished friends made by her before her widowhood. I went with Willis to the studio of Mr. Rothwell, who was engaged on a half-length portrait of her, which he never, I believe, completed, and was introduced to her. She said a few kind words in that winning and gracious manner which no woman's welcome can have ever surpassed; and from that moment till the day of her death in Paris, I experienced only a long course of kind constructions and good offices. She was a steady friend, through good report and evil report, for those to whom she professed friendship. Such faults as she had belonged to her position, to her past history, and to the disloyalty of many who paid court to her by paying court to her faults, and who then carried into the outer world depreciating reports of the wit, the banter, the sarcasm, and the epigram, which but for their urgings and incitements would have been always kindly, however mirthful.

She must have had originally the most sunny of sunny natures. As it was, I have never seen anything like her vivacity and sweet cheerfulness during the early years when I knew her. She had a singular power of entertaining herself by her own stories; the keenness of an Irishwoman in relishing fun and repartee, strange turns of language, and bright touches of character. A fairer, kinder, more universal recipient of everything that came within the possibilities of her mind, I have never known. I think the only genuine author whose merits she was averse to admit was Hood; and yet she knew Rabelais, and delighted in "Elia." It was her real disposition to dwell on beauties rather than faults. Critical she could be, and as judiciously critical as any woman I have ever known, but she never seemed to be so willingly. When a poem was read to her, or a book given to her, she could always touch on the best passage, the bright point; and rarely missed the purpose of the work, if purpose it had. When I think of the myriads I have known who, on such occasions, betwixt a desire to show sagacity, slowness to appreciate, or want of tact in expression, flounder on betwixt commonplace which is not complimentary, and disquisitions that are rather hard to bear, I return to her powers and ways of accepting as among the lost graces, which have been replaced (say the optimists) by something truer and more solid. I doubt it.

Her taste in everything was towards the gay, the superb, the luxurious; but, on the whole, excellently good. Her eye was as quick as lightning; her resources were many and original. It will not be forgotten how, twenty years ago, she astounded the Opera-goers by appearing in her box with a plain transparent cap, which the world in its ignorance, called a Quaker's cap; and the best of all likenesses of her, in date later than the lovely Lawrence portrait, is that drawing by Chalon, in which this "tire" is represented, with some additional loops of ribbon. So, too, her houses in Seamore Place and at Kensington Gore were full of fancies which have since passed into fashions, and which seemed all to belong and to agree with herself. Had she been the selfish Sybaritic woman whom many who hated her, without knowing her, delighted to represent her, she might have indulged these joyous and costly humors with impunity; but she was affectionately, inconsiderately liberal — liberal to those of her own flesh and blood who had misrepresented and maligned her, and who grasped at whatever of bounty she yielded them, with scarcely a show of cordiality in return, and who spread the old, envious, depreciating tales before the service had well been done an hour!

What her early life had been, I cannot pretend to say. I have heard her speak of it herself once or twice, when moved by very great emotion or injustice from without. And what woman, in speaking of past error, is unable to represent herself as more sinned against than sinning? I have heard, on the other hand, some who professed an intimate knowledge of her private concerns and past adventures (which profession is often more common than correct), attack her with a bitterness which left her no excuse, no virtue, no single redeeming quality — representing her as a cold-blooded and unscrupulous adventuress, only fit to figure in some novel by a Defoe, which women are not to read. That this cannot have been true, every friend of hers will bear me out in asserting — and she kept her friends. The courage with which she clung to her attachments long after they brought her only shame and sorrow, spoke for the affectionate heart, which no luxury could spoil and no vicissitude sour.

COUNT D'ORSAY.

The wit of Count d'Orsay was more quaint than anything I have heard from Frenchmen (there are touches of like quality in Rabelais) — more airy than the brightest London wit of my time, those of Sydney Smith and Mr. Fonblanque not excepted. It was an artist's wit, capable of touching off a character by one trait told in a few odd words. The best examples of such *esprit* when written down look pale and mechanical: something of the *aroma* dies on the lips of the speaker; but an anecdote or two may be tried, bringing up as they do the magnificent presence, and joyous, prosperous voice and charming temper of him to whom they belong.

When Sir Henry Bulwer was sent on a diplomatic mission to Constantinople, "*Quelle bêtise*," was the Count's exclamation, "to send him there among those Turks, with their beards and their shawls — those big handsome fellows — a little gray man like that! They might as well have sent one whitebait down the Dardanelles to give the Turks an idea of English fish."

I have heard the Count tell, how, when he was in England for the first time (very young, very handsome, and not abashed), he was placed at some dinner-party next the late Lady Holland. That singular woman, who adroitly succeeded in ruling and retaining a distinguished circle, longer than either fascination or tyranny might singly have accomplished, chanced that day to be in one of her imperious humors. She dropped her napkin; the Count picked it up gallantly; then her fan, then her fork, then her spoon, then her glass; and as often her neighbor stooped and restored the lost article. At last, however, the patience of the youth gave way, and on her dropping her napkin again, he turned and called one of the footmen behind him "Put my *couvert* on the floor," said he. "I will finish my dinner there; it will be so much more convenient to my Lady Holland."

There was every conceivable and inconceivable story current in London of the extravagance of the "King of the French" (as the Count d'Orsay was called among the sporting folk in the Vale of Aylesbury); but it was never told that he had been cradled as it were in an ignorance of the value of money, such as those will not believe possible who have been less indulged and less spoiled, and who have been less pleasant to indulge and to spoil than he was. But extravagance is like collection as a passion. Once let it be owned to exist, and there will be found people to forgive it, and to feed it, and to find it with new objects. When an American gentleman, the gifted Mr. Charles Sumner, was in England, his popularity in society became, justly, so great and so general, that his friends began to devise what circle there was to show him which he had not yet seen, what great house that he had not yet visited. And so it was with Count d'Orsay. His grandmother, Madame Crawford, delighted in his beauty, and his sauciness, and his magnificent tastes. When he joined his regiment, she fitted him out with a service of plate, which made the boy the laughingstock of his comrades. Whether it was broken up into bits, or played for at *lansquenet*, or sunk in a marsh, I cannot recollect; but one or other catastrophe happened, I do know. He was spoiled during most of his life by every one whom he came near; and to one like myself, endowed with many luxurious tastes, but whom the discipline of poverty had compelled prematurely to weigh and to count, it was a curious sight to see, as I often did in the early days of our acquaintance, how he seemed to take it for granted that everybody had any conceivable quantity of five-pound notes. To this fancy the Lichfield, Beaufort, Chesterfield, Massey Stanley set, among whom he was conversant, ministered largely. He spent their money for them royally, and made them fancy they were inventing all manner of sumptuous and original ways of spending it. When the crash and the downfall came, and the Count owned himself beaten, ruined, "done for at last" (as the familiar phrase runs), he said, "Well, at least, if I have nothing else, I will have the best umbrella that ever was." The wish was granted by a lady, who brought the immured man of pleasure in difficulties an umbrella from Paris, with a handle set in jewels. That was a type of Count d'Orsay's ideas of poverty and bad weather, and retrenchment!

But never was Sybarite so little selfish as he. He loved extravagance — waste, even. He would give half a sovereign to a box-keeper at a theatre as a matter of course, and not ostentation; but he could also bestow time, pains, money, and recollection, with a munificence and a delicacy such as showed what a real princely stuff there was in the nature of the man whom Fortune had so cruelly spoiled. He had "the memory of the heart" in perfection.

Theodore Hook.

Aug. 15*th*, 1835.—Last night Westmacott told a *Hookism* at Lady Blessington's worthy of being kept. He was at some large party or other where the lady of the house was more than usually coarsely anxious to get him to make sport for her guests. A ring formed round him of people only wanting a word's encouragement to burst out into a violent laugh. "Do, Mr. Hook; *do* favor us!" said the lady for the hundredth time. "Indeed, madam, I can't; I can't, indeed. I am like that little bird, the canary; can't lay my eggs when any one is looking at me."

Aug. 18*th*, 1835.—I must post one anecdote of Theodore Hook. . . . . He was dining at Powell's the other day, to meet Lord Canterbury, and the talk fell upon *feu* Jack Reeve. . . . . "Yes," said Theodore, when they were speaking of his funeral, "I was out that day: *I met him in his private box, going to the pit!*"

Anecdote of Byron.

The following anecdote of Byron, told on the authority of his travelling companion, Mr. Trelawney, a frequent visitor at

Gore House, is eminently characteristic. When Byron, Shelley, and Trelawney were in Italy together, some small secret (perhaps a bit of London scandal) had come over in an English letter, of which Shelley and Trelawney were the sole possessors. He (Byron) was most eager to discover this, and, when riding out with the latter, went to the childish length of jumping off his horse, declaring that he would kneel down in the middle of the road and never rise — that he would lie down and rot — and let his companion ride over him, etc., etc., if he was not satisfied. On which, Trelawney improvised some *historiette* or other, so that Lord Byron got up again contented. A few minutes afterwards, La Guiccioli's carriage appeared in sight. Lord Byron rode up to it, brimful of his secret, which he presently discharged upon his *donna.* When he rejoined his companion, Trelawney upbraided him with treachery. "Damn it! what's a secret good for else? Do you think I would have done as I did if I had not meant to tell it?" His chagrin and humiliation may be imagined on being made acquainted with the real state of the case.

Michael Angelo Drawings.

Just returned from looking at the Michael Angelo drawings. Here again one feels the difference — how strongly! — between those who work for immortality and those who manufacture for the hour. I expected anatomical precision and grandeur of conception, of course, but hardly that I should be able (so little experienced in old pictures) to throw myself loose enough of the conventionalisms of a taste nourished among modern drawing-room works, to be able to enjoy and appreciate as much as I did. One or two things struck me particularly. All the Christs have a divinity about them I never saw before in any painted idea of the Ecce Homo. One in particular, crucified between the two thieves, though sketchy compared with some others, affected me: the two outside figures were writhing in the agonies of *animal* death; in Him, the agonies of the last hour had no power over the patience and sweetness of his nature. The head is upturned almost with adoration; the limbs languid and stiffening, but still calm.

EDWIN FORREST.

However much Macready moves one at the time by the subtle intellect of his personifications, I never am much the better for it afterwards — never find a word, a look, an attitude written on my heart. There are certain points of Mr. Forrest's playing that I shall never forget to my dying day. There is a force, without violence, in his passionate parts, which he owes much to his physical conformation; but which, thrown into the body of an infirm old king (his Lear was very kingly), is most awful and withering; as, for instance, where he slides down upon his knees, with —

"For, as I am a man, I think this lady
To be my child, Cordelia."

WALTER SAVAGE LANDOR.

May 8th, 1838. — Yesterday evening, I had a very rare treat — a dinner at Kensington *tête-à-tête* with Lady Blessington and Mr. Landor; she talking her best, brilliant and kindly, and without that touch of self-consciousness which she sometimes displays when worked up to it by flatterers and gay companions. Landor, as usual, the very finest man's head I have ever seen, and with all his Johnsonian disposition to tyrannize and lay down the law in his talk, restrained and refined by an old-world courtesy and deference towards his bright hostess, for which *chivalry* is the only right word. There was never any one less of "a pretty man;" but his tale of having gone from Bristol to Bath, to find a moss-rose for a girl who had desired one (I suppose for some ball), was all natural and graceful, and charming enough.

ISAAC DISRAELI.

Well, this, with a thousand other delightful things which there is no use remembering, went by when Mr. Disraeli the elder was announced. I had never seen him before; and, as of course they talked and I heard, I had the luxury of undisturbed leisure wherein to use eyes and ears. An old gentleman, *strictly*, in his appearance ; a countenance which at first glance (owing, perhaps, to the mouth, which hangs) I fancied slightly chargeable with stolidity of expression, but which developed strong sense as it talked ; a rather *soigné* style of dress for so old a man, and a manner good-humored, complimentary (to Gebir), discursive and prosy, bespeaking that engrossment and interest in his own pursuits which might be expected to be found in a person so patient in research and collection. But there is a tone of the *philosophe* (or I fancied it), which I did not quite like ; and that tone (addressing the instinct rather than the judgment) which is felt or imagined to bespeak (how shall it be ?) absence of high principle. No one can be more hardy in his negation than Mr. Fonblanque ; in no one a sneer be more triumphantly incarnate — and it is sometimes very withering and painful ; but he gives you the impression of considering destruction and denial to be his mission ; whereas there is an easy optimism and expediency associated with my idea of Mr. Disraeli, which, while it makes his opinions less salient, increases their offense. This is very hardy in the way of generalization ! I did not like the manner, above all things, in which he talked about the Slave Trade and Wilberforce's life — how the latter was set down as a mere *canter*. (Curious to hear this by his own fireside !) Then he advanced a theory about Shakespeare's having been long in exciting the notice he deserved, as compared with Ben Jonson and other dramatists, which was either incompletely stated, or based on shallow premises — most probably the former. It gave occasion to a very fine thing by Landor: "Yes, Mr. Disraeli, the oak and the ebony take a long time to grow up and make wood, but they last forever."

M. Rio.

[As a final sketch, may be quoted a scene at which Landor was contrasted with M. Rio. This gentleman, the author of "Art Chrétien," Chorley describes as one of the most picturesque-looking men he had seen, and the first he had encountered of the honest and picturesque romanticists of the Middle Ages.] "An enthusiast but without that distressing measure of enthusiasm behind which I at least linger, and in proportion to the heat of which my mind, whether out of conceit or want of sincerity I know not, grows cold. On the occasion referred to, Landor was more petulant and paradoxical than I ever heard him, saying violent and odd rather than the clever and poetical things he is used to say; of all things in the world, choosing to attack the Psalms. M. Rio, who is an Ultramontane Catholic, winced under this, as any man of good taste must have done. Lady Blessington put a stop, however, to this very displeasing talk by saying, in her arch, inimitable way, '*Do* write something better, Mr. Landor.'"

Lord Lytton.

We walked home together (from Lady Blessington's), and in his cloak and in the dusk he unfolded more of himself to me than I had yet seen; though I may say that I had guessed pretty much of what I did see — an egotism — a vanity — *all* thrown up to the surface. Yes, he is a thoroughly *satin* character; but then it is the *richest* satin. Whether it will wear as well as other less glossy materials remains to be seen. There was something inconceivably strange to me in his dwelling, with a sort of hankering, upon the Count d'Orsay's physical advantages; something beneath the dignity of an author, my fastidiousness fancied, in the manner in which he spoke of his own works, saying that the new ones only interested him as far as they were *experiments*. It is a fine, energetic, inquisitive, romantic mind, if I mistake not, that has been blighted and opened too soon. There wants the repose, "the peace that passeth all understanding," which I must believe (and if it be a delusion, I hope I shall never cease to believe) is the accompaniment of the *highest* mind.

A little later, after a *tête-à-tête* dinner with Bulwer at the Reform Club, Chorley writes: "I found all my judgments confirmed by further experience, both as to cleverness and self-conceit. I am not quite sure about the *heart*, or its opposite;

but it is infinitely amusing to discover what there is no escaping from, that he makes personal appearance his idol, and values Voltaire as much on being a tall man as on his satires, or essays, etc. It is unlucky to make so many *valets de chambre* of all one's acquaintances, when a little reserve and calmness of mind might make a tolerable hero of a man.

[The differing estimates which he entertained of Lord Lytton's powers as a novelist, and as a dramatist, have been adverted to elsewhere. At one of these expressions of critical independence the author seems to have taken umbrage, and a stop was thus put to an acquaintance which did not promise to be prosperous.]

Sydney Smith.

Sydney Smith was the only wit, perhaps, on record, whom brilliant social success had done nothing to spoil or harden; a man who heartened himself up to enjoy, and to make others enjoy, by the sound of his own genial laugh; whose tongue was as keen as a Damascus blade when he had to deal with bigotry or falsehood or affectation; but whose forbearance and gentleness to those, however obscure, whom he deemed honest, were as healing as his sarcasm could be vitriolic. Of all that passed under Lady Blessington's roof, the wildest stories were current in the outer world, among women of genius especially, who hated with a quintessence of feminine bitterness, a woman able to turn to account, so brilliantly as Lady Blessington did, the difficulties of her position, inevitable because referable to the events of her early life. Lady Holland — who ruled her subjects with a rod of iron, and who, supported by her lord's urbanity, his literary distinction and political influence, ventured on an amount of capricious insolence to the obscure, such as counterbalanced the recorded deeds of munificence by which her name was known abroad and at home — had not a more distinguished court of men around her than Lady Blessington assembled. It was a duel betwixt gall at Kensington and wormwood at Gore House. Sydney Smith was one of Lady Holland's "court-cards," and was, naturally enough, prepared to receive her tales of what passed in the smaller but livelier Kensington household. On one occasion, at the house of a third person, I heard him, primed with her slander, speak of the high gambling by which Lady Blessington, at the instance of d'Orsay, lured foolish youths of cash and of quality to Gore House. The fact was, there never was such a thing there as play, or the shadow of play — not even a rubber of whist. I stayed in the house — I was there habitually and perpetually during many years, early and late, and as habitually and perpetually was driven to my own lodging at midnight, by Count d'Orsay, who had a schoolboy's delight in breaking the regulations of St. James's Park, which then excluded every one save royal personages from passing after midnight. After this he would go to Crockford's, and play; but with these matters Lady Blessington had nothing to do, beyond the original mistake of harboring so exhausting an inmate as he was. This is a digression necessary to that which is to follow. When I heard the scandal retailed as above by Sydney Smith — told as a fact by such a just and good man, and yet with a condiment of such mirth as makes scandal sweeter — I felt that I must speak out. It was cruelly hard to do so, but I did get out the real version of the story. "Thank you," said the old wit to the obscure penny-a-liner; "thank you for setting me right." And from that time till the day of his death his kindness to me was unbroken.

Before his death he called in his letters, with a view to their destruction; averse to the misuse which could be made, according to the flagrant fashion of our time, of every scrap of written paper, by the literary ghouls who fatten their purses in the guise of biographers. Before one series of such intimate and lively communications was delivered up to him, an intimate and a prized friend, to whom they were addressed, asked him whether he had any objection to my reading them. "No," was the answer; "he is a gentleman." The sanction gives a relish beyond all price to my recollection of the exquisite whimsies, the keen appreciation of character, and the justice in judgment which these letters contained.

George Grote.

The Historian of Greece, one of the few serious English men of letters who has made his mark all the world over, within the past half century, was for many years indulgently kind to me. A more noble-hearted and accomplished gentleman than he who has departed full of years, and rich in honors, I have never seen. When the word "gentleman" is used, it is with express reference to that courtesy and consideration of manner, which appears to me dying out of the world. Four men that I have known, the late Duc de Grâmont, the Duke of Ossuna, the late Duke of Beaufort, and Mr. Grote, in their high breeding and deference to women, in their instinctive avoidance of any topic or expression which could possibly give pain, recur to me as unparagoned. But the three men first named had little beyond their manner by way of charming or influencing society.[1] Mr. Grote, as a man holding those most advanced ideas which were at war with every aristocratic tradition and institution, a man with vigorous purposes, and ample and various stores of thought, might well have been allowed to dispense with form and smoothness and ceremony. But he showed how these could be combined with the most utter sincerity. If, at times, he was elaborate in conversation, with little humor of expression, though not without a sense of it in others, he was never overweening. He stands in a place of his own, among all the superior men to whom I have ever looked up.

He was a skeptic, as regards matters of religious faith, to the very core. But he was keenly alive to the truth, that to force extreme opinions, not called for, on those having other

[1] Yet the Spanish grandee could at once evade and rebuke a piece of noble English impertinence. Rumor had exaggerated the extent of the Duke's fortune and possessions; but they were notoriously very large — for Spain. I heard an Earl, whose name should have been a warrant for good taste and good breeding, ask him point blank, "What was the amount of his income?" — there being, if I remember rightly, a wager at Crockford's to be settled by the answer. 'My lord,'' said the Duke, with the most imperturbable politeness, "I do not know your English money."

convictions, is an abuse of freedom of thought and of speech which no large-minded man will permit himself. There was neither craft nor cowardice in this reticence. Had fortune, or worldly position, or life, depended on his falsifying his opinions, he is the last man I have ever known who would have done so. His uncompromising constancy to his peculiar opinions cost him all influence and support in Parliament, and was the cause of his early retirement from political life and action.

With all his vast stores of knowledge, and his habits of universal reading, were combined a taste for Art, and a certain amount of practical accomplishment not common among scholars so profound and so ripe. He was a lover rather than a judge of pictures; he was an intelligent opera-goer, and had made some proficiency in learning to play on the violoncello. But in everything he undertook, whether it was of grave importance or of slighter pastime, his modesty was as remarkable as his earnestness and his courtesy. The completeness of the scholar and the gentleman strikes me more forcibly on retrospect than it did at the time when I was frequently in his society. It is fit that he should lie among the high-minded and lettered men who have made England great among the nations. But even were there no stone in the Abbey to hand his merits down for scholars and politicians to come to imitate, I am satisfied that his reputation will only brighten and deepen as years pass on, and new men take up the studies in which his honorable life was spent; and the result of which has already a wide and lasting place in the world of letters.

SAMUEL ROGERS.

I used to meet Rogers frequently at the Grotes', at the Kembles', at the Procters'; and at the first house in very small parties, where I had an opportunity of hearing and seeing him closely. Few old men have ever shown a more mortifying behavior to a young one than Mr. Rogers, from the first to the last, displayed towards me. There was no doubting the dislike which he had conceived for me, and which he took every possible pains to make me feel. I do not recollect ever to have intruded myself on his notice, ever to have interrupted him in narration (an offense which he could not endure). In the society where I met him I never talked, for it was a delight to listen to Sydney Smith, and to Charles Austin, and to Mr. and Mrs. Grote. Perhaps Rogers thought my dress coxcombical, or my manner affected (an accusation under which I have lain all my life). Perhaps he did not forgive me for living as house-mate with a person for whom he openly professed antipathy. Whatever the cause might be, he did his best to make me feel small and uncomfortable; and it was often done by repeating the same discouragement. The scene would be a dinner of eight; at which he would say, loud enough to be heard, "Who is that young man with red hair?" (meaning me). The answer would be, "Mr. Chorley," *et cetera, et cetera.* "Never heard of him before," was the rejoinder; after which Rogers would turn to his dinner, like one who having disposed of a nuisance, might unfold his napkin, and eat his soup in peace.

It has been fortunate for me all my life that unprovoked rudeness of this sort has never had any power over me, has never added to a physical nervousness, of itself sufficiently disqualifying, nor to a shyness, which I don't think has included moral cowardice. Those to whom I have attached myself, and those in whom I have believed, have been able to give me any amount of pain. I have been hag-ridden all my life by an over-sensitiveness with respect to *friends*, and have suffered from my own jealous and exacting nature, from too much yearning for entire confidence and complete regard. But slights from acquaintances I have never heeded, more than I should heed a random call at my heels in the street. And thus the deliberate and avowed antipathy of Mr. Rogers (never provoked by want of respect on my part) served only to amuse me, as a trait of character, and did not prevent my profiting, as well as I could, by all that was more genial in his nature and manners. It still seems to me a doubtful matter which of the two attributes was reality, which affectation; the elegance and sympathy and delicacy he could throw into his intercourse with those whom he protected, or the acerbity, often displayed and directed without any conceivable reason, with which he pursued unaffected persons, or denounced everything in literature and art which did not suit him. His admiration, in some points showing a marvelous foresight, in others, hung so curiously far behind his time, as to puzzle all those who are apt to dream that liberality should exclude prejudice. As a young man collecting pictures, he showed an excellent courage in leaving all the beaten tracks of connoisseurship, to select, and enjoy, and recognize that which he felt to be good. He was one of the first in England who recognized ancient Italian painting, as having a beauty and an expression totally distinct from archæological value; not repelled by technical mistakes or audacities, provided the work was sincere. But as an old poet, who was ever so inhuman and perverse in sitting in judgment on the works of young poets as Rogers? I have heard him absolutely venomous and violent (as much as so low-voiced a man could be) in dissection, or in wholesale abuse, of the verses of Tennyson, Browning, Milnes; and end his task of "perverse industry" (as Moore has somewhere happily designated such exhibitions) with such a sigh of satisfaction as might befit one to whom the extermination of vermin is not a profession, but a pleasure.

In music, too, he was no less exclusive, no less vicious in reproof, but far more ignorant. How one, who had been hearing music for so many years, and who would never keep away from any place where it was going on, could have made so little progress in taste and knowledge as Rogers, used to excite my wonderment. Scott, it is said, used to profess that he was totally devoid of musical sense, save such as enabled him to bear the burden to Mrs. Lockhart's ballads, or to sing after supper (as Moore has told) over the quaigh of whiskey. But I cannot but imagine that Rogers, with all his profession, was as meagrely gifted by nature as Scott had been, and that his culture had merely been applied to the fostering of those old associative prejudices which, however precious as pleasures of memory, have nothing to do with the good or ill of music. The name of Beethoven used to make him singularly active and acrid in epithet: instrumental music, of any kind, was "*those fiddlers;*" though he would lavish gracious compliments on a Kemble, an Arkwright, or a Grisi, or any woman who sung, no matter what, small matter how she sung It was on the debatable land of music that I used to meet Mr. Rogers the most frequently since he came to many houses which I frequented, ostensibly to hear and to enjoy music; and, sometimes, for the sake of getting a name or a fact, would even lay by his antipathy and ignorance of me, and ask, "*What was going on?*" or, "*whereabouts we were?*" I remember one night in particular, his religiously sitting through a fine performance of Beethoven's Mass in C, and pertinaciously appealing to me, from movement to movement, "*Now is that good?—because I don't know!*" "*Now do you really understand that?*"

The temptation to retort was strong: "What need to sit?" —till one recollected the different world into which he had been born, the different atmosphere as regards Art, which he had breathed; and admitted that the good of his willingness to listen ought to outweigh the bad of his arrogance in knocking down all that he could not understand.

And very great and very bitter was that arrogance. One night Mrs. Sartoris had been singing a canzonet by Signor ———, who had accompanied her. When it was done, Rogers made the labor of crossing the room and going up to the pianoforte; "What was that you have been singing?" said he, in his low, clear voice. "A song of Signor ———," was the answer; "give me leave to introduce him to you." "I thought it was that man's!" was the gracious reply; "*there's no tune in it.*"

I have always considered myself the person to whom Rogers made his most gratuitously ill-natured speech, as under. It was at the *Antient Concerts*, on a night when the room was crowded, owing to a royal visit, and when every seat was occupied. Mine was at the end of a bench, by the side of the Dowager Lady Essex (Miss Stephens that had been). She was one of Rogers' prime favorites; even though she is in private as in public one of those gracious and gentle women against whom no exception can be taken. He loved to sit next her, and pay her those elegant and courteous compliments, the art of paying which is lost. When I saw the old gentleman creeping down the side avenue betwixt the benches, at a loss for a seat, I said, "*Now I shall give up my place to Mr. Rogers; good-night.*" While I was stooping for my hat, "Come," said she, in her cordial way, "come, Mr. Rogers, here is a seat for you by me." "Thank you," said the civil old gentleman, fixing his dead eyes on me, as I was doing my best to get out of the way; "thank you; *but I don't like your company.*"

I may tell you a companion story which I heard from the younger Westmacott the sculptor, who was rather a favorite with Rogers than otherwise. Westmacott had finished a bust, I believe, of Lord John Russell, and, being anxious that Lord John's friends should pronounce on the likeness, invited Mr. Rogers to his *studio* with that express view. The poet, I suppose, came on a bad day, for round and round the room he walked, and through and through the labyrinth of marbles, slowly and ponderingly, passing the bust in a marked manner. At last he paused, paused before one of those *hunches* of marble which have only begun to assume human semblance, by the drill holes and compass marks with which the sculptor's men prepare the block for the sculptor's own chisel. Here he stopped and pointed with his finger, "*I think,*" said he, "*that's the best likeness here.*"

Though I have done my best to produce a true picture of the humors of the Rogers I saw and met often, let me no less earnestly state my belief that the crookedness and the incivility of these had nothing to do with his heart and his hand. when the one told the other to give. Rogers' hospitality to poets might be pleasant to himself, and no less so his handsome reception of every handsome woman, but for the poor, struggling, suffering man of genius, and to the garret with its dirt and cold, without any charm or warmth or Southern picturesque, he was, I believe, a delicate almoner, a liberal distributor and a frequent visitor. Billious, vicious, *cruel* as he was with his tongue, Rogers was, I know, a kindly and indefatigable friend to many humble men, and to a few less humble ones; and at no period of his life, when his antipathy to me was the most rancorously expressed, should I have feared presenting to him the case of poor painter, poor poet, poor musician, or poor governess. Though I never *did* apply to Rogers for aid to others, I am personally cognizant of too many acts of munificence quietly done by him, and of which no trumpeting was or *is* possible, not to dwell on the good as warmly as I talk about the mischief unreservedly.

Lady Morgan.

One of the most peculiar and original literary characters whom I have ever known, was Sydney Lady Morgan, a composition of natural genius, acquired accomplishments, audacity that flew at the highest game, shrewd thought, and research at once intelligent and superficial; personal coquetries and affectations, balanced by sincere and strenuous family affections; extreme liberality of opinions, religious and political; extremely narrow literary sympathies, united with a delight in all the most tinsel pleasures and indulgences of the most inane aristocratic society; a genial love for Art, limited by the most inconceivable prejudices of ignorance; in brief, a compound of the most startling contradictions, impossible to be overlooked or forgotten, though possible to be described in two ways — both true, yet the one diametrically opposite to the other. Those whom she exasperated by her skepticism and her fearlessness of speech and action, could only dwell upon her frivolity and vanity, which were patent enough; those whose tempers were not heated by rivalry or antagonism could discern beneath all these fopperies a solidity of conviction, a sincerity of purpose, and a constancy of regard which could not fail to win appreciation of, though they could not always insure respect for their owner. Her life, were it thoroughly and truly told, would be one of the most singular contributions to the history of gifted woman that the world has ever seen. She tried to tell it herself, in a fragmentary fashion, from time to time; but the chapters of a strange story, however amusing, were like their writer, so made up and rouged for effect as not to have taken a permanent place in the library of Female Biographies. It may be doubted whether such a woman will be ever seen again, since many of her peculiarities were clearly ascribed to circumstances of birth and education, which, in our days of rapid intercourse and diffused instruction, can hardly be reproduced. The efforts of the young to acquire distinction must henceforth take other milder forms than they formerly wore, must be more speculative, less practical: on the other hand, perhaps, the distinction when gained will never be so original and direct in its manifestation, nor so racy in its expression, in any generation to come.

Lady Morgan, when touched too closely on the subject of her birth, was used to say, that she was born on the sea, betwixt Ireland and England. I have heard her declare in one breath that she had created the national Irish novel, while in another, with sublime inconsistency, she would assert that Miss Edgeworth was a grown woman when she was yet a child. Her father, Mr. Macowen (the name for gentility's sake legitimately transformed into Owenson) was a comic actor of some repute in Ireland, some eighty or a hundred years ago. I have always believed that Sydney, his daughter, was destined for public exhibition, as she was taught to sing, to dance, to recite, and to play on the harp. But in none of these accomplishments was she sufficiently tutored to make limited natural gifts and personal attractions presentable to that hard taskmaster, the Public, with any chance of great favor. And the girl early discovered that she had within herself better chances of asserting her individuality; a shrewd observation of character, a keen wit, a fearless tongue, a resolute desire and curiosity for instruction in the ways of the world. Anything but regularly pretty, she must at one time have been odd and piquant looking; in this more attractive than many a dull compound of lilies and roses.

The resolution to get on rarely fails to be its own fulfillment. From the moment when she was received into the Marquis of Abercorn's family, partly as a governess, partly as a household musician, her success in the life she coveted and was fittest for, became only a matter of time. She danced, she played on the harp; by her mother-wit she amused the inane persons of quality whom, in later years, she delighted so mercilessly to satirize in her novels. But all this time she was reading eagerly in a desultory fashion; getting some superficial knowledge of French and Italian; if without any very steady purpose, with that instinct of future success which contains the fulfillment of its own prophecy.

There is no need to dwell on Lady Morgan's first attempts at fiction; "Ida of Athens," "The Novice of St. Dominick," "The Wild Irish Girl," the last probably the least imitative, the one which gave to its writer her own pet name of Glorvina, after its heroine. All are as much forgotten as the tale "St Irvyne," by which Shelley began his literary career. A collection of Irish Melodies, long preceding those of Bunting and Moore, was of better promise. One of these, "Kate Kearney," still lives in cheap editions of popular songs.

It is as little my business to offer any judgment here on Lady Morgan's National Tales; neither on her travels in France and Italy, her "Life of Salvata Rosa," and the most serious and best of her works, "Woman and her Master." Whatever be their real merit, it is past doubt that they established for her a brilliant reputation in France and Italy, and this expressed in forms which were not calculated to give ballast to one of the most feather-brained, restless creatures who ever glittered in the world of female authorship. After her first book on "France" was published she became the *rage* in Paris; and I have been told, on good authority, that on one occasion, at some grand reception, she had a raised seat on the *dais*, only a little lower than that provided for the Duchesse de Berri. It is true that she had at her side a staid, shrewd, cynical, skeptical companion in Sir Charles Morgan, who was weary of bearing a part in perpetual glitter, his mind being bent on graver pursuits and speculations than ners. A strangely assorted pair they seemed to be, on a first glance; but the one suited the other admirably. He did something towards reducing the exuberances of her vanity, and directing her attention to courses of research. That he helped to write her books, as has been asserted, I do not believe. Her fame, for it amounted to fame, gave him access to circles of society which possibly he might never otherwise have entered. Both agreed in the expression of the most fearless skepticism (sometimes most painfully and needlessly expressed); both, like all the skeptics I have ever approached, were absurdly prejudiced and proof against new impressions. Neither of them, though both were literary and musical, could endure German literature or music, had got beyond the stale sarcasms of the "Anti-Jacobin," or could admit that there is a glory for such men as Weber, Beethoven, Mendelssohn, as well as for Cimarosa, Paiesiello, and Rossini. Prejudice such as theirs, professing liberalism, is a "sure card" to play. Party animosity is far more amusing than justice, the latter being apt to bear the bad name of phlegmatic indifference. He, however antipathetic his views might be to many persons, was, I have no doubt, thoroughly sincere in them; she was as much so as a spoilt woman of genius, who delighted in being thought a woman of fashion, could be.

Her familiar conversation was a series of brilliant, egotistic, shrewd, genial sallies. She could be caressing or impudent, as suited the moment, the purpose in hand, or the person she was addressing. At times the generous, hearty nature of the Irishwoman broke out, strangely alternating with her love of show and finery, and the bitter cynicism she showered on all practices and opinions which rebuked her own. I recollect her telling how, when she had been detained at some roadside country inn by an illness of her husband's, she sat on the bench beside the door, and treated a party of weary country laborers, who were there resting, to bread, cheese, and beer, having obviously taken a rich and real enjoyment in their homely talk. And the next moment she would fly off to some nonsense about dukes and duchesses, royal celebrities, at home and abroad, who had complimented her books, her conversation, or her toilette; for of her toilette, which was largely, during her life, made by her own hands, she was comically vain without concealment. I remember to have heard her describe a party at a *Mrs. Leo Hunter's* (who received all manner of celebrities at what she called "her morning *soirées*," without the slightest power of appreciating anything but the celebrity), — "There," said she, "was Miss Jane Porter, looking like a shabby canoness; there was Mrs. Somerville, in an astronomical cap. *I* dashed in, in my blue satin and point-lace, and showed them how an authoress should dress."

I remember her, at another of those wondrous gatherings, where the crowd was great, and the drawing-room was crammed, breaking through a company of men, who had perched on an upper staircase, sitting down, and crying out aloud, "Here I am in the midst of my seraglio!" In freedom of speech she proved herself the countrywoman of those renowned wits, Lady Norbury and Lady Aldborough; but, however free, she never shocked decorum, as they rather rejoiced in doing, to have their tales of *double entendre* carted over the town by diners-out, who found the second-hand indecency answer, as creating "a sensation."

What a blessing is self-approbation! In Lady Morgan's case I am satisfied it was sincere. She had no Statute of Limitations, and absolutely professed to have taught Taglioni to dance an Irish jig! How far Taglioni profited by the lesson is a secret.

Sometimes "her spirit and vivacity" (as the inimitable Lady Strange expressed it) carried Lady Morgan into strange lengths of freedom. I once met her in a literary *ménagerie*, where, among other guests, figured a large lady, but a small authoress, Mrs. Cornwell Baron Wilson. She displayed rather protuberantly, below the waist of her black dress, a awdry medal, half the size of a saucer, which had been awarded her for some prize poems by some provincial Della Cruscan literary society, probably as tawdry and of as little worth as the rhymes it was given to reward. "My — !" said Lady Morgan, using an exclamation more irreverent than the reverse, "only look at Grace Darling!" (the heroic daughter of the Northern Lighthouse-keeper). "Hush! hush!" said some one or other, "It is Mrs. Cornwell Baron Wilson." "Who? Oh, Mrs. Barry Cornwall." I do not believe that she ever took the trouble to set her knowledge right regarding a lady living and moving in her own literary world. Yet who could be so sarcastic as herself on the mistakes of others?

I heard her ask, in all sincerity and simplicity, at a literary party, "Who was Jeremy Taylor?" on the occasion of some reference to that distinguished divine. She may have, and I think had, some notion of the Taylors of Ongar! But more absurd still was her introduction to the stately, grave, and accomplished Mrs. Sarah Austin, on which occasion she complimented her sister authoress on having written "Pride and Prejudice."

Her resolution to assemble lions of all sorts and sexes was nothing short of dauntless. If a nobody happened to get into her circle, she made no scruple to pass him or her off as "the Cleopatra pears" were passed off by my relative. I think, could it have helped one of her parties, she would have fitted up a "Grace Darling." I know of one quiet and unobtrusive woman whom she had invited, and subsequently thought it necessary to ticket, who overheard how she was pointed out by the hostess "as a woman of extraordinary genius, who had written" — Well, the rest did not come easily, and so Lady Morgan fluttered off elsewhere, having mysteriously accounted for the presence of an anonymous guest.

Among the guests whom she received in her latter years, when the death of Sir Charles Morgan left her at liberty to consult her humors without restraint, was the last person one could have expected to meet within precincts such as hers — Cardinal Wiseman. Not long before had she written her pamphlets on St. Peter's chair at Rome, aimed at the immaculate immutability of Papal succession; papers controversial, as strong, and caustic, and conclusive, as possibly were ever written by a woman, in which she took great delight (for her avowed pleasure in her own works was wonderful). I believe *his* eminence and *her* eminence met on grounds of the most cordial good fellowship. Such an encounter tells well for the honest sense and real feeling of the conflicting parties. Such encounters, I have often had reason to think, are nowhere so frequent as in England.

She could be recklessly bitter in regard to other, especially other Irish, literary women. Her hatred to Lady Blessington had no bounds. In point and quality of authorship no sane person could for an instant think of comparing the two; and the writer of "Florence Macarthy," and the "Life of Salvator Rosa," might well have afforded to pass by the more colorless works of the lady of Gore House. But there Gore House was; and, in spite of the more austere and literary and political attractions of Holland House beyond it, Lady Blessington, by her grace, her sweetness, her admirable tact as the leader of society, and her no less admirable constancy, contrived, in spite of the most tremendous social disadvantages, to draw round her such a circle of men there, as I fancy will hardly be seen again. Lady Holland hated her badly, but, I think, let her alone. Lady Morgan could not let her alone. I have never heard venom, irony, and the implacable and caricatured statement of past mistakes heaped *Pelion-wise* on *Ossa*, even by woman on woman, so mercilessly, as by Lady Morgan in regard to Lady Blessington. And the former had the bad taste to assail the known friends of the latter with perpetual gibings and assaults. I have never been able (as other literary men can do) to partake of such miserable stories as these without a feeling of shame and discomfort; as unable as, I hope, unwilling, to spoil society by wrangling, which must merge in honest animosity should unprovoked scandals be circulated.

As life passed on, these follies in some measure fell away from, or were tempered, in Lady Morgan. She accepted what was becoming to advanced years with a grace almost amounting to dignity, hardly to have been expected from one who had so long defied time, and who found herself almost alone in the world. She became quieter, more considerate, very attentive to younger people, and to rising talent. She had been spoiled by having had to work her way under difficult circumstances into a position which she improved into a success. She had been flattered, and was more accessible to flattery than ninety-nine out of a hundred women are. She had the consciousness of having conquered a place for herself and her family, which was bright, and, to some degree, solid, in the best society of England and the Continent. Last and best of all, she had never to be appealed or apologized for, as a forlorn woman of genius under difficulties. The pension which was granted to her in her latter days, and justly, as one who had done her best to see after the redress of Irish abuses, had not, I have reason to believe, been solicited.

Paul de Kock.

I opened the door, and there stood a short, middle-aged man, with a very prepossessing countenance, but intelligent and melancholy rather than gay, very thin and longish black hair (he is, indeed, all but bald) — a fine forehead, and mild, but observant eyes. He was dressed in a black pelisse, faced and cuffed with plush. "Je suis Paul de Kock." I was thoroughly glad to see him, and welcomed him my best in my bad French; told him of the pleasure I had received from his writings, and we had some pleasant talk. His character seems to me true to the feeling, and simplicity, and shrewdness of his novels. I have yet to find whether it be true to those looser parts which (pity on them !) make so beautiful a series a sealed book to English readers in general. But, as he spoke with affection of a son ten years old (who plays the piano very well), I will believe him to be a good father at all events. He referred modestly to his books, disclaimed the praise usually given to him as a writer merely humorous, and seemed pleased and touched by my assuring him (which I could honestly do) that I found something in them far beyond the emptiness of mirth, and instanced the "Frère Jacques," and the last scenes of "Le Bon Enfant." He asked me whether I had read them in translation. I said, No; that I thought his humor untranslatable; and he seemed also much pleased. We spoke of Victor Hugo, whom we agreed in placing at the head of his school; of George Sand, whom we equally agreed in regarding as a hermaphrodite — a "*génie malade*." . . . . He spoke of Count d'Orsay, till tears came into his eyes, and asked me whether he was [still] a Frenchman! He spoke of his own manner of life pleasantly and well. He has a little cabin or cottage in the country, and there he goes *pour se distraire*, is his own mason, his own joiner; and, truly enough, said that a literary man has, beyond all his fellows, need of pursuits and occupations in which the mind can pleasantly unbend itself, and wander away from its fevers or its researches. He spoke strongly, but not with bitterness, of his critics. "They disliked him," he said, "because he belonged to no coterie, and would not do service for service." How I admired this! And he said that they called him the author of cooks, porters, and scullions. "Well," he said, "I console myself, and could silence them if I liked, by saying that I am content, so long as these people don't begin to admire the monsters and prodigies of human nature." But he seemed to feel to the full the comfort of knowing that no enemies or evil speakers can hinder that which is written to the heart of a people finding its answer there. He also spoke of the care and attention which his theatrical engagements required, as a reason for his not leaving Paris often, or to any great distance; and we parted, I full of the most agreeable impressions. I have never seen a literary man, whom I should better wish to have written works I am fond of studying as models than M. Paul de Kock.

[Some days afterwards Chorley called upon his new acquaintance.] I found him from home; but Madame de Kock, from an inner room, invited me to go in, and I am not sorry to have accepted the invitation, though, I hope, from something better than curiosity to see a literary man's *ménage* in Paris. First, the room was small and low, an *entresol*, I think, with a *parquet*, and no carpet; a tea-table set out in the midst; a cot tage-piano in one corner, and beside it a chair full of music; on the wall, opposite the fire-place, a portrait of M. de Kock's brother, whom Madame de Kock, if I remember right, spoke of as being connected with the Dutch Government; and an inner cabinet, shelved with books, where, I suppose, he sits to write. Madame de Kock was busy doing lace-work; a very little woman, *un peu déshabillée peut-être;* and though with, perhaps, not much of the grand lady in her *abord*, full of true and honest pride in her husband, speaking of his simple tastes with great pleasure; how fond he is of children, how much he hates money transactions with his publishers; that she is always obliged to be the *man* of business; and how thoroughly he is fond of the quiet habits which have retained him a tenant of his modest *ménage* (against her will) for nineteen years. She spoke of his unwillingness to quit Paris, even for a visit to his brother, whose portrait I saw; and we were getting on very pleasantly, when he entered. The more I see, the better I like him. He talked very interestingly of Paris, of the life of the people on the Boulevards and beyond the barriers, which he recommended me to see, and of the pleasantness of his situation of residence. I said, Yes, but that I was sure I never could work if I had a house on the Boulevards. "Well," said he, "I find physiognomies and figures, above all, costumes and groups in the streets, which are to me invaluable." He then charged me with a book for M. le Comte d'Orsay, and on my begging permission to read it on the way, said he would give me one for myself. It is "Gustave;" but why I note this is, as a trait, that the book bears as title-page an illustration, which I shall tear out ere I bind this; and I am sure that neither he nor she (whether from greater honesty of mind — whether from the lower tone of national taste, as regards the gross and the sufferable) found anything strange, or wrong, or objectionable. In England no author would have printed a book with such a picture — not even Byron. And yet, if I have any skill, this French novelist is twice the worth of Byron as a husband, a father, and a friend. It is odd to make these distinctions.

Alfred de Vigny.

[It was in his third visit to Paris (paid in 1839) that Chorley made the acquaintance of Alfred de Vigny, whom he found exceedingly pleasant, conversable, *tender*, and friendly — perhaps in too *pale a tone* for a man. "But what right have I, who have all my life been laughed at for like paleness, to object to this?" Their conversation chiefly turned upon French drama; one of de Vigny's remarks on which, Chorley notes as chiming in with his own preconceptions, viz., that the Oromanes and Coriolanus of Corneille and Voltaire were *words*, not *characters*, as distinguished from the beings of Shakespeare. On another occasion they talked of Molière, whom de Vigny defended against the charge of want of enthusiasm and passion sometimes brought against him; averring that the passion of "Le Misanthrope" "was none the less passion for its being hooped, petticoated, and wigged."]

Rachel.

[In de Vigny's company Chorley went, for the first time, to see Rachel's performance in Voltaire's "Tancrède." Though very much struck with the remarkable force and emphasis of her declamation, and the propriety of her by-play, he thought her deficient in action, and her attitudes too constantly in *ordonnance*, as though the *pose*, having been once found effective was repeated whenever invention fell short. Her acting on a subsequent occasion as Camille, in Corneille's "Horace," materially altered his estimate of her.] "It is a great triumph, and I am converted to her. In that wonderful scene with the soldier she was sublime; the quivering play of her hands, every fibre listening and yielding and struggling with despair, as one who would deal with it herself, and let it have its way with others; the sinking form, the horror-stricken countenance, were all in the best style of art; to me finer and more affecting than her tremendous taunts to her brother, every word of which was a heart-string broken, and a drop of heart's blood shed against him, to pile on his head 'the mountain of her curse.'

Mlle. Mars.

[On another occasion he was present at a performance by the great actress Mars, then in the golden sunset of her powers and fame.] "The piece was 'Marie.' To be sure, in the epoch of girlhood her physical powers would not second her conception; but as the young wife of the *financier*, all dressed out in diamonds and flowers, and trying to smother an old passion under the semblance of gayety and worldliness, she was admirable. One speech, the great speech wherein, on her old lover reproaching her with coldness, she turns and tells him of the agonies she has endured, the death that is in her heart, was more the language of anguish than anything I ever heard. Then what could exceed her acting in the last act, when, having thought all her trials were on the point of being rewarded, and looking forward to the future with a calm happiness, not so wholly meditative, as to show that all capacity for enjoyment is dead within her, she finds that her lover has transferred his affections — to her daughter! That charming, exquisite, girlish little Anais in the part of the daughter! with a beauty, a freshness, and a bird-like gayety! No: we have nothing like it in England!"

Louis Napoleon.

He used to drive me frequently from Kensington to Hyde Park Corner, when we left Gore House, and would make shrewd remarks, and ask searching questions about subjects concerning which he desired to have information. Mr. Reeve — whose keen interest and close participation in matters concerning foreign politics is no secret — was then in constant relation with M. Guizot, the French ambassador in London. It was on the Saturday before the Prince's attempt was made at Boulogne, that my house-mate, before going out for the day, left with me a note to be taken by our joint servant to the French embassy in Manchester Square. The servant aforesaid, Jonathan . . . . was a rough talkative man, not a little vain of the notoriety of some among our habitual guests.

While I was dressing for dinner, he began to tell me that, during his evening rounds, he had seen in the Mall in St. James's Park two carriages duly appointed, and to them came alone from Carlton Gardens, where Prince Louis was then residing, himself, his faithful friend, Count Persigny, and one or two other gentlemen. Jonathan had stayed to gossip with some of the servants, to whom he was well known, and brought, on their authority, the news that Prince Louis "was going to France to kick up a row." Treating the matter (who would not have done so ?) as a piece of pure fiction, and averse to anything like scandal proceeding from our house, especially in the case of one so delicately circumstanced as Prince Louis, I spoke angrily to the man, and charged him on no account to repeat the absurd tale, least of all at the French embassy, to which he was going that same evening with a note from Reeve. This he promised to do, and kept his promise. My dinner that day was at Gore House, *tête-à-tête* with Lady Blessington. When we were alone at dessert, our talk ran on English servants, and the liberties too frequently taken by them with the names of their masters and their masters' friends. I mentioned what had passed at home, as an instance. She treated the tale as I had done. "Why," she said, "I drove down to Carlton Gardens only yesterday to leave a parcel there, which Prince Louis had undertaken to send for me to Paris by Prince Baiocchi ; he came out and spoke to me." We passed on to something else. When I went home, I told the thing to Reeve, as a good story. After I had left Gore House, Lady Blessington told the same to Count d'Orsay, who got home late, also as an absurdity. Reeve went, according to his note, to breakfast with M. Guizot on the Sunday morning, and, of course, did not trouble the grave man in office with such a piece of nonsense. Monday passed, and Tuesday ; on Wednesday afternoon late, some one rode up to the carriage of Lady Blessington, who was driving in the park, open-mouthed with the news of the attempt at Boulogne, and the arrest of the pretender to the French throne. "Good God ! to be sure," she cried in her eager way, "know all about it ; Chorley told me on Saturday ! "

I have often speculated on the "ifs" and "ands" which might have happened, had we all four not disregarded the affair as a preposterous tale, and had M. Guizot been apprised on the Sunday morning. There have been days in which we might have been all accused, and with a fair show of circum stantial evidence, of complicity in the treason.

During the time when Prince Louis was imprisoned in Ham, by the failure of his attempt, covered with ridicule, I was in occasional communication with him, with the view of beguiling his hours of captivity, and heard of him constantly —from him more than once. When his "Idées Napoléon-iennes," written in his dungeon, were to be published by Colburn, I was invited, with his concurrence, to translate the book into English; and a set of proofs, corrected by himself, was sent me. I did not accept the task, mainly because I have never put my hand to a task of the kind, without some special knowledge of that which I professed to handle. For the same reason, whatever have been my prejudices or predilections, on yet stronger grounds, I would never take service as a political journalist; such subjects are too grave ones to be undertaken merely as the means of gaining a livelihood. Whether right or wrong, I kept the proofs of the book by me for a long time, and was very near being brought into trouble by them, as under.

I was going into France, before the Prince escaped from Ham, and while making the hasty provisions for my journey, totally overlooked the fact that my writing-book contained some of the sheets of this perilous production, annotated by the writer. Fortunately, the *douanier* at Calais knew my face, and did not open my bundle of travelling wares. I destroyed the proofs, not conceiving that one day they might become a literary curiosity, no matter what was the intrinsic poorness of the work.

When Prince Louis made his escape from Ham, I was one of the first persons whom he called on; and it seems as if it were but yesterday that he told me, from one of my easy-chairs, the particulars of the manner of his deliverance, too well known to the world for the tale to be told again here. To the last days of his residence in England, he continued to show a recollection of the very trifling services I could render him, such as has not been the rule with others on an equality with myself, to whom chance has enabled me to give important assistance at critical junctures of their lives.

The Misses Berry.

Horace Walpole's Miss Berrys. What luck to have met with them! They are more like one's notion of ancient Frenchwomen than anything I have ever seen; rouged, with the remains of some beauty, managing large fans like the Flirtillas, etc., etc., of Ranelagh, and besetting Macready about the womanly proprieties of the character of Pauline in the "Lady of Lyons," till one thought of the "Critique de l'Ecole des Femmes." It is not often that I have heard anything so brilliant and amusing.

When that most charming of modern antique books, Landor's "Pericles and Aspasia," appeared, subsequently to his "Gebir," his "Imaginary Conversations," and even (I think) his "Examination of Shakspeare," on his name being passed round in their circle by some enterprising guest, Miss Berry said, — "Mr. Landor? What has he written?"

Southey.

I never met any literary man who so thoroughly answered my expectations as Southey. His face is at once shrewd, thoughtful, and quick, if not irritable, in its expression; a singular deficiency of space in its lower portion, but no deficiency of feature or expression; his manner cold, but still; in conversation, bland and gentle, and not nearly so dogmatic as his writings would lead one to imagine. Talking, and talking well, a good deal about America.

He was speaking of Miss Martineau patiently, but without respect, describing her as "talking more glibly than any woman he had ever seen, and with such a notion of her own infallibility." I was more agreeably impressed by Southey than I have, for a long time, been by any stranger.

Mr. and Mrs. Haynes Bayly.

Till I saw them, I never understood the full force of the reproach of *Bath fashion;* tawdry, airy, sentimental, vulgar; he with a pen-and-red-ink complexion, and a hyacinthine Romeo wig, dancing, and behaving prettily to all the little girls in the room; she in an old French dress, rouged, *fade*, haggard: what a pair of shabby old butterflies!

Miss Sedgwick.

She is decidedly the pleasantest American woman I have ever seen, with more of a turn for humor, and less American sectarianism. The twang, to be sure, there is in plenty; and the toilette is the dowdiness (not the finery) of the backwoods; but then she is lively, kind, heart-warm; and I feel somehow or other, almost on friendly terms with her, though I never spoke more than twenty consecutive words to her.

Miss Sedgwick [1] has been returning the compliment of all English journalists, by putting us all round on paper to a degree which is too bad. She asked, it seems, poor dear Miss Mitford's servants what wages they received, and the like; and, I hear, has written that which is likely most sadly to compromise some of the Italian refugees in America, who were negotiating with the Austrian Government for a restoration to their families. I liked her so well in private, as an honest-minded, simple-mannered, cultivated woman, that I am really more vexed than there is any occasion for. I fear the next cage of Transatlantic birds will not run much chance of being very liberally dinnered and soirêed here; only every thing passes off like a nine-days' wonder!

Mrs. Browning.

Mrs. Browning and her writings claim affectionate commemoration on the part of those who knew her personally, and consider the high place she must ever hold among the recognized poetesses of this country. In the first class only

[1] In a volume of "Letters."

five can be named — Joanna Baillie and Miss Mitford, in right of their tragedies (the former, too, one of Great Britain's most exquisite lyrists); Mrs. Hemans, the musical, high-hearted, and impassioned; and herself, less complete in execution, it may be, than the three women of genius already named, but bolder in imagination and deeper in learning, with a wider (and wilder) flow of inspiration than any of those with whom she is here classed. She has a place of her own — rare, noble, daring, and pure beyond reproach — in the Golden Book of gifted women. There has been only one since, Adelaide Anne Procter, less ambitious, perhaps, than her predecessors, but, as a lyrist, more complete, more delicate, not less original therefore, than any among them, whose verses have a beauty and a finish that owe nothing to any model.

It must be at least thirty years ago that I was startled by a new pleasure — a published ballad, signed, I think, with only initials — in "The New Monthly Magazine" — "The Romaunt of Margret." I got it by heart: if I copied it once, I copied it ten times, and must have made myself a nuisance, as immature enthusiasts are apt to do, by talking of it, in season and out of season, as an appearance of a strange, seizing, original genius. I was doubted and put aside accordingly, in obedience to English law and usage, which (as it were) make us set our teeth and lean our backs against the door whenever the same is to be opened to a real novelty. The chance, however, that brought me to the knowledge of that munificent man and indulgent friend, John Kenyon, Miss Barrett's relative, brought me also the privilege of writing to one whom I so sincerely admired, and of being on the list of those to whom she was willing to write.

In those days, no other intercourse was possible; for she was an invalid — thought to be a hopeless one — as such, not to be intruded on (were the candidates as persevering, gifted, and charming as the American "interviewers"), save by a very few old friends.

Her letters ought to be published. In power, versatility,

liveliness, and *finesse;* in perfect originality of glance, and vigor of grasp at every topic of the hour; in their enthusiastic preferences, prejudices, and inconsistencies, I have never met with any, written by men or by women, more brilliant, spontaneous, and characteristic. This was *her* form of conversation. I have never done a duty more against the grain than in restoring those addressed to me to their rightful possessor — the true poet whom she married, after an intimacy suspected by none save a very few, under circumstances of no ordinary romance, and in marrying whom she secured for the residue of her life an emancipation from prison and an amount of happiness delightful to think of, as falling to the lot of one who, from a darkened chamber, had still exercised such a power of delighting others. It was more like a fairy tale than anything in real life I have ever known, to read, one morning, in the papers, of her marriage with the author of "Paracelsus," and to learn, in the course of the day, that not only was she married, but that she was absolutely on her way to Italy. The energy and resolution implied were amazing on the part of one who had long, as her own poems tell us, resigned herself to lie down and die. I cannot recollect when I have been more moved and excited by any surprise, beyond the circle of my immediate hopes and fears.

Every letter of hers from Florence told me of one prospect after another brightening, of one hope after another fulfilled — told with a piquant originality and prejudice not to be overstated nor under-praised.

I never met Mrs. Browning face to face till after her return to England. The time is too recent for me to tell *how* we met — as correspondents who had become friends. And her indulgent friendship never failed me to the last, in spite of serious differences of opinion concerning a matter which she took terribly to heart — the strange, weird question of mesmerism, including *clairvoyance.* To the marvels of these two *phenomena* (admitting both as incomplete discoveries) she lent an ear as credulous as her trust was sincere and her heart high-minded. But with women far more experienced in falsity than one so noble and one who had been so secluded from the world as herself, after they have once crossed the threshold, there is seldom chance of after-retreat. Only, they become bewildered by their tenacious notions of loyalty. It is over these very best and most generous of their sex that impostors have the most power. They are no matches, as men are, for those miserable creatures who creep about with insinuating manners, and would pass off legerdemain, the tricks of cup and ball, for real, portentous discoveries.

I have never seen one more nobly simple, more entirely guiltless of the feminine propensity of talking for effect, more earnest in assertion, more gentle yet pertinacious in difference, than she was. Like all whose early nurture has chiefly been from books, she had a child's curiosity regarding the life beyond her books, co-existing with opinions accepted as certainties concerning things of which (even with the intuition of genius) she could know little. She was at once forbearing and dogmatic, willing to accept differences, resolute to admit no argument; without any more practical knowledge of social life than a nun might have, when, after long years, she emerged from her cloister and her shroud. How she used her experiences as a great poetess, is to be felt and is evidenced in her "Aurora Leigh," after every allowance has been made for an extreme fearlessness in certain passages of the story and forms of expression, and that want of finish in execution with which almost all her efforts are chargeable.

The success of "Aurora Leigh" (with all its drawbacks) was immediate, wide, and, I conceive, is one likely to last. The noble and impassioned passages which printed themselves on memory as I hurried through the tale, carried along by its deep interest, the brilliancy of allusion, the felicity of description, separate it from any effort of the kind which I could name. Those who care for comparison may come to something like a right appreciation of this poem, on comparing it with efforts in the same form by M. de Lamartine, or an English novel in verse which followed it, by the accomplished but imitative author of "Lucille." In Mrs. Browning's ballad poems, the same preëminence in fantasy may be ascribed to her. I refer to the "Rhyme of the Duchess May," "The Brown Rosarie," "The Romaunt of the Page," "Lady Geraldine's Courtship," and "Bertha in the Lane." It is idle to talk of halting tones and occasional platitudes (what fertile writer has been exempt from them?), when so much vigor and variety are to be counted on the other side of the question. Some of Mrs. Browning's minor lyrics can hardly be exceeded in beauty and tenderness. The verse from one entitled "Sleeping and Watching," which begins,

"And God knows, who sees us twain,"

has a pathos which will speak to every one who has had experience in the darkened chambers of life.

Sir William Molesworth.

Among my betters, with whom it has been always my desire and my good fortune to live, I have known no man, as regards heart, head, and capacity, superior to Sir William Molesworth. Our acquaintance was strangely made; but it ripened into what I have a right to call a friendship, which lasted to the end of his life. That he trusted me I have good reason to know; and howsoever wide apart our pursuits were (one alone excepted — love of flowers and trees), I was never by him made to feel the inferiority of my flimsy knowledge to his massive command of the greatest subjects which can engage a serious man's attention. I was, from first to last, at ease when I was with him, and have not to remember a single depreciating word or doubtful look on his part.

Sir William Molesworth was in no respect brilliant, but earnest; perfect in mastery over every subject he took in hand, open to any testimony which interfered with his own views; a man of a high and truthful nature, under the cover of whose deeds and strong opinions, call them prejudices, the least gifted of those whom he met and harbored must have felt safe. He was just rather than habitually generous; but when he chose to be generous, he was munificent, and without regard to his good deeds being blazoned. He was well aware of his own value, as every sincere man must be who has any value at all; but in private life, never was any great man less self-asserting. He seemed to love to rest in it by way of enjoyment, not to show shows or to make speeches, on the strength of his position as a man of letters or a statesman.

It is curious to recall how, as a young leader in the Radical party, wealthy to boot, and with an honorable family name and estate, Sir William Molesworth was pursued by squadrons of strong-minded women, or terrible mothers, "shallow-hearted" (as Tennyson sings), having daughters to whom the name, and the fame, and the position of his wife would have been a promotion little short of heavenly advancement on earth. It is excellent to recollect how quietly he put aside everything like control or intrigue or suggestion; and, by choosing for himself, secured as complete a happiness for two married people as the world has ever seen. This could not have been more emphatically attested than by his testamentary dispositions.

A deliberation and persistence, not to say heaviness of nature, were among his remarkable characteristics, and had no small share in his success. Whatever he attempted to do he did thoroughly; let the thing be ever so great or ever so small, the shaping of a course of political service, the gathering together testimony as regarded Colonial affairs, in which field of action he has never been replaced, the fulfillment of a task no less dry than the editing of the philosophical works of Hobbes of Malmesbury, which called down on him that rancorous abuse of his opinions, then too fiercely used against all those suspected of Liberal heresies by the high Tory party—all that he did was thoroughly done. This peculiar characteristic was carried out to the most trifling occupation. I have seen him for a couple of hours absorbed in the solving of a chess problem; or in disentangling a skein of silk, while his mind was steadily pursuing some train of thought and speculation. But he never used his accuracy as an engine of oppression, as meaner men are too apt to do. When, at last, his worth and his weight could be no longer overlooked, and he entered the Ministry as responsible for the "Woods and Forests," the question of a new National Gallery was on the carpet. He was resolute not to move in it till he was in possession of the fullest information as to the merits and demerits of foreign picture-galleries. How carefully he received, and how patiently he sifted this, I am in case to record. He gathered specifications, working plans, and estimates of what had been the cost, of what was the nature, of what the success, of the great European establishments of the kind, and was preparing to present the result of his comparisons to the nation in a tangible form, when changes occurred in our administration, and he was promoted to the Secretaryship of the Colonies. According to certain established principles of English policy and private judgment, which imply English destructive waste at the expense of public money, his successor, as small as he was a great man, swept away all the fruits of his care and provision into some unseen official closet, where, probably, they may be mouldering at this day, and began anew a series of inquiries and perquisitions, just as if the subject was still a virgin subject. *Corollary.*—We have no National Gallery, save a building originally penurious and inefficiently patched up, even to this present day.

From all abominable waste like this, the experience and counsel of such men as Sir William Molesworth—were there many such—might have protected this country. But the name of such is *not* legion. When he came to be promoted, as was inevitable, to his legitimate sphere of action, as Colonial Secretary, the frame, by nature not a healthy one, was worn out. He had a very few days of consciousness of reward, due to a power and probity as priceless as they are uncommon, and died peacefully, with perfect consciousness that he was dying.

His sense of humor was not keen, but no man delighted in such quaint stories and conundrums as he seized and relished more thoroughly than himself. As has been often the case, he took a positive pleasure in hearing the same tale or jest told over and over again, let him know it ever so well by heart. He would begin it wrong, as children do, with the intention of hearing it corrected. He rarely produced or paraded the results of his grave thought and deep reading; but when he *did* speak, he was apt to close the question in debate.

It was curious to observe how one so mathematical, and so sparingly endowed with the poetic faculty of appreciation, had so strong a tendency to occupy himself with those recondite and mysterious subjects regarding which no clear conclusion can be arrived at. He had a theory of dreams of his own, which, I think, he put forward in the "Westminster Review" during his brief proprietorship of that periodical. He was patient and clear in investigating the pretensions of mesmerism, separating the phenomena of cataleptic sleep from those of pretended *clairvoyance*, with that resolution to sift evidence, and to discriminate betwixt truth and falsity, which the more mercurial and imaginative seldom retain. He was a willing and diligent reader of foreign novels. Without an atom of taste for music, or care about the drama above melodrama, he endured both, in indulgence to other persons, but not very willingly. It is comical to recall how, after the first performance of "Le Prophète," he never again entered his own opera box; driven thence, he said (and, I suspect, not averse to the excuse), by the psalmody of the Three Anabaptists!

But his real enjoyments, as apart from the pleasurable cares of ambition, were at home in Cornwall, in the place which he had decorated and beautified with the hand of a master.[1] The lovely Italian garden before his house, the plantations so choicely adjusted, the long descending avenue, flanked by a collection of rare firs and evergreens only equaled by those of the Pinetum at Dropmore; the hot-houses, with their strange, weird-looking orchidaceous plants, were a perpetual source of pleasure to him — the pleasure belonging to rich and accurate knowledge. He knew every tree he had set; the quickness of its growth and its chances of health or disease were duly noted by him in his garden diary; and his deliberate afternoon walks through his beautiful grounds were

[1] Pencarrow.

among his pleasantest solitary hours of the day — a whole some relief from the coil and cumber of state measures and treaties, the verbiage of blue-books to be fathomed, and the strong excitements of political ambition. I have often and again thus walked with him, and heard him talk — a pleasure and a privilege not to be forgotten. His indulgence and regard for me are among the most precious of my recollections. I must change more than I hope I ever shall before I cease to be aware of their distinction and their value.

THOMAS CAMPBELL.

Campbell was a little man, with a shrewd eye, and a sort of pedagoguish, *parboiled* voice ; plenty to say for himself, especially about other people, and not restrained from saying whatever seemed good to him by any caution ; speaking with a violent antipathy of Theodore Hook (by the way, the *new* editor of the " New Monthly Magazine "), and yet not more violently than the latter deserves ; dressing up his good stories. and looking about him while he *did them*, with the unmistakable air of a diner-out, which is so amusing — more amusing, by the way, than agreeable. To myself he was very complaisant.

It would be hard to name an English poet of greater refinement and sweetness, alternating with outbreaks of the most manly vigor and high heroic spirit, than Thomas Campbell. It would be equally hard to name an author of any country whose personality was more entirely at variance with his poetry than his — at least, during the second half of his life. A man, be his habits what they may, does not deteriorate uniformly and steadily from every promise and sign of grace which he may have shown in earlier years, without showing, from time to time, some flashes of the olden brightness, let them be ever so few and far between. What I saw and knew of Campbell, at least, made it very hard to credit the possibility of there having been days much better essentially. If such had been the case, his latter state was not one so much of enfeeblement as of metamorphosis — of what was pure having become gross — of what was intellectual and appreciative losing itself in a prosy and commonplace stupidity.

I first heard of him when he was delivering his lectures on Poetry at Liverpool, more than forty years ago. The extent to which these were overrated, in consequence of the beauty, power, and finish of the poet's poetry, only revealed itself when the poet's prose came to be published. They are as completely forgotten to-day as if they had never been — the fate, perhaps, of all lectures ; but Campbell was prodigiously lionized in circles which, I have always felt, were too prone to lionize. How all ease, grace, and nature of intercourse are destroyed by the extravagance of social idolatry ; how talk for effect must be the consequence of

"Wonder with a foolish face of praise,"

have been truths as clear as day to me, ever since I was in a case to observe and compare. Then, I could but stare, as a very young boy, and remark how the best, and most refined, and most beautiful of men and women laid themselves at the lecturer's feet. Of himself, at that time, I recollect nothing ; but he must have had something, in show, at least, better to offer in return than the gifts and graces displayed by him later in London — the paltry conversation, when it was not coarsened by convivial excesses to a point which would not to-day be endured, were the poet thrice as godlike as he was. In fact, as years went on, Campbell slipped out of society as steadily as though he had been a false prophet and not the author of "The Pleasures of Hope," "Hohenlinden," "The Battle of the Baltic," "Ye Mariners of England," "The Exile of Erin," "O'Conner's Child," and "The Last Man" — poems which will endure so long as a single lover of imperishable thought, feeling, and fancy, enshrined in most musical verse, shall be left in England. Their spell is strong now, even in this age of jargon, this time when "whitings' eyes" by so many are permitted to pass as "pearls."

He was my neighbor in Victoria Square, Pimlico, during the last years passed by him in England, and was willing to bestow much of his leisure on a poetaster so much younger a man as I was. I can hardly describe how painful it was to be sought by one whose notice should have been such an honor, but whom it was hardly possible for youthful fastidiousness and want of charity to endure as a companion. It was woeful, weary work, unredeemed, so far as I recollect, by one passing flash of the spirit which had shone with such brilliancy and beauty in the verse; and great was the relief when he withdrew from London, — to die, in all but utter neglect, at Boulogne.

One friend, however, Campbell retained, who believed in and ministered to him till the end came — the friend, as I have grateful reason to commemorate, of many more obscure literary men — Dr. Beattie, himself an author of modest pretensions, and who, in the fullness of sincere admiration, wrote the only English biography of the poet which has appeared. It must not be forgotten, when writing about Campbell, that the poet of "The Pleasures of Hope," like the poet of "The Pleasures of Memory," was from first to last fond of children. So it should be with those alike who look forward or look back.

Professor Bendemann.

Bendemann is reputed to be the first of German modern artists. He has a thin face, of a sweet and melancholy expression, large, intense thoughtful eyes, of a painter's keenness and poetry — a countenance not wholly unlike Weber's in its pattern, with mild, gentlemanly manners. I found him in his *atelier* at the great hall of the palace, which he has been employed to decorate with frescoes. He was at work on a very high scaffolding, without a cravat, in a blue blouse, and with a long pipe. I had an exceedingly pleasant half hour of conversation with him, though I could not, I fear, come far enough upon his own ground to be acceptable to him; and I will never talk more than I understand There is a sort of frieze in compartments running round the room, which he is filling with a series of paintings imaging the progress of human life, beginning with the Paradise of Nature, when there was no death, and ending with the Paradise of Redemption, when life eternal shall be restored, and between the two, embracing the ages of man from the cradle to the grave. Some of these were not complete, but those which were, were very beautiful — a dance of children, for instance, and a group representing a wedding, all youth and joy, and motion and hope. Besides this, he showed me two very noble cartoons of single figures of sages, lawgivers, etc., with which he is going to surround the hall. Zoroaster and Solomon were the subjects. The one, with the Magian censer in his hand, was very grand and Chaldaic and imposing, and, if forcibly wrought out, will make the breath stop of those who look at it. But dare I say that it is this very want of forcible working-out which makes the long step between the modern Germans and the great ancients whom they so nobly aspire to approach? They make "shadows of beauty, shadows of power;" the others called up real kings and apostles, and the real Divinity who needs but touch the hills to make them smoke! I know next to nothing of the works of modern German painters; but the few I have seen appear to me, with all their beauty of drawing and sentiment, to want *body*. I like Bendemann very much. He was very patient with my platitudes; and I liked him, who bears the reputation of being among the first painters, telling me that Kaulbach, of Munich, was their first man, and speaking of his works with such enthusiasm.

KAULBACH.

He is a very thin man, with a little long, glossy, black hair smoothed over his forehead, with deep, tender, shining, humorous eyes. In his manner a mixture of simplicity, friendliness, fun, and enthusiasm. He was painting a man handsomer than himself, but not so much of a genius. Several magnificent full-length portraits were about; one of a falconer. The one on which he was occupied was the chief of a company of Lanz-knechts. Their originals were young artists who, with their wives, had, last winter, appeared to the number of two hundred in a pageant at the theatre, on the return of Prince Max; and the king had commanded three of their portraits for Schleissheim. "After all," said Kaulbach, "it was an honor to paint such fine fellows." One that was finished struck me more than any modern portrait I have ever seen; the full-length of a knight, with sanguine complexion and red hair; a metal bonnet on the head, a cuirass, a scarlet dress slashed with white, and a gorgeous furred mantle. When Kaulbach drew up the blind, and let in the light upon it, it seemed to float out of the canvas with its force and brilliancy. We saw some illustrations to "Faust," which I did not like. They were clever, but grim and ungraceful compared with those by Retszch — and yet the one has no honor here! We saw, too, three admirable designs for a new edition of "Reinecke der Fuchs." But the most remarkable picture of all was an enormous cartoon of the Destruction of Jerusalem. Above are the three prophets watching the angels, who are sounding the trumpets and pouring out the vials of wrath at their feet — noble winged figures of a superb Apocalyptic sublimity. In the centre, to the left, the Jews, in all the agonies of terror, distress, famine, dissension, murder, and blasphemy; the degrees being indicated by a mother entreated of her children, the high-priest about to slay himself, and the Wandering Jew spurred on his way by fiends above his head — the last free Israelite who will issue from that scene. To the extreme left, Titus riding calmly into the city with an air of solemn astonishment at the frenzy around him, and the portents which attend his conquest. The most magnificent subject of all time, done (may we not say it?) full justice to. All the effete and pedantic efforts which good King Louis has called forth are assuredly well bestowed, if they have formed and fostered a school of Art of which such a noble work was the sole result.

Nathaniel Hawthorne.

[For the creative genius of Hawthorne, Chorley had always entertained the highest admiration, and was proud, as he had a right to be, of having been the first English critic who drew attention to its manifestation in the "Twice-Told Tales." The novelist's subsequent works had received his lavish praise, both in public and private; especially the "Scarlet Letter," which he commended to a friend at Liverpool as "the most powerful and most painful story of modern times — the only tale in its argument in which the *purity* overtops the *passion*. It has struck me prodigiously; and I think will end in taking a very remarkable place among stories of its quality." This impression of Hawthorne's power was confirmed by the personal intercourse with him elsewhere referred to, the terms of which were extremely cordial. Chorley was therefore disappointed, when a new work by Hawthorne was published soon after their acquaintance had been established, to find himself unable to render it as high a tribute as he had rendered to its predecessors. The shortcomings of "Transformation" were accordingly criticised in the "Athenæum" of March 3d, 1860, with some keenness; ample praise being accorded to its subtlety and beauty, but a marked stress laid upon the poverty of invention which the author had shown in repeating the types of his former fictions: Hilda, for example, being "own cousin" to Phœbe in the "House of the Seven Gables." Other faults, too, were found, whether justly or unjustly matters little, since it was well worth being mistaken to be set right so charmingly. It will be understood that the following letters were written on the same sheet; Mrs. Hawthorne occupying all but the last leaf, which was reserved for her husband.]

"My dear Mr. Chorley,

"Why do you run with your fine lance directly into the face of Hilda? You were so fierce and wrathful at being shut out from the mysteries (for which we are all disappointed), that you struck in your spurs and plunged with your visor down. For indeed and in truth Hilda is not Phœbe, no more than a wild rose is a calla lily. They are alike only in purity and innocence; and I am sure you will see this whenever you read the romance a second time. I am very much grieved that *Mr. Chorley* should seem not to be nicely discriminating; for what are we to do in that case? The artistic, pensive, reserved, contemplative, delicately appreciative Hilda can in no wise be related to the enchanting little housewife, whose energy, radiance, and eglantine sweetness fill her daily homely duties with joy, animation, and fragrance. Tell me, then, is it not so? I utterly protest against being supposed partial because I am Mrs. Hawthorne. But it is so very naughty of you to demolish this new growth in such a hurry, that I cannot help a disclaimer; and I am so sure of your friendliness and largeness, that I am not in the least afraid. You took all the fright out of me by that exquisite, gem-like, æsthetic dinner and tea that you gave us at the fairiest of houses last summer. It was a prettier and more *mignonne* thing than I thought could happen in London; so safe, and so quiet, and so very satisfactory, with the light of thought playing all about. I have a good deal of fight left in me still about Kenyon, and the 'of course' union of Kenyon and Hilda; but I will not say more, except that Mr. Hawthorne had no idea that they were destined for each other. Mr. Hawthorne is driven by his Muse, but does not drive her; and I have known him to be in inextricable doubt in the midst of a book or sketch as to its probable issue, waiting upon the Muse for the rounding in of the sphere which every work of true art is. I am surprised to find that Mr. Hawthorne was so absorbed in Italy that he had no idea that the story, as such, was interesting! and, therefore, is somewhat absolved from having ruthlessly 'excited our interest to voracity.'

"We are much troubled that you have been suffering this winter. We also have had a great deal of illness, and I am only just lifting up my head after seven weeks of serious struggle with acute bronchitis. I dare say you are laughing (gently) at my explosion of small muskets. But I feel more comfortable now I have discharged a little of my opposition.

"With sincere regard, I am, dear Mr. Chorley, yours,

"SOPHIA HAWTHORNE.

"Leamington, March 5th, 1860.
"21 Bath Street."

"DEAR MR. CHORLEY, —

"You see how fortunate I am in having a critic close at hand, whose favorable verdict consoles me for any lack of appreciation in other quarters. Really, I think you were wrong in assaulting the individuality of my poor Hilda. If her portrait bears any resemblance to that of Phœbe, it must be the fault of my mannerism as a painter. But I thank you for the kind spirit of your notice; and if you had found ten times as much fault, you are amply entitled to do so, by the quantity of generous praise heretofore bestowed.

"Sincerely yours,

"NATH. HAWTHORNE.

"21 Bath Street, Leamington."

March, 1870. — At the instant of closing this chapter of recollections I read of the death of the widow of the greatest and choicest author of fiction whom America has till now produced, Nathaniel Hawthorne. This sets me free to write concerning that singular original man what I know and have seen of him in England.

From the first appearance, in an American magazine, of those delicious and individual stories, subsequently collected and given forth as "Twice Told Tales," it was evident that something as exquisite as it was finished was added to the world's stores of fiction. I am bold to say that there could not be two opinions among open-minded persons, be the English ever so "slow to move" (as the author of "De Vere" has it). They were quicker, however, in Hawthorne's case than they were in America. But it is one of my greatest pleasures, as a journalist, to recollect that I was the first who had the honor of calling attention to these tales when they appeared in the form of periodical articles. What Hawthorne's reputation has since grown into — a universal fame — I need not recount. From the first, I followed its growth at a distance, step by step, with the pleasure which one has of seeing dawn brightening into day, and day ripening into noon, without the slightest idea that I should ever see or ever be known to him. That I wished to form some idea of the man, as distinct from the author, is no less true. The sole idea I could "realize" (as the Americans say) was one of his invincible shyness. No one had seen him, or met him, or known him; so ran the legend. It was a clear case of mystery, in its way, I have since come to think, as fondly promoted and cherished by the romancer as that of the "Great Unknown."

There is small need to recall how, subsequently, appeared a second miscellany, "Mosses from an old Manse" (among other legends, containing that ghastliest of stories, "Rapaccini's Daughter"), then "The Scarlet Letter," and the yet more original "House of Seven Gables," "The Blithedale Romance," and, lastly, "Transformation." Such works of art as these, like all real creations, *must* make their way. It was then with no common interest I heard that his own country, by way of paying due honor to Hawthorne, was doing its utmost for him by appointing him to the consulate at Liverpool. At the same time it was told me that, on accepting the appointment, he inquired whether the American consul would, *ex officio*, be obliged to talk much, and on being told *not*, in reply, laconically said, "Thank God!"

When I heard that Hawthorne was to live at Liverpool as American consul, it seemed clear that, with some knowledge of the best, most liberal, and most delicately-minded of those who then, as now, dispensed public hospitality and private kindliness in the town, I might justifiably write to him, and refer him to them, in case he should stand in need of society and private sympathy, totally apart from anything like the tinseled folly of *lionism*. I did so, and received no answer to my letter. Hawthorne established himself, as his Memoirs have told us, at Rock Ferry, in Cheshire, enjoyed as much as he cared to enjoy, and afterwards retired into that sulky, suspicious mood (of a consul taking pay?) which befits a misunderstood hero. To myself, and those to whom I sent him, he responded by neither "look, word, nor sign."

After some natural disappointment, I naturally came to forget the man, and to think only of his admirable books. It was, then, with surprise that, some years later, I received a note from a boarding-house in Golden Square, in which Hawthorne announced his arrival in London, and his *great* desire to see me before he returned home ("as one," *etc.*, *etc.*, *etcetera*) I answered this in person, and found, what I might have been sure of, a most genial and original man, full of life, full of humor, in no respect shy. He agreed at once to pass a day with me. I gave him the option of a party or no party. He chose the latter alternative. A pleasanter day than the one in question is not in my "Golden Book." I think I have never heard any one, save my honored friend Carlyle, laugh so heartily as did Hawthorne. It is generally a nervous business to receive those to whom one has long looked up; but it was not the least so in his case. The impression I received was one of a man genial, and not over sensitive, even when we could make merry on the subject of national differences and susceptibilities.

This experience, it may well be believed, has made me read with an amazement almost approaching distress the book Hawthorne published on his return home, and, later, the selections from his manuscript journals, put forward by his widow. It is hard to conceive the existence of so much pettishness in a man so great and real; of such a resolution to brood over fancied slights and strange formalities, yet, withal, to generalize so widely on such narrow premises; of such vulgarity in one who had written for the public so exquisitely. It is difficult to accept such a writer's criticisms on "the steaks and sirloins" of English ladies. I still remember Hester Prynne and Pearl, in the "Scarlet Letter," and Phœbe and Hepzibah, in the "House of the Seven Gables," and ask myself how far the case in point proves the adage that there is nothing so essentially nasty as refinement. The tone of these English journals is as small and peevish as if their writer had been thwarted and overlooked, instead of waited on by hearty offers of service, which in most cases were declined almost as persistently as if they had been so many affronts. A more puzzling case of inconsistency and duality has never come before me.

Spiritualism.

I have always, on principle, resisted swelling the crowd of those, professedly anxious to wait on experiments, in reality hungerers and thirsters after "sensation;" the more since, when the imagination is once engaged, those as nervous as myself may well mistrust that which by way of term is so largely abused — "the evidence of the senses." What do our keenest powers of observation avail, when they are brought to bear on the legerdemain of a Robert Houdin, a Bosco (that distasteful, fat old Italian, who executed his wonders by the aid of hands ending arms naked to the shoulder)? What, still more, when they attempt to unravel the sorceries of such a conjuror as the Chevalier de Caston — the man who could name the cards which distant persons had silently taken from an unbroken pack, with his back turned and blindfolded, and at the distance of a drawing-room and a half? This, further, I saw him do. There were three of us sitting on an ottoman in the front room, he, as I have said, with his back to us, and thoroughly blindfolded. Two opaque porcelain slates, to all appearance entirely new, were brought. On one of these, each of the three wrote, in pencil, a question, without uttering a word. The slates were laid face to face, and bound together with a broad ribbon, thus totally clear of transparency. My question was, in French, "What was the color of Cleopatra's hair?" I forget the other two. The Chevalier put his hands behind his chair. I placed the slates so bound in the two hands. He retained them a moment without stirring or turning, and to my amazement, said, "Cleopatra dyed her hair, so wore all colors." The other two questions, which I have forgotten, were no less pertinently and explicitly answered. Now, even on the theory of complicitly, it would be by no means easy to explain this feat. I can only say that I am satisfied I have recounted it accurately.[1]

When one Alexis was here, who was guarantied to read

[1] This Chevalier de Caston, by the way, was the only professor of his art who succeeded in puzzling Charles Dickens, himself a consummate and experienced conjuror.

everything, no matter how far off, however hermetically sealed up,[1] a friend of mine called on his way to a *séance* — no willing co-juggler with Alexis, I am persuaded, but leaning towards his marvels. He was anxious that I should bear him company. I declined, on the argument I have stated. "Well," said he, "what *would* satisfy you?" Said I, "Supposing I were to write an odd word — such a one as 'orchestra' — and seal it, and satisfy myself that no one could read it without breaking the seal, and be equally satisfied that no one would mention it who was honestly disposed" — "Well?" "Well, then, *if* it was read, I should say the guess was a good one — nothing more." "Let us try." I went into an adjoining room for writing materials, and thought, as an odd word, of "Pondicherry." I wrote down this; I satisfied my eyes that no one could read it unless it was tampered with. It was signed, sealed and delivered. I am, at this day of writing, as satisfied of my friend's honor as I am of my own. He was to come back to dine with me and to report what had happened. He did come back, scared considerably, but in no respect disabused. "Well," said I, "did he read my note?" "Oh, yes, immediately; but he read it wrong. He read *orchestra*." That my friend may have whispered, "Chorley's test-word" into some ear can hardly be doubted by those who are, as Hood says, "with small belief encumbered;" but, of his honest self he took the performance as a brilliant illustration of *thought-reading*.

Almost enough of these pitiful matters. One more experience, however, is not unworthy of being told, as showing how the agitation was kept up, and, when denounced, how those denouncing it were treated. I was in the house of an old friend given to divers amusements and sensations, who, one evening, having a society rather credulous, mesmeric, and supernaturally disposed around her, bethought herself, by way of the evening's amusement, "to turn tables;" if rappings came, so much the better. I was about to leave, in the full-

[1] Yet the reading of the number of the historical bank note of £1,000, payable to him who could pronounce it, has never, I believe, been accomplished.

ness, or emptiness (which ?) of my unbelief, when I was especially asked to remain and be convinced. I felt that inquiry was impossible, and I said so; but in answer I was asked, "What form of inquiry would satisfy me? If I would stay, I might inquire to the utmost." The answer was, a row of candles on the floor and my seat underneath the table. All this was cordially, kindly granted to the unbeliever, who had been persuaded to stay. Down sat the believers; almost on the floor sat the unbeliever. The above made a chain of hands; the low man watched their feet. The table, which I am assured bore a fair reputation among wooden oracles, was steadfast not to stir. I sat, and they sat, and we sat for nearly a good half-hour. (Happily, the abominable pretext at a prayer had been omitted.) At length, the eight believers became tired; and the most enthusiastic among them broke up the *séance* in "a temper." "There can be no experiments," said he, "where an infidel spirit prevails." And so I went forth, branded as a "spoil-sport;" and, as such, in a certain world, have never recovered the place before that time allowed me.

Long live legerdemain as a useless combination of ingenuity, memory, and mechanical appliances — owned as such! But when, after seeing its perfect marvels, exhibited by way of dramatic show and paid for by money, one is invited and expected to believe in revelations which have never told one secret — in oracles from the dead, the best of which amount to the sweet spring saying, "Grass is green" — it is not wholly unnatural that with some, be they ever so prosaic, be they ever so imaginative, the gorge *will* rise, and the dogmatism (it may be) become strong, if only because it is the inevitable descendant of the superstition. To play with the deepest and most sacred mysteries of the heart and brain, of love beyond the grave, of that yearning affection which takes a thousand shapes when distance and suspense divide it from its object, is a fearful and unholy work. If this dreary chapter, which expresses almost the sincerest of convictions that can influence a man towards the decline of his life, can make any one disposed to tamper with "wandering thoughts and vain imaginations" consider, without cant or pedantry, the argument endeavored to be illustrated, it will not have been written in vain.

Chorley at Gad's Hill.

"Mr. Chorley used to come constantly to Gad's Hill, used often to invite himself, and was always most welcome. People who were in the habit of seeing him only in London would hardly have known him at Gad's Hill, I think. He was a brighter and younger being altogether there. He would be down punctually to breakfast by nine o'clock, very often earlier; would occupy himself writing, or reading, etc., all the morning, and, after luncheon, set off for a long walk with my father. I remember one day our going for a picnic a long way off; some of our party driving, some walking. When we started to return, we all took it for granted that Mr. Chorley would drive. But my father walking, *he* walked too. It was a hot summer's day, and they did eighteen miles — walking, as my father always did, at a good pace; and Mr. Chorley came down to dinner as bright and as fresh as possible. This sort of thing for most men, is of course, no matter for surprise; but to those who knew Mr. Chorley, and his apparently weak *physique*, it was quite wonderful to see how much he could do. He was always ready for any game, charade, or impromptu amusement of any sort and was capital at it. One Christmas my father proposed, quite suddenly, that we should have some charades. They were to be in dumb pantomine, and Mr. Chorley was to play the piano. He immediately began to practice music suitable for the different scenes. And when the evening arrived, he came down dressed up in the queerest way, and sat down to the piano, in a meek and unobtrusive manner, being a poor old musician, and very shy, and very shabby, and very hungry, and wretched-looking altogether. He played this part admirably the whole evening, and his get-up was excellent. A great many of the audience didn't know him at first. He had made a secret about this dressing-up, and had done it all by himself; and I met him on the stairs and didn't know him! He was most innocently proud of the success of his self-invented part.

"I think he was a truly kind and charitable man, doing all sorts of good and generous deeds in a quiet, unostentatious way. I do not suppose anybody really in need ever applied to him in vain. And I know he has given a helping hand to several young musicians, who, without the aid of his kind hand, could not have risen to be what they now are. He was very grateful for any love and attention shown to him, and never forgot a kindness done to him. I believe he loved my father better than any man in the world; was grateful to him for his friendship, and truly proud of possessing it, which he certainly did to a very large amount. My father was very fond of him, and had the greatest respect for his honest, straightforward, upright, and generous character. I think, and am very glad to think, that the happiest days of Mr. Chorley's life — his later life, that is to say — were passed at Gad's Hill.

"After my father's death, and before we left the dear old home, Mr. Chorley wrote and asked me if I would send him a branch off each of our large cedar-trees, as a remembrance of the place. My friend, and *his* dear friend, Mrs. Lehmann, saw him lying calm and peaceful in his coffin, with a large green branch on each side of him. She did not understand what this meant, but I did, and was much touched, as, of course, he had given orders that these branches should be laid with him in his coffin. So a piece of the place he loved so much, for its dear master's sake, went down to the grave with him."

MAMIE DICKENS.

J. ROBINSON PLANCHÉ.

J. ROBINSON PLANCHÉ.

ELLISTON.

ELLISTON had become proprietor of the Olympic Pavilion, as it was then called, in Wych Street, built originally by old Astley for equestrian performances. At his suggestion I wrote a speaking harlequinade, with songs for the columbine, the subject being "Little Red Riding Hood." On the first night of its representation (December 21, 1818), every trick failed, not a scene could be induced to close or to open properly, and the curtain fell at length amid a storm of disapprobation. I was with Mr. Ellison and his family in a private box. He sent round an order to the prompter, that not one of the carpenters, scene-shifters, or property-men were to leave the theatre until he had spoken to them. As soon as the house was cleared, the curtain was raised, and all the culprits assembled on the stage in front of one of the scenes in the piece representing the interior of a cottage, having a door in one half and a latticed window in the other. Elliston led me forward, and standing in the centre, with his back to the foot-lights, harangued them in the most grandiloquent language — expatiated on the enormity of their offense, their ingratitude to the man whose bread they were eating, the disgrace they had brought upon the theatre, the cruel injury they had inflicted on the young and promising author by his side ; then pointing in the most tragical attitude to his wife and daughters, who remained in the box, bade them look upon the family they had ruined, and burying his face in his handkerchief to stifle his sobs, passed slowly through the door in the scene, leaving his auditors silent, abashed, and somewhat affected, yet rather relieved by being let off with a lecture. The next minute the casement in the other flat was thrown violently open, and thrusting in his head, his face scarlet with fury, he roared out, "I discharge you all!" I feel my utter incapacity to convey an idea of this ludicrous scene, and I question whether any one unacquainted with the man, his voice, action, and wonderful facial expression, could thoroughly realize the glorious absurdity of it from verbal description. With Elliston I was extremely intimate for several years, and had great respect for his amiable wife and charming daughters, but our mutual friend, the late George Raymond, has written so exhaustive a life of this "Napoleon of the Drama," — so thoroughly described the man, and so industriously collected every scrap of information concerning him, every anecdote connected with him, — that there is only one little incident that I do not find he has mentioned, at least in the edition I possess, and it is so characteristic, that it deserves recording. Within a few hours of his death he objected to take some medicine, and, in order to induce him to do so, he was told he should have some brandy and water afterwards. A faint smile stole over his face, the old roguish light gleamed for a moment in his glazing eye, as he murmured, "Bribery and *corruption*." They were almost the last intelligible words he uttered. Elliston was one of the best general actors I have ever seen; but the parts in which he has remained unrivaled to this day were the gentlemanly rakes and agreeable rattles in high comedy. His Ranger, Archer, Marlow, Doricourt, Charles Surface, Rover, Tangent, and many other such characters, he made his own — and no wonder, for these characters reflected his own.

SAMUEL BEAZLEY.

Dear, good-tempered, clever, generous, eccentric, Sam Beazley! He died in Tonbridge Castle, where he resided for the few last years of his life, having a professional appointment in connection with the South Eastern Railway. Many years before, he wrote his own epitaph : —

> "Here lies Samuel Beazley,
> Who lived hard and died easily."

Alas! the latter declaration was not prophetic. He suffered considerably a short time before his decease, and his usual spirits occasionally forsaking him, he one day wrote so melancholy a letter, that the friend to whom it was addressed, observed, in his reply, that it was "like the first chapter of Jeremiah." "You are mistaken, my dear fellow," retorted the wit; "it is the last chapter of Samuel."

Beazley never had five shillings for himself, but he could always find five pounds for a friend. Returning with him, in his carriage, from a Greenwich dinner, I casually alluded to the comfort of being independent of public conveyances. "Yes," he said ; "but I'm rather a remarkable man. I have a carriage. and a cabriolet, and three horses, and a coachman, and a footman, and a large house, and a cook and three maid-servants, and a mother and a sister, and — half-a-crown."

It was scarcely an exaggeration, and yet he was never known to be in debt, and left many little legacies to friends, besides providing for his widow and only daughter. He was truly "a remarkable man." The work he got through was something astounding. He appeared to take no rest. He built theatres and wrote for them with the same rapidity; had always "just arrived by the mail" in time to see the fish removed from the table, or was going off by the early coach after the last dance at four in the morning. At dinner, or at ball, was there a lady who appeared neglected, because she was old, ill-favored, or uninteresting, Beazley was sure to pay her the most respectful and delicate attentions. Not a breath of scandal ever escaped his lips ; not an unkind word did I ever hear him utter. There were two men whom he held in horror, but he never abused them ; his brow darkened if their names were mentioned, but by that, and his silence alone could you have surmised that he entertained the least feeling against them. His pleasant sayings would fill a volume. The wit was, perhaps, not particularly pungent, but it was always playful. Building a staircase for Sir Henry Meux, he called it a new "Gradus ad Parnassum," because it was steps for the *Muses*. Some very old brandy, pathetically pointed out by George Robins as having been left to him by his father, he proposed should be called, "Spirit of my Sainted Sire!" and when the question arose of how the title of Herold's charming Opera, "Le Pré aux Clercs,' should be rendered in English, he quietly suggested "Parson's Green." Beazley was essentially a gentleman, and it is, therefore, a greater gratification to me to record him as one of the first to take me by the hand in the society to which I had been so suddenly and unexpectedly introduced.

Sir Lumley Skeffington.

There was another *habitué* with whom I became acquainted at the same period; one of the last of that peculiar style of fop whose dress and manners were unsparingly caricatured in the print-shops, and became conventional on the stage. But with all his extravagance of attire, his various-colored under waistcoats, his rouged cheeks, and coal-black wig, with portentous *toupée*, poor old Sir Lumley Skeffington was a perfect gentleman, a most agreeable companion, and bore "the stings and arrows of outrageous fortune" with Spartan courage and Christian resignation. Though his fair-weather friends had deserted him, no complaint or reproach ever passed his lips. But once only, during the many years we were acquainted, did I hear him allude to the misery of his position. We were the only two guests at the dinner-table of a mutual friend, and Sir Lumley had been particularly lively and entertaining. Our host being called out of the room to speak to some one on business, I congratulated the old baronet on his excellent spirits. "Ah! my dear Mr. Planché," he replied, "it's all very well while I am in society; but I give you my honor, I should heartily rejoice if I felt certain that after leaving this house to-night I should be found dead on my own doorstep.' I shall never forget the deep but quiet pathos of these sad words. I am happy to add that he lived to inherit a small property, and ended his days in peace and comfort.

PEAKE, THE DRAMATIST.

I have spoken of Peake as "a humorist," for I know no epithet that would so accurately describe him. He was not a wit in the true sense of the word. There is not a scintilla of wit that I can remember in any of his dramas or in his conversation; but there was some good fun in a few of his farces, and he had a happy knack of "fitting" his actors, a memorable example of which is Geoffrey Muffincap, the charity school-boy, in "Amateurs and Actors," which was expressly written to suit the peculiarities of person, voice, and manner of Wilkinson. Peake's humor consisted in a grotesque combination of ideas, such as the following: Calling with him one summer day on a mutual friend, the fire-place in the drawing-room was *ornamented* with a mass of long slips of white paper falling over the bright bars of the stove. Peake's first question was, "What do you keep your macaroni in the grate for?" At a party at Beazley's his black servant entered to make up the fire. Peake whispered to me, "Beazley's nigger has been scratching his head, and got a scuttle of coals out." I could fill a page or two with such *concetti*, which, spurted out in his peculiar manner, were perhaps more comical to hear than to repeat. His farces were usually damned the first night, and recovered themselves wonderfully afterwards. A striking instance of this was "A Hundred-Pound Note," at Covent Garden, in which the conundrums, bandied between Power and Keeley, were violently hissed on the first representation, and received with roars of laughter subsequently. Indeed they may be said to have popularized, if not originated, the "why and because" style of jesting, which forms a principal feature in our comic journals and Christy Minstrel entertainments. His failures I consider were attributable to a strange misapprehension of the principles of dramatic composition. Any absurdity which had made *him* laugh, he assumed must necessarily produce a similar effect on a general audience; a most fatal mistake for any one to fall into who caters for that "many-headed monster," the public. Poor Dicky's misfortunes rarely came alone. He was wont to pace Waterloo Bridge during the performance of a new piece, and on returning to the theatre received, with the account of its failure, the tidings on more than one occasion that his wife had presented him with twins. His extreme good temper and obliging nature made him a universal favorite. He was devotedly attached to Mr. Arnold, whose bond for 200*l*., in acknowledgment of his long and faithful service, he generously thrust into the breakfast-room fire before him, the morning after the burning down of the Lyceum Theatre (February 16th, 1830), saying, "You have lost all by fire, let this go too." Richard Brinsley Peake died a poor man—a singular circumstance considering that he had been for so many years the treasurer of a theatre.

VON WEBER'S "OBERON."

The year 1826 is memorable in the annals of music, for it is that in which Carl Maria von Weber produced his last great opera, "Oberon," on the English stage. The deathless work of a dying man. Mr. Charles Kemble having engaged the celebrated composer of "Der Freischütz" to write an opera expressly for the Theatre Royal, Covent Garden, I had the honor of being selected to furnish the libretto, the subject having been chosen by Weber himself. An immense responsibility was placed upon my shoulders. The fortunes of the season were staked upon the success of the piece. Had I constructed it in the form which would have been most agreeable to me and acceptable to Weber, it could not have been performed by the company at Covent Garden, and if attempted must have proved a complete fiasco. None of our actors could sing, and but one singer could act—Madame Vestris—who made a charming Fatima. A young lady who subsequently became one of the most popular actresses in my recollection was certainly included in the cast; but she had not a line to speak, and was pressed into the service in consequence of the paucity of vocalists, as she had a sweet though not very powerful voice, and was even then artist enough to be intrusted with anything. That young lady was Miss Goward, now Mrs. Keeley, and to her was assigned the exquisite Mermaid Song in the finale of the second act. At the first general rehearsal with full band, scenery, etc., the effect was not satisfactory, and Fawcett, in his usual brusque manner, exclaimed, "That must come out!—it won't go!" Weber, who was standing in the pit, leaning on the back of the orchestra, so feeble that he could scarcely stand without such support, shouted, "Wherefore shall it not go?" and leaping over the partition like a boy, snatched the baton from the hand of the conductor, and saved from excision one of the most delicious *morceaux* in the opera. No vocalist could be found equal to the part of Sherasmin. It was, therefore, acted by Fawcett, and a bass singer, named Isaacs, was lugged in head and shoulders to eke out the charming quatuor, "Over the Dark Blue Waters." Braham, the greatest English tenor perhaps ever known, was about the worst actor ever seen, and the most unromantic person in appearance that can well be imagined. His deserved popularity as a vocalist induced the audience to overlook his deficiencies in other qualifications, but they were not the less fatal to the dramatic effect of the character of Huon de Bordeaux, the dauntless paladin who had undertaken to pull a hair out of the Caliph's beard, slay the man who sat on his right hand, and kiss his daughter! Miss Paton, with a grand soprano voice, and sufficiently prepossessing person, was equally destitute of histrionic ability, and consequently of the four principal parts in the opera only one was adequately represented, that of Fatima by Madame Vestris. Amongst the minor characters, Miss Harriet Cawse, a pupil of Sir George Smart's, distinguished herself as an arch and melodious Puck, and did her "spiriting gently," and Mr. Charles Bland, brother of James the future king of extravaganza, was happily gifted with a voice which enabled him to execute at least respectably the airs assigned to the King of the Fairies. The composer therefore had justice fairly done to *him*, and any short-comings, as far as the drama was concerned, were of secondary importance. My great object was to land Weber safe amidst an unmusical public, and I therefore wrote a melodrama with songs, instead of an opera, such as would be required at the present day. I am happy to say that I succeeded in that object, and had the great gratification of feeling that he fully appreciated my motives, and approved of my labors. On the morning after the production of the opera (April 12), I met him on the stage. He embraced me most affectionately, and exultingly exclaimed, "Now we will go to work and write another opera together, and *then* they they shall see what we can do!" "Man proposes and Heaven disposes." In a few weeks after I followed him to his grave! ("Oberon" was the song of the dying swan.) The hand of death was upon him before he commenced it, and the increasing weight upon his spirit is unmistakably evident in the latter portion of his work.

According to the courteous custom which has prevailed time out of mind in English theatricals, an Easter piece on the subject of "Oberon" had been rushed out at Drury Lane in anticipation of Weber's opera, and, in addition to this, Bishop was engaged to write an opera to be produced in opposition to it, the libretto by George Soane being founded on the popular story of "Aladdin, or the Wonderful Lamp." It was not very favorably received, and the delicious warbling of Miss Stephens could not secure for it more than a lingering existence of a few nights. Tom Cooke, the leader of the orchestra at Drury Lane, one of the cleverest musicians and most amusing of men, met Braham in Bow Street, and asked him how his opera ("Oberon") was going. "Magnificently!" replied the great tenor, and added, in a fit of what he used to call *enthoosemusy*, "not to speak it profanely, it will run to the day of judgment!"—"My dear fellow," rejoined Cooke, "that's nothing! Ours has run five nights afterwards!"

WILLIAM JERDAN.

His unvarying kindness to me and mine for upwards of thirty years imperatively demands this brief but sincere acknowledgment. He was my near neighbor, occupying a large house, with a long garden attached to it, in what was Brompton Grove, and is now Ovington Square. There I met Crofton Croker and his clever wife, Tom Hood and his brother-in-law, John Hamilton Reynolds, whose dawning genius had attracted the notice of Byron; the Rev. George Croly, author of the "Angel of the World," and the comedy of "Pride shall have a Fall," which latter work, produced at Covent Garden, not meeting with much success, Poole, who hated him, invariably spoke of, as "'Croly shall have a Fall, by the Rev. George Pride," and Miss Landon — poor L. E. L. — whose early death in the fatal region of Sierra Leone caused a painful excitement in literary circles. A melancholy roll-call — not one remains to answer "Here!" Jerdan, himself the earliest born, was the latest who left us. He attained the patriarchal age of eighty-eight, dying only two years ago, June 11th, 1869, having retired from the editorship of the "Literary Gazette," in 1850. In a notice of his decease in the "Times" newspaper, it was remarked that "his kindly help was always afforded to young aspirants in literature and art, and his memory will be cherished by many whom he helped to rise to positions of honor and independence. As one who specially enjoyed that "kindly help," and was a frequent witness of its ready extension to others, it is my gratifying duty to testify to the truth of that honorable record. His buoyant spirits enabled him to bear up against "a sea of troubles," which would have overwhelmed an ordinary man. Mr. Moyes, his printer, "a canny Scot," being asked by a mutual acquaintance, "Has our friend Jerdan got through his difficulties?" characteristically exclaimed, "Difficulties! I never knew he was in any."

Thomas Hood.

The genius of Tom Hood has been so generally acknowledged, his humor and his pathos so highly appreciated, and so many anecdotes recorded of him, that I shall only cite a few of his sallies, which I believe have never been chronicled. At a large dinner party at Jerdan's one of the guests indulged in some wonderful accounts of his shooting. The number of birds he had killed, and the distances at which he had brought them down, were extraordinary. Hood quietly remarked,—

"What he hit is history,
What he missed is mystery."

Anything more happily conceived and expressed I contend it would be difficult to discover.

At the same house, on another occasion, when Power the actor was present, Hood was asked to propose his health. After enumerating the various talents that popular comedian possessed, he requested the company to observe that such a combination was a remarkable illustration of the old proverb, "It never rains but it *powers*."

In his last illness, reduced as he was to a skeleton, he noticed a very large mustard poultice which Mrs. Hood was making for him, and exclaimed, "O Mary! Mary!—that will be a great deal of mustard to a very little meat!"

Shortly before his death, being visited by a clergyman whose features as well as language were more lugubrious than consoling, Hood looked up at him compassionately and said, "My dear sir! I'm afraid your religion doesn't agree with you.'

There seemed to be a mint in his mind in which the coining of puns was incessantly and almost unconsciously in process, not with the mere object of raising a laugh, but because his marvelous command of language enabled him to use words in every possible sense in which they could be understood; and he could not help playing upon them, even in his most serious moods. For instance, in that pathetic appeal to the benevolence of the public on behalf of the widow and children of poor Elton, the actor, who was drowned on his passage from Leith to Hull, in 1843, after most touchingly describing the lifeless hand idly playing with the tangled weed, he concludes with a parallel between the dead and the living, by imploring assistance for the latter, who is struggling "'mid *breakers* huge enough to *break* the heart." Admirably delivered as I heard it, by Mrs. Sterling, the power of the line told upon the audience with increased effect from the play on the word, which

I question if any other writer would have hazarded under such circumstances.

When the water broke into the Thames Tunnel, during the progress of the work, he said to me, "They've been laboring at that affair for a long time, and now the Thames has filled up their leisure." On my repeating this to Charles Kemble, the same afternoon, he said, "Well, Planché, I can't see anything in that so"—— laughable, he would have added; but he began to laugh before he could finish the sentence.

John Hamilton Reynolds.

John Hamilton Reynolds, his brother-in-law, and *collaborateur* in some of his works, less generally known to the public, was only inferior to his celebrated connection as a wit, a poet, and if I may be allowed the expression, a philosophical punster.

He was specially distinguished for the aptness of his quotations. Finding him one day lunching at the "Garrick," I asked him if the beef he was eating was good. "It would have been," he answered, "if damned custom had not *brazed* it so."

Not long before his death, he was appointed treasurer of a County Court in the Isle of Wight. It was absolute exile for a man of his town tastes and habits, and he lost no opportunity of running up, if only for a few hours, to London. Expatiating on the dullness of the locality to which he was relegated, and the absence of that class of society to which he had been all his life accustomed, he told me how that, one evening he had attended a tea-party, and noticing a pretty, bright-looking girl, he entered into conversation with her, and elicited from her, to his great gratification, that she was very fond of poetry. "Then, of course, you admire, as much as I do, Shakespeare's exquisite comedy of 'As you like it.'" "I have read it," she answered; "but I don't understand it —." "Not understand it! Then I am afraid you don't understand a tree." This was infinitely beyond her, and with a look of blank astonishment, she replied, "I don't know what you mean." "Upon which," said Reynolds, "I took my leave of her 'under the shade of melancholy *bows*.'" The happiness of this quotation from the play itself, might have induced even Doctor Johnson to pardon the pun it inevitably suggested.

L. E. L.

Of Lætitia Elizabeth Landon, Mr. and Mrs. Carter Hall have given so minute and interesting an account in their "Book of Memories," that it leaves me little to say, beyond adding my testimony to the truth of all they have asserted in defense of that most cruelly maligned lady, and my tribute of regret at her miserable and unmerited fate. I was her constant visitor in Hans Place, and have preserved some letters of hers, and of her friend Miss Emma Roberts ; but they contain no passages that would justify quotation. I remember "L. E. L.," however, saying to me one day, when congratulating me on some recent success in the theatre, "I would give all the reputation I have gained, or am ever likely to gain, by writing books, for one great triumph on the stage. The praise of critics or friends may be more or less sincere ; but the spontaneous thunder of applause of a mixed multitude of utter strangers, uninfluenced by any feelings but those excited at the moment, is an acknowledgment of gratification surpassing, in my opinion, any other description of approbation."

The Superannuated General Postman.

Oh happy days of England, when babies were really born with gold spoons in their mouths, and could be made colonels of regiments, commissioners of excise, or masters of the Mint, in their cradles, and without competitive examination ! The great-grandfather of a friend of mine affords a remarkable example of this precocity of preferment. The lady of a cabinet minister (I purposely suppress names) had promised to stand godmother to the infant, and calling on his parents a day or two previous to the ceremony, expressed her regret that Lord ——— had nothing left at his disposal of any importance ; and that the only thing he could do for her godson was to put his name on the pension-list as a superannuated general postman. The offer was accepted. The pension was regularly paid to the parents during the minority of their son, and to him afterwards as long as he lived. He thrived in the world, became an alderman of Chichester, and attained a considerable age, often declaring that he had more pleasure in pocketing the few pounds he drew half-yearly from this source, than he derived from the receipt of any other portion of his income. He died a few days after one payment was due, and one of his executors came to town to receive the money and announce his decease. On asking the clerk who paid him if it were necessary to produce a certificate of the death, he was answered, "Oh no, not in the least — I will take your word for it. My father paid this pension as long as he lived, and I have paid it myself for the last thirty years. I'm quite sure Mr. ——— must be dead by this time." He had been a superannuated general postman for upwards of eighty years! His descendant is now a baronet and a member of parliament; and I had the story from his father at his own dinner-table.

THE PEACE OF AMIENS.

Dining recently with an old friend and schoolfellow, the conversation turned upon the ages of the persons present, and each was asked what was the earliest public event he could remember. My answer was, "The general illumination for the peace of Amiens." "The peace of Amiens? Why, that was in 1801!" exclaimed a learned judge who sat near to me. "Exactly; but I remember it perfectly." He turned to his next neighbor, and, in an audible whisper, said, "The wandering Jew!" In support of my assertion I then related the following circumstance. Monsieur Otto, the French Minister, resided, at that time, in Portman Square, and my father having moved from Old Burlington Street into Park Street, Grosvenor Square, took me to see the illumination at the French Embassy, which was exceedingly magnificent. The house was one blaze of colored lamps from parlor to parapet. Green olive-branches with red berries — not natural, but effective — and other pacific emblems surrounded the windows; and above those of the drawing-room, occupying the whole breadth of the building, glittered in golden-colored lamps the word "Concorde." Though as nearly English as a French word could well be, it was misinterpreted by a number of sailors in the crowd, who began shouting, "We are not conquered! Pull it down!" The mob, always ripe for a row, took up the cry, and was proceeding from uproar to violence, when some one announced from the doorsteps that the obnoxious word should be altered; and a host of lamplighters were speedily seen busily employed in removing and substituting for it "Amitié." Unfortunately this was also misunderstood by the ignorant masses for "Enmity," and the storm again raged with redoubled fury. Ultimately was done what should have been done at first. The word "Peace" was displayed, and peace was restored to Portman Square for the rest of the evening. The peace itself was of not much longer duration. What a different thing was a general illumination in those days to one at the present time! True, there was no gas, nor so much picturesque effect as modern art has, by the means of cut glass, produced in such decorations as have delighted the public at Poole's; but, on the other hand, the former illuminations were really general. Not a window in the smallest court or blindest alley but had its candle stuck in a lump of clay, while in houses of more pretension one blazed in every pane. Rows of flambeaux fastened to the area railings flared in every direction, and long lines of variegated lamps bordered every balcony, or, arranged in graceful festoons, valanced each verandah. There was not a dark street to be found in London. Mobs paraded the metropolis, from Hyde Park Corner to Whitechapel, with shouts of "Light up! Light up!" and smashed every window that did not swiftly display a humble dip in obedience to the summons. Since the rejoicings for the crowning victory of Waterloo, nothing like a general illumination has been seen in London.

Manager Morris.

Mr. David Morris was a great character. A thoroughly honorable gentleman and a shrewd man of business, by no means illiberal in his dealings with authors and actors, and scrupulously punctual in his payments ; had Providence added to these very valuable qualifications for a theatrical manager, the talent of a theatrical management, he would have been the most perfect specimen of his class in England : but, unhappily, he was lamentably deficient in that one rather important article, and, what was more unfortunate, he was not in the least aware of the deficiency. On the contrary, he prided himself particularly on his managerial abilities, and was extremely surprised at the expression of any doubts, however delicately hinted, of the soundness of his judgment or the accuracy of his taste. Such a delusion is by no means uncommon. An anecdote or two will enable the reader to form a tolerably fair estimate of his capacity for the position which had been previously held by Macklin, Samuel Foote, and the two Colmans. Fulfilling faithfully all his own obligations, he expected, justly enough, equal rectitude on the part of others. Observing, one morning at the rehearsal of some music, that one of the band was quiescent, he leant over from the pit in which he was standing, and touched him on the shoulder — "Why are you not playing, sir ?" — "I have twelve bars rest, sir," answered the musician. "Rest ! Don't talk to me about rest, sir ! Don't you get your salary, sir ? I pay you to play and not to rest, sir ! Rest when you've done your work, and not in the middle of it !"[1]

Alexander Lee, who had the musical direction of the Haymarket the following season — when my "Green-Eyed Monster" was produced, complained to him of the unsatisfactory state of the orchestra. "Unsatisfactory ! Pray what fault have you to find with my orchestra ?" Every man having been engaged by himself he considered the attack personal. "Some of the principal members are extremely inefficient. "Name one, sir !" — "Well, there is Mr. ——— the first clarionet — really of no use at all." "Mr. ——— ! Do you know who he is, sir ? Are you aware that he was for more than twenty years first clarionet at His Majesty's Thea-

[1] A similar story is told about old Astley, and there is no reason why both should not be true. "Great wits jump," they say, and it may be equally true of the reverse.

tre?" It was quite true, and naturally the poor old gentleman had scarcely any breath left in his body.

It was one of the absurd ideas of managers in general at that period that the stage should never be unoccupied; and Mr. Morris was especially a martinet in this matter. If he found no one upon it after the clock had struck eleven at the latest, he would immediately cause a rehearsal to be called of something, no matter what. He paid his people, and he was determined they should earn their money. So the poor stage-manager had a pleasant time of it. Tom Dibdin, one of the sons of the celebrated nautical poet, and himself the author of many popular dramatic pieces, held that responsible position at the Haymarket in 1823, and had engaged to write a comedy for that theatre. Some weeks having elapsed, and no portion of it being forthcoming, Morris attacked him one day as he was coming through the box-office. "Mr. Dibdin! Where is the comedy you promised me?—"My dear sir, what opportunity have I for writing? I am on the stage all day from ten or eleven in the morning till four in the afternoon. Run home to my dinner, and back again to see the curtain up, and remain till it finally falls, long after midnight. I never have any time for composition." "No time! What do you do on Sundays?"

Poole and Kenny.

They were equally witty; but in Poole's wit there was too frequently a mixture of gall, while Kenny's never left a taste of bitterness behind it. I appreciated Poole's talent, but I loved Kenny. The former was, perhaps, the most humorous as well as the most satirical; the latter more refined and more genial. Dining one day where the host became exceedingly excited and angry at not being able to find any stuffing in a roasted leg of pork, Poole quietly suggested, "Perhaps it is in *the other leg.*" Dining in his company on another occasion, the conversation turned on the comedy of "The School for Scandal." A city knight who was present inquired, "Who wrote 'The School for Scandal?'" Poole, with the greatest *sang froid,* and a glance of infinite contempt, replied, "Miss

Chambers, the banker's daughter." "Ah! indeed," said Sir J———, "clever girl! *very* clever girl!" Almost immediately afterwards, Poole said, "Pray, Sir J———, are you a knight bachelor or a knight errant?" "Well now — I really can't say — I don't think I ever was asked that question. I'll make it a point to inquire." It was as good as a play to watch Poole's countenance, but I confess his audacity made me shiver.

Kenny would have had too much respect for the friend he was dining with, to have shown up one of his guests so unmercifully. I do not remember his saying a severe thing of or to any one. Even in moments of irritation he would give a graceful turn to his reproof. One evening when I was playing whist with him at his own house, Mrs. Kenny burst suddenly into the room, followed by three or four ladies who had been dining with us, all in fits of laughter at some ludicrous incident that had occurred, and startled Kenny (a very nervous man) so greatly that he let drop some of his cards, and exclaimed, "Is —*Heaven* broke loose?"

Thomas Hill.

He might have sat to Mrs. Centlivre for the portrait of Marplot in "The Busy Body," and if not the original of Poole's "Paul Pry," which Poole always denied, though nobody believed him, he certainly sat for the portrait of Mr. Hull, in Theodore Hook's novel "Gilbert Gurney." He knew, or was supposed to know, everything about everybody, and was asked to dine everywhere in order that he might tell it. Scandal was, of course, the great staple of his conversation; but in general defamatory gossip he might have been equaled by too many. His *specialité* was the accurate information he could impart to those whom it concerned, or whom it did not concern, of all the petty details of the domestic economy of his *friends*, the contents of their wardrobes, their pantries, the number of pots of preserves in their store-closets, and of table napkins in their linen-presses, the dates of their births and marriages, the amounts of their tradesmen's bills, and whether they paid them weekly or quarterly, or when they could -- and he always "happened to know," and never failed to inform you when they couldn't. He had been "on the Press" in former times, and particularly connected with the "Morning Chronicle," and used to drive Mathews crazy by ferreting out his whereabouts whenever he left London, though but for a short private visit, popping the address in some paper, and causing his letters to be sent to houses after he had left them, sometimes to the obstruction of business, and always to the doubling of postage — no small matter in those days.

But while so communicative respecting others, he was rigidly reticent with regard to himself. Nobody knew when or where he was born, or could form the slightest conjecture respecting his age or connections. Fawcett and Farley, and others still more advanced in years, remembered finding him established in London when they entered it as young men, looking much the same as he did when I knew him, and no one had ever been able to elicit from him the least morsel of evidence that would lead them to a probable conclusion. This was the cause of much amusing banter amongst his acquaintances, who used to ask him questions concerning the Norman Conquest, the Spanish Armada, and other ancient historical events, which they insisted he must have been contemporary with; and some one, less extravagantly, identified him with a Mr. Thomas Hill, who is mentioned by Pepys in his Diary, as giving musical parties in the City in the reign of Charles II. He bore all this with the greatest equanimity, and was never observed to wince but upon two occasions; once when Theodore Hook declared that Tommy had stood godfather to old Mrs. Davenport, which was just within the bounds of possibility, and again when Charles Dance maintained that it was quite clear Hill could not have been, as reported, in the ark with Noah, because the animals were all in pairs, and there never was another beast of Tommy's kind.

It was surely his thus being the cause of wit in others that occasioned him to be so constantly the guest of many of the most brilliant men of the time; for he was certainly not witty himself, and I will not do them the injustice to believe that the extremely small tittle-tattle of which he was the ceaseless retailer could have had any particular attraction for them, although it occasionally provoked laughter from its contemptible triviality. I never heard any one express the least regard for him while living, or regret for him when he died; for I believe, but would by no means affirm, that he *is* dead, and "kills characters no longer."

Novelists and Dramatists.

Walter Scott was devoted to the theatre, but quite incapable of dramatizing his very dramatic novels and romances, and gladly contributed his valuable aid to his friend Terry in their adaptation as operas, by writing for him many charming characteristic lyrics. Dickens tried "his 'prentice hand," and never repeated the experiment. Thackeray sadly disappointed the manager to whom he had promised a comedy, and which, when presented, was pronounced unactable.

Mrs. Charles Gore and Lord Lytton are the only examples, so far as I can recollect, of novelists who have obtained any success on the stage; and it is worthy of remark that they have never attempted to dramatize their own most popular novels; but sought in history or the French drama for plots better suited to the purpose. Mr. Wilkie Collins appears likely to add his name as a third; but these are quite the exceptions that prove the rule, and I am aware of none other; for Mr. Charles Reed was a dramatist before he was a novelist, having written for the stage at the commencement of his literary career, in conjunction with a master of his art, Tom Taylor. He cannot, therefore, be included in the category. On the other hand, I should be the last to dispute the right of the novelist to the full benefit of his own property, or think he should not be "courteously entreated" previous to any meddling with it. He may have contemplated attempting to dramatize it himself, or be desirous to intrust another with the task, or have strong objections to its being dramatized at all, as Dickens had to the adaptation of his Pickwick Papers; and no one with a grain of delicacy would disregard such objections. I simply contend that, except in special cases such as above mentioned, the complaint of injury to the interest of the novelist which has been recently so loudly expressed, is utterly without foundation. And in any case who is the greatest criminal? The adapter, who violates the right of property and the courtesies of society, or the manager who rewards him for the act, even if he have not, as is the case in nine instances out of ten, suggested and tempted him to commit it? Surely if the receiver be worse than the thief, the encourager of literary larceny is more blamable than the perpetrator. Were there not ready markets for stolen goods, depredation would speedily cease to be a trade worth following. Were there no theatres at which such pieces were acceptable, the least scrupulous dramatist would soon find honesty the best policy.

Revival of "King John."

In 1823, a casual conversation with Mr. Kemble respecting the play of "King John," which he was about to revive for Young, who had returned to Covent Garden, led to a step, the consequences of which have been of immense importance to the English stage — and not the less valuable because, as in all other great changes, excess and abuse have occasionally entailed misfortune and merited reprobation. I complained to Mr. Kemble that a thousand pounds were frequently lavished on a Christmas pantomime or an Easter spectacle, while the plays of Shakespeare were put upon the stage with make-shift scenery, and, at the best, a new dress or two for the principal characters. That although his brother John, whose classical mind revolted from the barbarisms which even a Garrick had tolerated, had abolished the bag-wig of Brutus and the gold-laced suit of Macbeth, the alterations made in the costumes of the plays founded upon English history in particular, while they rendered them more picturesque, added but little to their propriety; the whole series, King Lear included, being dressed in habits of the Elizabethan era, the third reign after its termination with Henry VIII., and, strictly speaking, very inaccurately representing the costume even of that period. At that time I had turned my attention but little to the subject of costume, which afterwards became my most absorbing study; but the slightest reflection was sufficient to convince any one that some change of fashion must have taken place in the civil and military habits of the people of England during several hundred years. I remembered our Life Guards in cocked hats, powder, and pigtails, and they were at that moment wearing helmets and cuirasses. It was not requisite to be an antiquary to see the absurdity of the soldiers before Angiers, at the beginning of the thirteenth century, being clothed precisely the same as those fighting at Bosworth at the end of the fifteenth. If one style of dress was right, the other must be wrong. Mr. Kemble admitted the fact, and perceived the pecuniary advantage that might result from the experiment. It was decided that I should make the necessary researches, design the dresses, and superintend the production of "King John," *gratuitously*, I beg leave to say; solely and purely for that love of the stage, which has ever induced me to sacrifice all personal considerations to what I sincerely believed would tend to elevate as well as adorn it. Fortunately I obtained, through a mutual friend, an introduction to Doctor, afterwards Sir Samuel Meyrick, who had just published his elaborate and valuable work, "A Critical Inquiry into Ancient Arms and Armor," and was forming that magnificent and instructive collection now exhibiting at South Kensington. How little did I dream at that time that I should ever be called on to arrange it twice for public exhibition! — at Manchester, in 1857, and at South Kensington, in 1868. He entered most warmly and kindly into my views, pointed out to me the best authorities, and gave me a letter of introduction to Mr. Francis Douce, the eminent antiquary, from whom also I met with the most cordial reception.

This gentleman had assisted Mr. John Kemble when he introduced several alterations in the costume of Shakespeare's plays, particularly those founded on Roman history; for which latter, however, he drew his materials from the columns and arches of the emperors, and not from contemporaneous republican authorities. When urged to do so, and to "reform it altogether," he exclaimed to Mr. Douce, in a tone almost of horror, "Why, if I did, sir, they would call me an antiquary." "And this to me, sir!" said the dear old man, when he told me of this circumstance, "to *me*, who flattered myself I *was* an antiquary." Mr. Douce speedily discovered that, so far from having any objection to incur the risk of such a reproach, it was my ambition to deserve the appellation, and most liberally placed the whole of his invaluable collection of illuminated MSS. (now in the Bodleian Library, to which he bequeathed them) at my disposal. He paid me also the great compliment of lending me his fine copy of Strutt's "Dress and Habits of the People of England," colored expressly for him by its author. "I will lend *you* books, sir, because you love them and will take care of them;" I think he added, "and will return them"—a more uncommon virtue to possess than the two former. At any rate, I can honestly say that I justified his confidence. Dr. Meyrick was equally kind and of great assistance to me, for of armor our artists and actors in those days knew even less than of civil costume. In the theatre, however, my innovations were regarded with distrust and jealousy. Mr. Fawcett, the stage-manager, considered his dignity offended by the production of the play being placed under my direction. He did not speak to me, except when obliged by business, for, I think, nearly three years; but I lived it down, and remained very good friends with that excellent actor to the day of his death. Mr. Farley—dear old Charles Farley—also took huff. He was the recognized purveyor and director of spectacle, and dreaded "the dimming of his shining star." The expenditure of a few hundred pounds on any drama, except an Easter piece or a Christmas pantomime, was not to be tolerated. "Besides," he piteously exclaimed, "if Shakespeare is to be produced with such splendor and attention to costume, what am I to do for the holidays?" He was not quite so openly rude to me as Fawcett, but he didn't like me a bit the better *then*, though he also came round in the end, and was one of the warmest admirers of *my* Easter pieces. Never shall I forget the dismay of some of the performers when they looked upon the flat-topped *chapeaux de fer* (*fer blanc*, I confess) of the 12th century, which they irreverently stigmatized as *stewpans!* Nothing but the fact that the classical features of a Kemble were to be surmounted by a precisely similar abomination would, I think, have induced one of the rebellious barons to have appeared in it. They had no faith in me, and sulkily assumed their new and strange habiliments, in the full belief that they should be roared at by the audience. They *were* roared at; but in a much more agreeable way than they had contemplated. When the curtain rose and discovered King John dressed as his effigy appears in Worcester Cathedral, surrounded by his barons sheathed in mail, with cylindrical helmets and correct armorial shields, and his courtiers in the long tunics and mantles of the 13th century, there was a roar of approbation, accompanied by four distinct rounds of applause, so general and so hearty, that the actors were astonished, and I felt amply rewarded for all the trouble, anxiety, and annoyance I had experienced during my labors. Receipts of from £400 to £600 nightly soon reimbursed the management for the expense of the production, and a complete reformation of dramatic costume became from that moment inevitable upon the English stage.

That I was the original cause of this movement is certain. That without fee or reward, and in defiance of every obstacle that could be thrown in my path by rooted prejudice and hostile interest, I succeeded in the object I had honestly at heart, I am proud to declare; but if propriety be pushed to extravagance, if what should be mere accessories are occasionally elevated by short-sighted managers into the principal features of their productions, I am not answerable for their suicidal folly.

One ludicrous result I must needs chronicle. A melodrama, *quasi* historical, was announced for production at the Coburg Theatre, now known as the "Victoria," under the title of

"William the Conqueror, or the Battle of Hastings." In imitation of the Covent Garden playbill, a long and imposing (very imposing in this instance) list of authorities was quoted for the new dresses and decorations, most of them being those general works on costume and armor which I had enumerated in the announcement of "King John." Curious to observe the effect of such a representation on a transpontine public, I obtained a private box, and was seated in it long before the rising of the curtain. The house was crammed to the ceiling; and in the very centre of the pit, a most conspicuous object amongst the dingy denizens of the New Cut and St. George's Fields, who filled it to suffocation, arose the snow-white powdered head of the learned and highly respected Dr. Coombe, the Keeper of the Medals at the British Museum, who, attracted as I had been by the "promissory note" of preparation, had unfortunately neglected to provide himself, as I had done, with a "coin of vantage" from whence he could witness the performance in ease and comfort, without peril to his best black suit and immaculate neckcloth. There was no possibility of extricating him from the spot in which he was wedged; and I could only hope, therefore, that the brilliancy of the spectacle would atone for the discomfort of his position.

The hope was fallacious. I will not attempt to describe dresses that were indescribable, even by the indefinite term of conventional, and in which I could not detect the faintest resemblance to any portrayed in the works so unblushingly cited; but the banners of the rival hosts had obviously been painted from authorities which would have been admitted indisputable by the whole College of Heralds. Armorial bearings, it is true, were not known in the days of the Conqueror, but overlooking that slight anachronism, and the rather important fact that the arms were not even those borne by the direct descendants of the contending chieftains, the coats, crests, and supporters displayed were heraldically correct, and undeniably those of departed English worthies, noble and gentle, for they were nothing less than the funeral hatchments of some score of lords, ladies, baronets, and members of parliament, which having hung for the usual period on the walls of their family mansions, had reverted to the undertaker, and been "furnished" by him, for a consideration, to the liberal and enterprising lessee of "the Coburg." There they were, and no mistake. Simply taken out of their frames, and without any alteration of the well-known lozenge form, hoisted on poles, some surmounted by cherubims, others by skulls with crossbones. A wicked wag might have managed, by the exercise of a little ingenuity, to have appropriated the "hatchments" to the principal personages. The ambitious Norman duke, who aspired to a kingly crown, might have been preceded by one which bore for motto, "Spero Meliora." A hint might have been conveyed to the bellicose Bishop of Bayeux by another, with "In Cœlo quies;" and the royal Saxon standard might have drooped over the prostrate Harold, with "Requiescat in pace." I can scarcely hope to be believed when I assert that this ridiculous and disgraceful exhibition excited neither shouts of derision nor symptoms of disgust amongst the general audience. I certainly cannot say that the piece was received with enthusiasm; but it escaped the condign punishment which its absurdity and bad taste richly deserved.

JAMES WALLACK IN "THE BRIGAND."

The production of "Der Vampyr" was followed by that of "The Brigand" at Drury Lane, in which that great melodramatic favorite, James Wallack, increased his popularity so immensely by his performance of the hero, "Alessandro Mazzaroni," that the public would scarcely receive him in Tragedy or Comedy, the leading parts in which he was ambitious of sustaining. This unlooked-for consequence so nettled him, that he has frequently said to me, quite savagely, 'D——n your "Brigand," sir! It has been the ruin of me.' Nevertheless, he was not best pleased with his brother Henry, a very inferior actor, anticipating him in the character all over the country, and advertising himself as "Mr. Wallack of the

Theatre Royal, Drury Lane," omitting the distinguishing baptismal appellation.

In this melodrama I introduced three tableaux from Eastlake's well-known pictures, "An Italian Brigand Chief reposing," "The Wife of a Brigand Chief watching the result of a Battle," and "The Dying Brigand," engravings of which had been just published by Messrs. Moon, Boys, & Graves, and were in all the printshop windows. They were very effective, and led to the adoption of this attractive feature in several subsequent dramas, Douglas Jerrold's "Rent Day," founded on Wilkie's celebrated picture, in particular. Perhaps one of the most unexpected hits in the piece was the extraordinary success of the song, "Gentle Zitella," which I wrote for Wallack to sing, who was no singer. Assisted by the situation, he got through it very creditably, and it told well with the audience; but the extraordinary part of the business was the enormous popularity of the song out of the theatre. The late Mr. Chappell, of New Bond Street, who was at that moment in treaty for the purchase of the business of Mr. Latour, had agreed to give, as I was credibly informed, £500 more for it on the strength of the sale of that song alone, which brought him upwards of £1,000 the first year, and continued for many to produce a considerable income.

By this bit of good fortune I profited not one shilling. Mr. T. Cooke received £25 for his arrangement of the air (which was mine as well as the words), and some further benefit in the exchange of a piano; but when, on hearing of the wonderful sale of the song, I appealed to Mr. Latour for some recognition, however trifling, of my property in the work, he referred me to Mr. Chappell, to whom he had sold the business, and who would reap all the profits of the song; and on applying to Mr. Chappell, he assured me that Mr. Latour had exacted so large a sum from him in consideration of the value of that song, that he really could not afford to pay anything more for it. He had bought it of Mr. Latour, and to Mr. Latour I must look for remuneration.

Musical Copyrights.

This set me a-thinking. It had been a custom of long standing for an author to allow the composer of his opera to publish the words with the music. They were not considered of any value, and in a literary point of view there might, in too many instances, have been some truth in the assertion. Still, without the words, however poor they might be, the music of a new opera could not be published. That fact never appeared to have occurred to any one, or, if it had, no author had thought it worth his while to moot the question. In those days successful dramas had a certain sale, and there were actually booksellers who would give a very fair price for a new play, and a much larger one for an opera, as the sale of the book of the songs in the house would alone net a sufficient sum to pay the author and the expenses of printing at the least, without reckoning the money taken over the counter for the complete libretto. But those days were fast disappearing, and booksellers were becoming chary of purchasing the copyrights of any dramatic pieces whatever, unless at such low prices that they were able to publish them in a small size at sixpence or a shilling, instead of, as formerly, in 8vo, at three or five shillings. The lyrical drama also, assuming gradually a more strictly operatic form, "the book of the songs" no longer consisted of a few ballads and duets, a glee and two or three choruses. It contained the greater part of the whole piece, and every word of it was printed and published by the music-seller, without the least compensation to the bookseller who had purchased the copyright of the author. Mr. Miller, Mr. Dolby, and other theatrical booksellers, had paid me fifty, sixty, and a hundred pounds for copyrights, but such offers were "getting few by degrees and beautifully less." Meanwhile, the music-publishers were making large fortunes by the sale of songs for the words of which they had not paid sixpence. The case of "Gentle Zitella," though the most flagrant, was by no means the first. The ballad of "Rise, gentle Moon," in "Charles XIIth," had been published by the composer as a matter of course, and had commanded an extensive sale without my receiving the slightest consideration for it. I determined to be the victim of "tyrant custom" no longer, and told George Rodwell, who was just about to publish the vocal pieces of my operetta, "The Mason of Buda," of which he had arranged the music, that I should expect some payment, I cared not about the amount, provided it was a sufficient recognition of my right as author of the libretto.

My protest was contemptuously disregarded, and the music was published in defiance of it. I walked into the city, not to my lawyer, but to Mr. Cumberland, who was then publishing his "Theatre," explained to him the case, and sold and assigned to him, in due form, all my rights and interests, vested and contingent, in the operetta of "The Mason of Buda."

On my return home, I informed Messrs. D'Almaine & Co. of the step I had taken, and that, as they had declined to deal with me, they would now have to deal with Mr. Cumberland. My letter was speedily followed by one from Mr. Cumberland's solicitor, prohibiting the further sale of the music, and demanding an account. How they compromised matters with Cumberland, I forget, if I ever knew, but I recollect being warmly thanked by my old acquaintance FitzBall, to whom D'Almaine had sent in a great pucker, and paid him for a host of things for which otherwise he would not have received a farthing; and from that time I have been fairly paid by the music-publishers for the right of printing the words of my operas, without injury to the composers, who commanded the same prices as they did previously. I had the gratification also of feeling in this case, as well as in that of the Dramatic Authors' Act, that I was not simply struggling for my own benefit, but for that of all my extremely ill-treated brethren, whose claims were invariably the last considered by managers or publishers.

STEPHEN PRICE.

Mr. Price was not a highly educated man, nor the possessor of a very refined taste; but he was a straightforward, sensible man of business, thoroughly understood the practical working of a theatre, having been many years the manager of one of the principal theatres in New York. He had no favorites but such as experience proved to him were favorites of the public; no prejudices to warp his judgment, and was perfectly free from that common and fatal weakness of managers — the encouragement of talebearers and mischief-makers. He had his likings and his dislikings, as other men; but he never suffered them to bias him in matters of business, never allowed private feeling to influence his conduct to a performer, or affect the interest of the public. At the same time he ruled with a strong hand, and could neither be coaxed nor coerced into taking any step which his natural shrewdness warned him might be hazardous. An eminent tragedian once suggested to him the omission of Locke's music in the tragedy of "Macbeth," as it was an interpolation, the words sung to it being taken from Middleton's "Witch." Price listened attentively to his arguments, and after a few minutes of apparent consideration, said, "Well, look here, sir, I don't think it would do to omit the music; but, if you think it would be an improvement, I've no objection to leave out the Macbeth."

Price was very fond of a rubber, and not more irritable than whist-players in general, when a partner makes a mistake. A gentleman, apologizing for an inadvertence by saying, "I beg your pardon, Mr. Price, I thought the queen was out," he replied, "I'll bet you five pounds, sir, you didn't think any such thing."

THE BEEF-STEAK CLUB.

A Beef-steak Club had been established at Drury Lane, in 1826, in imitation of the original at the English Opera House. The meetings took place in the painting room of the theatre, a portion of which was partitioned off by scenery. The lessee for the time being was the president, and the treasurer of the theatre ("Billy Dunn," as he was familiarly called — a great character) acted in the same capacity, as well as secretary, for the club, having the assistance of a deputy in the collection of the subscriptions, fines, etc., who was Kean's friend John Hughes I was not a member of the club, but occasionally dined with it as a guest. There was much good fun, as may be imagined, at these dinners, and not a little practical joking. A rather strong example of the latter may be worth recording. By one of the rules of the club the fine of half a crown was imposed upon all members using certain expressions or doing certain things most natural and inoffensive, and which, from general and constant custom, it was almost impossible to avoid. One evening the company appeared strangely oblivious or pertinaciously defiant of their regulation. Everybody was fined over and over again, and little Jack Hughes was kept constantly on his legs during the dinner, rushing from one end of the table to another to collect the half-crowns of the unwary or willful offenders. Shortly after the cloth was drawn, the messenger of the theatre was sent up by the stage-doorkeeper, to tell Mr. Hughes a gentleman wished to speak with him directly on important business. Hughes followed the messenger down to the hall, and was ushered into the little room on the right of the entrance, used sometimes as a manager's room, and therein found L——, a Bow Street officer, who was perfectly well known to him. On inquiring the object of his visit, the officer gravely replied that he was extremely sorry to say, having known and respected Mr. Hughes for several years, that an information had been laid against him for the uttering of base coin, and that a warrant had been issued, which it was his painful duty to be the bearer of. Poor little Hughes, conscious of his innocence, was nevertheless horror-struck at the intelligence, and, while indignantly repudiating the charge, implored the officer not to take him into custody, pledging his honor that he would attend at Bow Street the next morning, and meet any accusation that could be brought against him. The officer said it would be at his own peril if he acceded to such a proposition ; but having known Mr. Hughes so long, and feeling confident there must be some mistake, he would run the risk, provided Mr. Hughes would not object to his searching him on the spot. Hughes assented eagerly, little thinking what would follow. In a few minutes the officer was in possession of between two and three dozen of bad half-crowns, which Jack had unsuspiciously stuffed into his pockets as fast as he could take them, without examination. In vain did he offer the easy explanation, and request the officer to go up-stairs with him, or to send for Dunn to corroborate his statement. Under such suspicious circumstances, he was told, he must be locked up for the night, and send for the witnesses in the morning. At this point, however, it was considered that the joke had been carried far enough; and Dunn, the chief conspirator, who had been on the watch, made his appearance and relieved his half-distracted deputy from apprehension of any description. He was a good-natured little fellow, and generously forgave the perpetrators the trick they had played him, which was rather beyond a joke, and even extended his clemency to the Bow Street officer, whose conduct in lending himself to the imposition was highly reprehensible, and, if reported, would have been severely visited.

BILLY DUNN.

He was a dry fellow, that Billy Dunn, a great character, as I have already observed. During the many years he was treasurer of Drury Lane I don't suppose he once witnessed a performance; but regularly after the curtain had fallen on a new piece, it mattered not of what description, he would let himself through with his pass-key from the front of the house, as if he had sat it out, and on being asked his opinion, invariably answer, after a long pause and a proportionate pinch of snuff, "Wants cutting." Nine times out of ten he was right, and if wrong it would have been difficult to prove that he was so, as he never entered into any discussion of the subject. The trouble of extracting a direct reply from him at any time or concerning anything, was remarkable. I called one morning at the theatre, on my way to the city, to ask him a question about writing orders on some particular night. I was told he was in the treasury, and accordingly ran up to it. He was alone at his desk, counting checks. "Would there be any objection, Dunn, to my sending a friend or two to the boxes on such a night?" He looked at me, but made no answer and continued to count his checks. I waited patiently till he had finished and replaced them in the bags. Still no answer. He turned to his books. I waited perhaps five more minutes, and then, without repeating my inquiry, or speaking another word, walked quietly out of the room and went about my other business. Returning between two and three in the afternoon, I ascertained from the hall-keeper that Mr. Dunn was still in the theatre. I mounted the stairs again, entered the treasury, and found him, as before, alone. I stood perfectly silent while he looked at me and took the customary pinch of snuff, after which he drawled out, "No, I should think not;" some four hours having elapsed since I asked him the question.

The Garrick.

It was a vastly pleasant club, receiving constant additions of the most desirable members. Since the days of "Will's" and "Button's," I question if such an assemblage as could be daily met with there, between four and six in the afternoon, had ever been seen in a coffee-room. James Smith, Poole, and Charles Mathews the elder, were original members. The Rev. Richard Harris Barham (Tom Ingoldsby), Theodore Hook, Thackeray, Charles Dickens, and a host of memorable names, were gradually added to the list; and the club being formed upon the principle that membership was a sufficient introduction, the social intercourse between men of all ranks was an attractive feature in "The Garrick," distinguishing it agreeably from the generality of such establishments, wherein, as a friend of mine observed of one of the most celebrated, "it was as much as your life was worth to ask a stranger to poke the fire."

Amongst the earlier members was a very amiable and accomplished gentleman, who, perfectly sane upon all other topics, had what the Scotch call "a bee in his bonnet" on the subject of the "Millennium." If this were touched upon he would start up from his chair, pace the room agitatedly, and declaim in the most vehement manner on the approach of that momentous epoch. One day, when he was more than ordinarily excited, he assured us that the world would be at an end within three years from that date. Hook looked up from his newspaper, and said, "Come, L———, if you are inclined to back your opinion, give me five pounds now, and I will undertake to pay you fifty if it occurs." L——— was not quite mad enough to close with the whimsical offer.

Theodore Hook.

I had often met Hook in society without being introduced to him; but our acquaintance and intimacy dated simultaneously from the evening of a dinner at Horace Twiss's in Park Place, St. James's, the precise period of which has escaped me, but not the circumstances connected with it. It was a very merry party. Mr. John Murray (the great Murray of Albemarle Street), James Smith, and two or three others, remained till very late in the dining-room, some of us singing and giving imitations. Hook being pressed to sing another of his wonderful extemporary songs, consented, with a declaration that the subject should be John Murray. Murray objected vehemently, and a ludicrous contention took place, during which Hook dodged him round the table, placing chairs in his path, which was sufficiently devious without them, and singing all the while a sort of recitative, of which I remember only the commencement: —

"My friend, John Murray, I see has arrived at the head of the table,
And the wonder is, at this time of night, that John Murray should be able.
He's an excellent hand at a dinner, and not a bad one at a lunch,
But the devil of John Murray is that he never will pass the punch."

It was daybreak — broad daylight, in fact, before we separated. I had given an imitation of Edmund Kean and Holland, in Mathurin's tragedy of "Bertram," which had amused Hook; and, as we were getting our hats, he asked me where I lived. On my answering "At Brompton," he said, "Brompton! — why that's in my way home — I live at Fulham. Jump into my cabriolet, and I will set you down." The sun of a fine summer morning was rising as we passed Hyde Park Corner. "I have been very ill," said Hook, "for some time, and my doctors told me never to be out of doors after dark, as the night air was the worst thing for me. I have taken their advice. I drive into town at four o'clock every afternoon, dine at 'Crockford's,' or wherever I may be invited, and never go home till this time in the morning. I have not breathed the night air for the last two months." From that day to the latest of his life, Hook's attachment to me was so remarkable, that, knowing his irresistible passion for hoaxing and practical jokes of all descriptions, I was at first a little alarmed occasionally at the peculiar and marked attention he paid to me, accompanied as it was by respect, which from one of his age and celebrity was as singular as, if sincere, it was flattering. That it *was* sincere I had many gratifying proofs, some of which I still treasure, in his handwriting. His fame as an *improvisatore* is a matter of social history; but I cannot refrain from giving one instance of his powers which is as creditable to his heart as his head. There had been a large party at the house of some mutual friends of ours and Hook's neighbors at Fulham. It was late, but many still remained, and before separating another song was requested of him. He was weary, and really suffering, but good-naturedly consented on condition that somebody would suggest a subject. No one volunteering, he said, "Well, I think the most proper subject at this hour would be 'Good-night.'" And accordingly he sat down to the piano, and sang several verses, each ending with "Good-night," composed with his usual facility, but lacking the fun and brilliancy which had characterized his former effusions. Some oddity of expression, however, in the middle of one of his verses, elicited a ringing laugh from a fine handsome boy, son of Captain the Hon. Montague Stopford, who was staying with his parents in the house, and who had planted himself close to the piano. Hook stopped short, looked at him admiringly for an instant, then, completing the verse, added with an intensity of expression I can never forget, —

"You laugh! and you are quite right,
For yours is the dawn of the morning,
And God send you a good-night!"

The effect was electrical, and brought tears into the eyes of more than one of the company, while cheer upon cheer arose in recognition of that charming and touching burst of feeling.

Other versions of this remarkable incident are in print, but I have confidence in the accuracy of my own, for one particular reason. Supposing that I had imperfectly heard the words, I could not have mistaken the emphasis in their utterance, and the fervor with which God's blessing was invoked upon that beautiful and joyous boy, could not by any possibility have accompanied such words as "For me, is the solemn good-night," nor the applause that followed, loud and long, been caused by so melancholy a farewell. I know the tears that filled my eyes were not those of sorrow, but of pleasurable emotion.

William Makepeace Thackeray.

My acquaintance with Thackeray commenced some time before he joined "The Garrick," and while I was the guest of his cousin, Captain Thomas James Thackeray, in the Rue du Faubourg St. Honoré, during one of my many visits to Paris. He was at that time a slim young man, rather taciturn, and not displaying any particular love or talent for literature. Drawing appeared to be his favorite amusement; and he often sat by my side while I was reading, or writing, covering any scrap of paper lying about with the most spirited sketches and amusing caricatures. I have one of Charles IX. firing at the Huguenots out of the windows of the Louvre, which he dashed off in a few minutes beside me on the blank portion of the yellow paper cover of a French drama. A member of "The Garrick," who was specially unpopular with the majority of the members, was literally *drawn* out of the club by Thackeray. His figure, being very peculiar, was sketched in pen and ink by his implacable persecutor. On every pad on the writing-tables, or whatever paper he could venture to appropriate, he represented him in the most ridiculous and derogatory situation that could be imagined, always with his back towards you: but unmistakable. His victim, it must be admitted, bore this desecration of his "lively effigies" with great equanimity for a considerable period; but at length, one very strong — perhaps too strong — example of the artist's graphic and satirical abilities, combined with the conviction that he was generally objectionable, induced him to retire from the club, and leave the pungent pen of Michael Angelo Titmarsh to punish more serious offenders than bores and toadies.

JAMES SMITH.

Of my old friend James Smith I have many gratifying recollections; but they are too purely personal for introduction in these pages. I may be allowed, however, to testify, perhaps, to the utter absence of that desire to "play first fiddle," which is too often remarkable in celebrities of his description. He was the heartiest laugher at another's joke, and generally prefaced his own by the question of, "Have you heard what a man said when," etc. On hearing a song of mine which I had written in humble imitation of his style, he good-naturedly and gracefully said, —

> "Let old Timotheus yield the prize,
> Or both divide the crown."

This song I shall take the liberty of introducing here, as it has never been printed in its original form, but only as altered for Charles Mathews to sing in my classical extravaganza, "Theseus and Ariadne," and because some verses, entitled "A Medley, for a Young Lady's Album," written about a year later by Barham, appear to have been suggested by it, some few lines being actually identical.

A DREAM.

I'm quite in a flutter,
I scarcely can utter
The words to my tongue that come dancing —
come dancing.
I've had such a dream,
That I'm sure it must seem
To incredulous ears like romancing —
romancing.
There can be no question
'Twas sheer indigestion,

Occasioned by supping on chine, Sir —
on chine, Sir;
But if such vagaries
Portend their contraries,
Pray what's the contrary of mine, Sir? —
of mine, Sir?
I dreamed I was walking
With Homer, and talking
The very best Greek I was able —
was able,
When Lord Liverpool, he
Came in very coolly,
And danced a Scotch jig on the table —
the table.
Then Hannibal rising,
Declared 'twas surprising
That gentlemen couldn't sit quiet —
sit quiet,
And sent his attorney
For Sir Richard Birney [1]
To hasten and put down the riot —
the riot.
He came, and found Cato
At cribbage with Plato,
And Washington playing the fiddle —
the fiddle;
Snatched a dirk in the dark
From the ex-Sheriff Park-
ins,[2] and ran Peter Moore [3] through the middle —
the middle.
Then Dido turned paler,
And looked at John Taylor,[4]
Who sat by her side like a mummy —
a mummy,
But Mr. MacAdam [5]
Said, Really dear Madam,
I never play whist with a dummy —
a dummy.

[1] Chief Magistrate at Bow Street. [2] A civic dignitary of that day
[3] An unpopular member of the Drury Lane Committee.
[4] Editor of the *Sun* [5] The Colossus of *Roads*

I'm rather perplext
To say what I saw next,
But I think it was Poniatowski —
atowski,
Came driving Queen Sheba,
With Reginald Heber,[1]
Through Portugal Place, in a drosky —
a drosky.
When Nebuchanazar,
In his witty way, Sir,
Observed it was very cold weather —
cold weather,
And flinging his jasey
At Prince Esterhazy,
They both began waltzing together —
together.
The news next was spread
That Pope Pius was dead,
And Elliston, fearing the worst, Sir —
the worst, Sir.
Proclaimed, in a hurry,
Himself at "the Surrey,"
As Pope Robert William the First, Sir
the First, Sir
He hanged Master Burke,[2]
And alarmed the Grand Turk,
By a bull of excommunication —
nication,
And cutting the rake,
For his family's sake,
Vowed he'd walk in his own coronation -
ronation.
But Mr. O'Connell,
Æneas McDonell,
And two or three more who were Roman
were Roman

[1] The Rev. Reginald Heber, of Bibliographical celebrity.
[2] A second "young Roscius."

Came o'er in a jiffy,
And swore by the Liffey,
The Pope should be Cobbett, or no man —
or no man.
Poor Robert, they stripped him,
And in the Thames dipped him,
And thought they were rid of the pest, Sir —
the pest, Sir,
When pop — up he rose,
In a new suit of clothes,
With his hair neatly powdered and drest, Sir —
and drest, Sir.
To laugh I began,
When a good-looking man,
With a handsome bald head and a cane, Sir,—
a cane, Sir,
Came and hit me a whack
On the broad of my back,
Saying, What! you are at it again, Sir —
again, Sir!"[1]
I woke in a fright,
And I found it was light,
By my bed-side, tea, toast, eggs, and cresses —
and cresses,
And down on the floor,
From a shelf o'er the door,
Had fallen — "Rejected Addresses" —
"Addresses!"

His brother Horace lived at Brighton, and of him I knew less, but quite enough to admire his talent and respect his character; and I have the pleasure still to include amongst my friends his two surviving and accomplished daughters.

[1] Alluding to another song, "Farewell to the Lilies and Roses," previously written and afterwards published at Hook's request in Colburn's *New Monthly Magazine.* In a note to Mrs. Orger, dated Saturday, 30th May (1835), Smith refers to it thus: "On Thursday last there was a great supper at Twiss's, at which I could not attend. Twiss addressed the company, stating that Mr. James Smith had just arrived, and would favor the company with a song. Whereupon Planché started off with one in mitation of me, to the great gratification of a candid and enlightened audience."

SIR HENRY WEBB.

I will mention here, a very amusing member of the club in early days, with whom I was on terms of great intimacy as long as he remained in England — Sir Henry Webb, a baronet, and formerly in the Life Guards. He was a man of refined taste, perfect manners, and great good-nature, and possessed the peculiarly happy art of saying agreeable things without forfeiting the independence of his judgment, or incurring the reproach of insincerity. There was a vein of humor also in his observations, of the most original and whimsical description. He was passionately fond of music, and a great patron of Eliason, who first started the "Promenade Concerts" in London, which were afterwards made so popular by Jullien. On my asking him how his *protégé* was going on, he replied, "He is going on so well that he will carry everything before him, or" — after a pause and a pinch of snuff — "he will leave nothing behind him — which is precisely the same thing." As of course it is; and the musician verified the prediction; for he omitted leaving behind him even the violin (a real Cremona) which he had pledged to Mr. Frederick Gye for money advanced to him.

MALIBRAN.

As a privilege of my office, I had a small private box in the proscenium of the theatre, which I had the pleasure of frequently placing at the disposal of Madame Malibran Garcia, who delighted in the rich humor of John Reeve — certainly, when he was sober or as nearly so as could be expected — one of the finest low comedians on the stage at that, or perhaps any other period. Often when I arrived at the theatre, I was told, "Madame Malibran is in your box, sir;" for almost every evening she was disengaged she would run down on the chance of finding a place in it. Our mere bowing acquaintance rapidly ripened into intimacy; and some of the most enjoyable evenings of my life were passed in the society of that brilliant and fascinating woman. One, in particular, can never be forgotten. I had dined with Bunn at Eagle Lodge, Brompton, the only other guests being Malibran, De Beriot, and Thalberg. After dinner, the latter sat down to the piano and extemporized several charming melodies, to which Malibran sang — not words, of course, but notes — while De Beriot played an accompaniment on the violin. Subsequently to these enchanting "Lieder öhne Worte," De Beriot gave us an amusing description of the performance he had once witnessed of a woman who had danced on the tight-rope to her own playing of the French horn. Fastening a bunch of keys to the strings of his violin, he chalked a line on the carpet, and went through all the evolutions of a rope-dancer, imitating the French horn on his own instrument to perfection. One "*tour de force*" suggested another — the night rapidly and unheededly passed, and a lovely summer morning saw us seated eating mulberries in the garden, under a fine old tree that was the pride of it.

At Madame Malibran's request, I translated an operetta for her, the music by Chelard, which was performed at Drury Lane, June 4th, 1833, under the title of "The Students of Jena;" and when she was discontented with the effusions of "the Poet Bunn," as "Punch" delighted to call him, she would send me her music, superscribed, "Betterer words here." Her early death was a fatal loss to English opera: her genius imparting a vitality to the most mediocre compositions; and upon our stage it is improbable that we shall ever see her like again. I transcribe here her letter to Bunn on the subject of the aforesaid opera, being the only relic of her handwriting I possess: —

"Mr. Planché has just been reading to me his delightful little opera, and I think, *sans meilleur avis*, nothing can be better; therefore I am satisfied *complètement*; but that is only harlequin's marriage, if my advice stands single, and is not ratified by yours.

"I remain,
"Your Columbine,
"MALIBRAN."

Rogers and Luttrell.

It was at the table of the Duchess-Countess of Sutherland that I had the gratification of meeting Mr. Samuel Rogers ("that anomalous personage, a rich poet," as Leigh Hunt used to call him), and that brilliant conversationalist, Mr. Luttrell, with both of whom I remained on terms of the greatest friendship to the end of their lives. The latter was at that period my near neighbor, residing in Brompton Square ; and shortly after our dining together in Hamilton Place, I asked Mr. Rogers, with whom I had breakfasted the following morning, to favor Mrs. Planché and myself by breakfasting with us in Brompton Crescent. I had just previously been subpœnaed as a witness in the case of Jerrold *v.* Morris, which was tried in the Court of Common Pleas ; and instead of writing a note to Mr. Luttrell, to ask him to meet Mr. Rogers, I sent him over-night the subpœna altered to suit the circumstances, with which in his hand he punctually made his appearance at ten in the morning. These two celebrated men, without whom few dinner parties in high life were considered complete, were very differently gifted. Rogers had an inexhaustible fund of anecdote of the most interesting, as well as amusing description, and told his stories in the fewest words possible, so that not only did they never weary you, but they might have been printed without the slightest verbal alteration. Luttrell rarely recounted anything he had heard or seen, but charmed you by the sparkle of his language, and the felicity of his epithets. One evening at a party, having accepted a verbal invitation to dinner, under the idea that his son, who was present, would also be asked, and finding subsequently that he was not, he said, "Then who is going to dine there?" "I really don't know, but I believe the Bishop of —— for one." "The Bishop of ——!" exclaimed Luttrell. "Mercy upon me! I don't mix well with the Dean, and I shall positively effervesce with the Bishop."

Though great friends, for many years, and almost constant companions, they would occasionally comment on each other's peculiarities with humorous freedom. At an assembly at Grosvenor House Mr. Luttrell informed me Mr. Rogers had hurt his foot. On expressing my regret at the cause of his absence, "Oh!" said Luttrell, "he'll be here to-night for all that; that old man would go out with the rattles in his throat!" I don't think Rogers was five years his senior.

Rogers had the reputation of being very ill-natured, and many instances have been given to me by others. I am bound to declare that during all the time I knew him I never heard him say a really ill-natured thing of any one; but he by no means denied the accusation. "When I was young," he observed to me, "I used to say good-natured things, and nobody listened to me. Now that I am old I say ill-natured things and everybody listens to me." So much has been written about the "Poet of Memory," and so many of his anecdotes circulated, both in print and conversation, that I shall limit my contribution to the "Table-talk" I heard from his own lips, and two or three anecdotes kindly communicated to me by Mrs. Procter. The following, which he told me himself, I give as nearly as I can recollect in his precise words: —

"My old friend Maltby, the brother of the Bishop, was a very absent man. One day at Paris, in the Louvre, we were looking at the pictures, when a lady entered who spoke to me and kept me some minutes in conversation. On rejoining Maltby I said, 'That was Mrs. ——. We have not met so long she had almost forgotten me, and asked me if my name was Rogers." Maltby, still looking at the pictures, said, "And was it?"

"A man stopped me one day in Piccadilly and said, 'How do you do, Mr. Rogers?' I didn't know him. 'You don't remember me, sir. I had the pleasure of seeing you at Bath.' I said, 'Delighted to see you again — at Bath.'"

"It was the fashion formerly to make your guests drunk; and there was a gentleman staying in a country house, and they made him very drunk, and they tarred and feathered him, and put him to bed. In the morning he woke, and he wasn't sober then. He rose and went to a cheval-glass, and he looked at himself and said, 'A bird, by ——!'"

Mrs. Procter's reminiscences I shall also give verbatim, from the notes with which she has favored me.

"Driving out with him," she writes, "I asked him after Lady Matheson, who was continually making him presents, and he said, 'I don't know Lady Matheson.' He then pulled the check-string and said, 'Henry, do I know Lady Matheson?' The servant replied, 'Law, Sir! my lady comes to see you, and sends you presents nearly every day.' We drove on, I feeling very uncomfortable, and wishing I had never mentioned the lady. Mr. Rogers took my hand, and raising it to his lips said, 'At any rate, I have not forgotten you.' Once breakfasting with him, a man was spoken of, and the whole party said, one after another, what a nice man he was, etc., etc., etc. When it came to me, I said, 'I don't like him.' 'No more do I,' said Rogers, 'only I had not courage enough to say so.'"

"At his table the conversation never degenerated into small gossip. He always gave it a good tone. I once said, 'I wonder how it is that the —— are able to keep a carriage?' He immediately turned to his man Edmond and said, 'Go to —— Square, with Mrs. Procter's and Mr. Rogers's compliments, and they wish to know how they contrive to pay for their carriage.' I felt this a very proper rebuke."

Rogers had very peculiar notions respecting poetry. The highly imaginative had no charm for him. He could not appreciate the grandeur of oriental language of the Old Testament, and constantly contrasted it with the simple pathos of the New. He would quote the celebrated description of the Horse in the Book of Job, "His neck is clothed with thunder, and he crieth Ha! ha! to the lightning." "That's nonsense," he said to me — then turning to the 11th chapter of St. John, he pointed to the two words which form the 35th verse, "Jesus wept." "*That's* poetry!"

The same taste induced him, whilst he admired the plays of Shakespeare, to speak contemptuously of his sonnets. At breakfast one morning, Mr. Procter and I undertook their defense. Rogers challenged us to repeat a line of them, and to his infinite amusement neither of us were able. I got as far as "Oh how much more doth beauty," and there I stuck. Procter could not remember a word. He who had sung the "Pleasures of Memory" chuckled triumphantly. We whom it had treacherously deserted sat humiliated, but "of the same opinion still."

It was much the same with respect to music. Simplicity and brevity alone had charms for him. "Is not that delightful," I asked him one evening at Mrs. Sartoris's. It was an air by Sebastian Bach. "Yes, and so short," was the reply With Dr. Johnson, he wished that everything "wonderful" in the way of execution or ornamentation was "impossible." During the performance of a "grand scena," no matter who was the singer, it was his custom to ask any one who sat near him, "If you heard those sounds in a hospital wouldn't you suppose some horrible operation was going on?"

The jokes on his personal appearance never seemed to disturb his tranquillity. "Rogers, you're rich enough, why don't you keep your hearse?" is a well-known question addressed to him by some wicked wag — I think Lord Alvanley; but he was as hard upon himself. He tried to cheer my wife, who was becoming a confirmed invalid, by assuring her that he never knew what health was till he was fifty, and that when he was a young man he wore a yellow coat, and was called the Dead Dandy. Singularly enough, after the accident which deprived him of the power of walking, it might truly have been said he kept his hearse, for he was carried in his chair and put into his carriage by a door made at the back of it, in perfect conformity with that vehicle which drives us to the bourne from which no traveller returns. The last time I breakfasted with him, the other guests were Lord Glenelg, Sir David Brewster, and Mr. Babbage; but his strength and memory were fast failing him, and he survived his old friend Luttrell but a few years. London society has yet to seek their successors.

LADY SALISBURY.

On the occasion of the first great Handel Festival in Westminster Abbey, May, 1784, at which Mr. Grenville was present, Lady Salisbury arrived very late. The King (George III.), Queen Charlotte, and all the royal family were in their places, and the performance had begun. In the midst of a piece of music, a loud hammering was heard, which disturbed and offended the audience, who expressed their displeasure promptly and vehemently; but in vain. On went the hammering without intermission. The music ceased; the assembly rose in an uproar; and their Majesties dispatched Lord Salisbury — at that time Lord Chamberlain — to ascertain the cause of so indecent a disturbance. It proved to be his own wife. On entering the box reserved for the Lord Chamberlain and his family, her ladyship found it had been divided, to accommodate another party, and had insisted on carpenters being sent for and compelled to pull down the partition, in utter disregard of King, Queen, Lords, and Commons, singers, fiddlers, and the awful British public!

Going with her daughters to the Chapel Royal St. James's, one Sunday morning, and not being able to find a seat, she said, in answer to the question of "Where shall we go, mamma?" "Home again, to be sure! If we can't get in, it's no fault of ours. We've done the civil thing."

Mr. Grenville survived the Duchess-Countess, and occupied the house in Hamilton Place, where he died, leaving the whole of his magnificent library to the British Museum. Her Grace was my warm friend to the end of her life, never losing an opportunity of showing me a courtesy or doing me a service. Rogers always spoke of her to me as "Our Friend — that very great lady." And she was as gracious as she was great. Lord Byron, who was introduced to her in Paris when she was Marchioness of Stafford, says in one of his letters, "Her manners are princessly;" and the term happily conveys the idea of that natural dignity of demeanor combined with the most charming affability which was her peculiar characteristic.

The Sketching Society.

At the choice little dinners of my friend Thomas George Fonnereau, in the Albany — a great lover and liberal patron of art — I constantly met Eastlake, Stanfield, Roberts, Maclise, and Decimus Burton, the architect, the latter of whom, I am happy to say, I can still number among surviving friends. There was a sketching society existing about that period (1836), held at the houses of the members alternately, to the meetings of which I was frequently invited, and most pleasant and interesting evenings I found them. The two brothers Alfred and John Chalon were constant attendants, and exceedingly amiable men they were. A subject was given by the host of the evening, and each member was allowed a certain time — an hour, I think — to treat it according to his own fancy.

It was extremely interesting to walk round the table and notice the variety of manner in which the same incident was illustrated, according to the peculiar taste and style of each of these eminent men. On one occasion I remember the subject was the seizure of Jaffier's goods and chattels by "the sons of public rapine," as described by Pierre, in Otway's tragedy of "Venice Preserved," act I., scene 1.

While one depicted the chambers and staircases of the Palazzo, swarming with "filthy dungeon villains," dragging out or staggering under the weight of costly furniture,

> "Ancient and domestic ornaments,
> Rich hangings intermixed and wrought with gold."

and another portrayed

> "A ruffian with a horrid face,
> Lording it o'er a pile of massy plate
> Tumbled into a heap for public sale."

Alfred Chalon contented himself with the single figure of Belvidera, gazing sadly from a window "jour à gauche" on the scene of spoliation supposed to be passing below; while Stanfield, true to his instincts, made a spirited drawing of a canal alive with gondolas, and just indicated the removal of the goods from the water-gate of the mansion.

When the allotted time had expired, each sketch was set up in its turn, finished or not finished, on the table, with two candles before it, and subjected to the criticism of the members — a process which was as productive of good-natured fun and banter as of valuable opinions and suggestions. After this came supper, rigorously restricted to bread, cheese, butter, and lettuce ; beer and brandy, or whiskey and water, and fortunately for me, no smoking.

I considered it a great privilege to be one of the very few visitors admitted to these noctes, and my recollection of them is only saddened by the reflection that not one of that gifted and genial company is now in existence. As the sketches of the evening became the property of the member at whose house they were made, it is probable that some night's work may have been preserved in its integrity. What an art treasure it would be now !

Historic Accuracy.

It may surprise many persons to learn that forty or fifty years ago our greatest painters, poets, and novelists were, as far as regarded a correct idea of the civil and military costume of our ancestors, involved in Cimmerian darkness. To Sir Walter Scott the honor is due of having first attracted public attention to the advantages derivable from the study of such subjects, as a new source of effect as well as of historical illustration ; and though his descriptions of the dress, armor, and architecture of the Anglo-Norman and mediæval periods are far from correct, those in the romances and poems, the scenes of which are laid in his own country or elsewhere during the sixteenth and seventeenth centuries, are admirable for their truth and graphic delineation ; but though writers of fiction, inspired by his example, took more pains to acquire information on these points, painters continued to perpetrate the grossest absurdities and anachronisms, often knowingly, under the mistaken idea that they were rendering their productions more picturesque. Did

West, the President of the Royal Academy, render his composition more picturesque by representing Paris in the Roman instead of the Phrygian costume? Did Etty gain anything by placing a helmet of the reign of James or Charles I. by the bedside of Holofernes? As I have remarked elsewhere, "Is it pardonable in a man of genius and information to perpetuate errors upon the ground that they may pass undiscovered by the million? Does not the historical painter voluntarily offer himself to the public as an illustrator of habits and manners, and is he wantonly to abuse the faith accorded to him?"

As an example of the extraordinary hallucinations which occasionally possess artists of first-rate ability, my old friend John Liston called on me one day and flattered me by expressing the request of Sir David Wilkie, who was a connection of his, that I would pay him a visit at Kensington and see his great picture (now so well known) of "Knox preaching to his Congregation," before it was sent to the Royal Academy for exhibition, in order that I might point out to him any little inaccuracy in the costume of the figures he had introduced. I accompanied Liston with great pleasure, and on being shown the picture, immediately pointed out to Sir David that the armed men in the gallery were depicted in helmets of the time of Charles I. or Cromwell, instead of those of the period of his subject. His answer was that he intended to represent persons who were curious to hear the discourse of the preacher, but did not wish to be recognized, and therefore came in armor. I could not help smiling at this explanation, and asked him wherefore, as such was his intention, he had not given them the helmet of the sixteenth century, which, when the vizor was closed, effectually concealed every feature, in preference to that of the seventeenth, with its simple nose-guard or slender triple bars, which allowed the face clearly to be seen? He mused a little, and then half promised to make the alteration; but he didn't; and there is the picture and the engravings from it handed down to posterity with a willful anachronism which diminishes the effect, whilst it utterly defeats the object of the painter!

But, it may be argued, the dresses of some periods would detract from the expression of the figure, which is the higher object of the painter's ambition. Such and such colors are wanted for peculiar purposes, and these might be the very tints prohibited by the critical antiquary. To these and other similar objections my answer has always been that the exertion of a tithe of the study and ingenuity exercised in the invention of dresses to satisfy the painter's fancy would enable him to be perfectly correct, and often, indeed, more effective, from the mere necessity of introducing some hues and forms which otherwise had never entered into his imagination. Take for example a circumstance related to me by Sir Samuel Meyrick, many years ago. Shortly after the publication of his "Critical Inquiry into Ancient Arms and Armor," in which the landmarks were first laid down for the guidance of all future antiquaries, Mr. Abraham Cooper, so well known for his spirited battle scenes, called on him with the request that he would kindly inform him what sort of caparisons were used for horses in the reign of Richard III., as he was painting the "Battle of Bosworth Field," and wished the details to be as accurate as possible. Meyrick explained to him that at that period the king's horse would have been covered with housings of silk, embroidered with the royal arms of France and England quarterly. "Oh!" exclaimed Cooper, in consternation, "that will never do! My principal object is to paint 'White Surrey,' and if he is to be muffled up in that manner there will be nothing seen of him but his hoofs!" "Stop," said the antiquary; "what particular incident in the battle do you propose to represent?" "The last desperate charge of Richard," replied the artist, "in which he slew Richmond's standard-bearer and unhorsed Sir John Cheney." "Then," suggested Meyrick, "it would be fair to suppose that in so fierce a conflict the silken housings of the horse would by that time have been almost in tatters, and display as much of his body as would be necessary." The painter seized the idea. The blue and scarlet housings, slashed to pieces and streaming in the wind, increased the effect of action in the steed, and contrasted admir ably with his color. The picture was most successful, and is, I believe, considered to this day one of the best examples of our English Wouvermans

Louis Napoleon.

I had been dining at Notting Hill, and was walking home to Brompton between ten and eleven. On arriving opposite Gore House, I thought I would avail myself of my pleasant privilege, and "drop in" for half an hour. There had been a small dinner party, and only four gentlemen were remaining. Two of them I knew, Lord Nugent and the Hon. Frederick Byng (familiarly called "Poodle"); the other two were strangers to me; but the youngest immediately engaged my attention. It was the fashion in that day to wear black satin kerchiefs for evening dress; and that of the gentleman in question was fastened by a large spread eagle in diamonds clutching a thunderbolt of rubies. There was but one man in England at that period who, without the impeachment of coxcombry, could have sported so magnificent a jewel; and, though I had never to my knowledge seen him before, I felt convinced that he could be no other than Prince Louis Napoleon. Such was the fact; and his companion was Count Montholon. There was a general conversation on indifferent subjects for some twenty minutes, during which the Prince spoke but little, and then took his departure with the Count. Shortly afterwards Lord Nugent, Mr. Byng, and I said, "Good-night," and walked townward together. As we went along one of my companions said to the other, "What could Louis Napoleon mean by asking us to dine with him this day twelve-months at the Tuileries?" Four days afterwards the question was answered. The news arrived of the abortive landing at Boulogne and the captivity of the Prince, who had fallen into the trap so astutely laid for him. After his escape from Ham, the Prince, as is well known, returned to England, and continued to be a welcome guest at Gore House. "Time's whirlgig" upset the throne of the Citizen King, who landed at Newhaven as "a party of the name of Smith;" — and, "Hey presto, pass!" Louis Napoleon was once more in France—and, this time, "President of the Republic." While the sun shone for him, a cloud came over his friends at Gore House. D'Orsay, "the glass of fashion and the mould of form," took refuge, in his turn, in Paris, and was soon followed by Lady Blessington. I heard by accident of her intended departure, called, and sat with her two hours alone on the day before she left. It is a great gratification to me that I had the opportunity of paying the last attention in my power to one who, whatever may have been her errors, was uniformly kind to me, and under whose roof I have passed so many enjoyable hours in the society of the most distinguished "men of the time," foreign as well as English. Naturally enough both Count D'Orsay and Lady Blessington calculated that the President would rejoice in his power to repay the hospitality and kindness he had received from them in his exile; but, unfortunately, they did not make sufficient allowance for the extremely delicate position in which he was placed. For D'Orsay he did what he could, and would doubtless have neglected no opportunity of serving him, compatible with his responsible situation. But what could he do for Lady Blessington? Receive her at the Tuileries? Impossible! and yet that was the thorn that rankled in her breast. Driving one day in the Champs Elysées, she was overtaken by the President on horseback. After the first salutations and the exchange of a few sentences, the Prince, unfortunately, asked, "Comptez-vous rester long-temps ici?" "Et vous?" was the bitter retort, by which "more Hibernice," she answered a question by a question. Her Irish blood was roused, and, like a true Celt, reason was disregarded.

Lablache.

On the occasion of the visit of Her Majesty and the Prince Consort to Paris, strict orders were issued respecting the admission of strangers to the Park of St. Cloud during the promenade of the Imperial and Royal Party. Amongst the select few admitted was the late most popular vocalist, Signo

Lablache. His remarkable person immediately caught the eye of the Emperor, who is said to have exclaimed, "There is Lablache! I only know him by sight. I should like to speak to him." And the Queen and Prince Albert being well acquainted with him, one of the gentlemen in attendance was sent for him. After presentation, the Emperor said, "You have a son, I believe, in my army?" "I have, sire." "What is his rank?" "He is a sous-lieutenant in the —— Regiment, sire." The Emperor of the French turned to the Queen of England, and said, "*Would not your Majesty like to make Lablache's son a captain?*" — and a captain, of course, he became. Not having been present, I can only "say the tale as 'twas said to me;" but it is highly characteristic of the Emperor's taste and tact, and I have every reason to believe it substantially true for the reason I have already given.

Apropos of Lablache, it was after dinner at Gore House that I witnessed his extraordinary representation of a thunder-storm simply by facial expression. The gloom that gradually overspread his countenance appeared to deepen into actual darkness, and the terrific frown indicated the angry lowering of the tempest. The lightning commenced by winks of the eyes, and twitchings of the muscles of the face, succeeded by rapid sidelong movements of the mouth, which wonderfully recalled to you the forked flashes that seem to rend the sky, the notion of thunder being conveyed by the shaking of his head. By degrees the lightning became less vivid, the frown relaxed, the gloom departed, and a broad smile illuminating his expansive face assured you that the sun had broken through the clouds and the storm was over. He told me the idea occurred to him in the Champs Elysées, where one day, in company with Signor de Begnis, he witnessed a distant thunder-storm above the Arc de Triomphe.

HAYNES BAYLY'S WIDOW.

My poor friend, Haynes Bayly, whose health had been failing for some time past, died at Cheltenham on the 22d of April, 1839, leaving his widow and two little girls, the eldest a cripple, in sadly straitened circumstances. Mrs. Bayly wrote to ask me if I thought the music-publishers would raise a subscription for her. I replied that it was possible a small sum might be collected from them and private friends; but that if she would allow me to get up a public representation at one of the great theatres, avowedly for "the benefit of the widow and children of the late Thomas Haynes Bayly," I was inclined to hope for much better results than could be expected from personal solicitation. She shrunk at first from the publicity of such an appeal, but at length consented; and with the ready and zealous coöperation of Charles Dance and the majority of my brother-dramatists, a most attractive bill of fare was speedily advertised; Bunn giving us the use of Drury Lane, and the *élite* of the dramatic and musical professions their gratuitous services.

In this good work I was greatly assisted by a most kind-hearted but singular man, with whom I had been long intimate, not only in consequence of his being a constant frequenter of the green-rooms at all the principal theatres, but from the circumstance of one of my brothers-in-law being a principal clerk in his department, which was a branch of the Audit Office. This was the Hon. Edmund Byng. He not only collected for me a good round sum in subscriptions, but gave a dinner to the Duchess of Bedford and some half dozen other ladies of high rank, in order to secure their personal attendance at the theatre, and thereby that of a large proportion of their acquaintance. Mr. Lockhart, Theodore Hook, Captain Marryat, and other private friends also exerted themselves most laudably. Miss Burdett Coutts, with her usual large-heartedness, on my application for her private box, sent me £20 in order to retain it for herself. A characteristic note of Hook is worth recording: —

"FULHAM, Tuesday.

"I send you a bit more for our poor widow, and hope to do more to-morrow. I will, and I can. One of my friends, whose taste is theatrical, but whose disposition is *thrifty*, would like four tickets for the performance as a set-off for his *mite*. I suppose he may or *must* have them; if so, perhaps you would put them under cover to me, directed hither per post. I have often heard of the golden *mean*. I now know what it is.

"Yours very truly,

"THEODORE E. HOOK."

We had a brilliant and overflowing house, and cleared between four and five hundred pounds. But most useful and important to her as was such a sum at the moment, it was, as Mrs. Charles Gore wrote to me, "little enough for a widow and two children,"[1] as a provision for the future, and with the greatest economy would soon be exhausted.

By Mrs. Bayly's desire it was placed in the hands of Lord Nugent and myself as trustees, to be drawn upon by her as circumstances might require; but now comes the most gratifying part of the story.

Mrs. Bayly possessed in her own right a small estate in Ireland, which was in the hands of what is called in that country "a middleman," and from whom she not only received no remittances, but continual demands for money for repairs and every imaginable purpose. Of this Lord Nugent and I knew nothing; but it occurred to Mrs. Bayly that if she could contrive to repay this gentleman, into whose debt she was daily getting to an extent which threatened the absorption of the whole property, she could go and live in Ireland in a house of her own, and on her own land, comfortably. Most providentially the proceeds of the benefit enabled her to do this, and fifteen years afterwards I had the pleasure of escorting her to Her Majesty's drawing-room to present her youngest daughter. The substantial "benefit" which thus resulted to my old friend's wife and family is an event I look back upon with the greatest gratification. Charles Kemble used to tell a far different story about some poor foreigner, dancer, or pantomimist in the country, who, after many annual attempts to clear his expenses, came forward one evening with a face beaming with pleasure and gratitude, and addressed the

[1] "I wrote," she added, in a postcript, "to two fine ladies, begging them to patronize the representation, but most likely without success, for during the London season, and especially in such very hot weather, *nobody cares for his fellow creatures*."

audience in these words: — "Dear Public! moche oblige Ver good benefice — only lose half a crown — I come again!

EDMUND BYNG.

I have incidentally mentioned Mr. Edmund Byng, and his kind exertions on behalf of Mrs. Haynes Bayly. As my ntimacy with this gentleman extended over very many years to the day of his death, I will take this opportunity of expressing my regard for one whom I ever found foremost in the cause of charity and kindness of every description.

I do this the more because he was, from infirmity of temper and other peculiarities — I may say eccentricities — extremely unpopular in many circles; even, unfortunately, with his own family. Amongst his numerous praiseworthy actions was the interest he took in cheering the last years of the veteran, Thomas Dibdin. An annual dinner was established by Mr. Byng at Evans's Hotel, Covent Garden, the tickets one guinea each; and the guests through his personal influence rarely fell short of a hundred. Half the money went to pay for the dinner; but it was a good fifty pounds per annum to the old man, and procured him many comforts he might otherwise have stood sorely in need of. The day fixed for the dinner was the 21st of March, the anniversary of the birthday of "the last of the three Dibdins," and the author, as it has been asserted, of 800 dramatic pieces. The first took place in 1837. He died in 1841, at the age of seventy.

I had the pleasure of acting as Mr. Byng's lieutenant on these occasions, and the gratification of receiving from the veteran dramatist the following proof of his appreciation of my earnest, however humble, exertions in the good cause: —

"DEAR SIR, —

"If words could express genuine thanks, you should have a specimen of more than common eloquence from a pen that can only plainly acknowledge your repeated and persevering kindness exhibited on the birthday anniversaries of, Dear Sir,

"Your truly obliged Servant,

"THOMAS DIBDIN."

King Street, March 24, 1839.
"R. Planché, Esq."

Mr. Byng's own dinners were things to remember. Lord Blessington, by no means a bad judge, used to say, "Byng, I often go out to dinner; but when I desire to *dine* I come to you." They were first-rate old English dinners. No soups; no *kickshaws;* large dishes of magnificent fish; a haunch of four-year-old Southdown; a pheasant pie; a coursed hare; or other equally excellent edibles, according to the season, and nothing *out* of it. No *forced* asparagus; no *house* lamb; and in the centre of the table stood always a large wooden bowl, as white as milk, filled with the finest potatoes perfectly boiled in their "*jackets!*" He kept an Irish kitchen-maid expressly for that purpose; and palled must have been the palates, and morbid the appetites, of those who could not enjoy such fare as was always to be found in Clarges Street. As to the company, it was as good as the dinner. By no means *select* in one sense of the word, as his guests were rarely selected. The first eight or ten men he met with as he walked down to his club, or found there, peers, poets, players, painters, soldiers, sailors, doctors of law, medicine, or divinity — "the three black graces," as James Smith called them; for Mr. Byng's acquaintance was most miscellaneous: any friends or agreeable persons whom gentlemen could not object to meet, were verbally invited for the next or an early day, "to dine and go to the play," for such was the usual programme. Here I met the Duke of Gordon, the late Marquis of Hertford, Lord Milford, Lord Methuen, Sir John Conroy, the Hobhouses, and many other men of note or "about town;" and passed many a pleasant evening, adjourning all together to a theatre or its green-room, and occasionally winding up with a supper at Evans's. Latterly Mr. Byng's eyesight became seriously affected, and his natural irritability increased with his years. I visited him to the last — one of the few who did so of "those his former bounty fed" — and shall ever cherish a grateful recollection of his many kindnesses. Apropos of dinners, Mr. Luttrell once said to me, "Sir, the man who says he does not like a good dinner is either a fool or a liar."

CHARLES MAYNE YOUNG.

I had been exceedingly amused, I might say interested, by watching at the Zoölogical Gardens the attention of an old monkey to a poor little sick young one. How related I had not ascertained. But describing the scenes I had witnessed one day in Young's company, he was so tickled with my imitation of the little invalid, that he immediately commenced one of the elder monkey, and whenever we met, in public or private, for many years afterwards kept up the joke. Upon one occasion I was talking to Sloman, the carpenter, on the stage at Covent Garden at the time Sheridan Knowles was reading one of his plays ("Old Maids," I think) in the Green-room, when Young entered the theatre, and, seeing me, commenced his usual antics, to which, of course, I immediately responded. Sloman, who was a valuable old servant of the establishment and on very familiar terms with every one in the theatre, rushed into the Green-room and announced that Mr. Young and Mr. Planché were "playing at monkeys" on the stage. In a moment the room was deserted, the whole of the company, Mr. and Mrs. Charles Mathews at their head, poured out of it to witness the exhibition, to the extreme and very natural annoyance of poor Knowles, whose reading was thus unceremoniously interrupted. Another day, as I was strolling westward through Coventry Street, Piccadilly, I became aware that a hackney coach was intentionally keeping pace with me and attracting the attention of passing strangers. On turning my head to see what was the cause, I observed what appeared to be the face of a large baboon, occupying nearly all the glass of the coach window, the eyes fixed on me with the most intensely serious expression. Startled for the moment, I speedily recognized Young, and laughingly nodded to him, but not a muscle of his features relaxed, and the face remained at the window, with the awful eyes bent upon me, as long as our course was in the same direction. His letters to me, consequently, about this period, frequently concluded with some allusion to this absurd practice of ours, as in the following note, without date.

"DEAR PLANCHÉ,

"Is there? that is, do YOU know of any picture or engraving of a cavalier in the reign of Charles II. wherein said person wore his *own* hair *short*, and not a wig?

"I anticipate that you *do not;* but I fear I must ask you to say *aye or no*, and either will answer.

"Your loving, constant brother,
"THE OLD MONKEY."

To many persons this may appear very silly, and unworthy of a great tragedian; but the charm of Young's character was the boyish spirit with which he entered into or appreciated any fun or frolic, harmless in its nature, and which made him as great a favorite in the profession as his noble acting did with the public, and his polished manners and intellectual acquirements in the highest circles of society.

One of the noblest tragedians on the stage, and a most perfect gentleman in private society, Young was an irrepressible *farceur*, constantly playing with imperturbable gravity the most whimsical pranks in public. He undertook to drive Charles Mathews (*fils*) to Cassiobury on a visit to the Earl of Essex. Having passed through a turnpike and paid the toll, he pulled up at the next gate he came to, and, addressing himself most politely to a woman who issued from the toll-house, inquired if Mr. ——, the toll-taker, whose name he saw on a board above the door, happened to be in the way. The woman answered that he was not in the house, but she would send for him if the gentleman wished to see him particularly. "Well, I'm sorry to trouble you, madam, but I certainly should like to have a few minutes' conversation with him," rejoined Young. Upon which the woman called to a little boy, "Tommy! run and tell your father a gentleman wants to speak to him." Away ran Tommy, down a straight, long path in the grounds of a nursery and seedsman, the entrance to which was close to the turnpike, —Young sitting bolt upright in the tilbury, solemn and silent, to the astonishment of Mathews, who asked him what on earth he wanted with the man. "I want to consult him on a matter of business," was the reply. After some five or six minutes the boy, who had entered a building at the extreme end of the path, reappeared, followed by a man putting on a jacket as he walked, and in due time both of them stood beside the tilbury. The man touched his hat to Young. "You wished to see me, sir?" "Are you Mr. ——?" "Yes, sir." "The Mr. —— who is intrusted to take the toll at this gate?" "Yes, sir." "Then you are precisely the person who can give me the information I require. You see, Mr. ——, I paid sixpence at the gate at ——, and the man who took it gave me this little bit of paper" (producing a ticket from his waistcoat-pocket), "and assured me that if I showed it to the proper authorities at this gate I should be allowed to drive through without payment." "Why, of course," said the man, staring with amazement at Young. "That ticket clears this gate." "Then you do not require me to pay anything here?" "No! Why, any fool ——" "My dear Mr. ——, I'm so much obliged to you. I should have been so sorry to have done anything wrong, and therefore wished to have your opinion on the subject. A thousand thanks. Good morning, Mr. ——." And on drove Young, followed, as the reader may easily imagine, by a volley of imprecations and epithets of anything but a flattering description, so long as he was within hearing.

One of his chief delights was to abuse Meadows for residing at so great a distance from the theatre. As soon as he caught sight of him, wherever it might be, he would shout, "Meadows! where do you live?" "No. —, Barnsbury Terrace, Islington," was the invariable answer, which as invariably brought down upon the respondent a torrent of whimsical invective, such as Young alone could extemporize, and uttered with a volubility and a vehemence as startling as humorous. One day, leisurely riding his well-known white cob up Regent Street, he espied Meadows walking in the same direction, considerably ahead of him. Fearing he might escape him, Young exerted all his magnificent power of voice in putting the usual question, "Meadows! where do you live?" Meadows turned at the sound of his name, and, to the utter discomfiture of his persecutor, bawled in reply, "No. —, Belgrave Square," rapidly disappearing round the corner of Jermyn Street, before a most emphatic impeachment of his veracity rolled like thunder over the heads of the amazed but amused pedestrians from Waterloo Place to Piccadilly.

Young was a special favorite with the late Lord Essex, and they were so much together, and on such familiar terms, that Poole being asked what Englishmen he had seen in Paris, said, "Only Lord Young and Mr. Essex." The last time Young called on me at Brompton he left his card, inscribed, "'Tis I, my lord—the early village cock." The last time I called on him was at Brighton, a few months before he died. He gave me a miserable account of himself, and wound up by saying, "I am seventy-nine, and seventy-nine is telling its tale." I never saw him again.

Practical Joking.

As long as I can remember, the peculiar style of joking of which I have related an example has been popular in the dramatic profession, and, strange to say, some of the most humorous and audacious pranks have been perpetrated by actors who would never have been suspected of such a propensity. Such as Egerton, a dull, heavy man in society; and Liston, who was an extremely shy man. Munden never saw me in the street, that he did not get astride his great cotton umbrella, and ride up to me like a boy on a stick. Wallack and Tom Cooke would gravely meet, remove with stolid countenances *each other's* hat, bow ceremoniously, replace it, and pass on without exchanging a word, to the astonishment of the beholders. Meadows continually would seat himself on the curb-stone opposite my house after we became neighbors, in Michael's Grove, Brompton, with his hat in his hand, like a beggar, utterly regardless of passing strangers, and remain in that attitude till I or some of my family caught sight of him, and threw him a halfpenny, or threatened him with the police. The peculiarity of these absurdities was that they were never premeditated, but were the offspring of mere "gaieté de cœur"—prompted by the whim of the moment. Unlike the elaborately planned hoaxes of Theodore Hook and other "mad wags,' at one time so much the folly of the day, or the later mischievous and dangerous *escapades*, the removal of signs, the wrenching off of knockers and bell-handles, and other more reprehensible outrages in which young men of rank and fashion were weak enough to find amusement.

LISTON.

Liston had taken his formal farewell of the public after the close of the Olympic in 1837 by a benefit at the Lyceum Theatre. The extreme depression under which that great comic actor occasionally labored has often been recorded ; and there was also, no doubt, a strong romantic and sentimental side to his character ; but his love of fun was great, and his humor, on and off the stage, irresistible. Like Young and others, his contemporaries, he delighted, as I have already premised, in practical joking in the public streets. Walking one day through Leicester Square with Mr. Miller, the theatrical bookseller of Bow Street, Liston happened to mention casually that he was going to have tripe for dinner, a dish of which he was particularly fond. Miller, who hated it, said, "Tripe ! Beastly stuff ! How can you eat it ?" That was enough for Liston. He stopped suddenly in the crowded thoroughfare in front of Leicester House, and holding Miller by the arm, exclaimed, in a loud voice, "What, sir ! So you mean to assert that you don't like tripe ?" "Hush !" muttered Miller, "don't talk so loud ; people are staring at us." "I ask you, sir," continued Liston, in still louder tones, "do you not like tripe ?" "For Heaven's sake, hold your tongue !" cried Miller ; "you'll have a crowd round us." And naturally people began to stop and wonder what was the matter. This was exactly what Liston wanted, and again he shouted, "Do you mean to say you don't like tripe ?" Miller, making a desperate effort, broke from him, and hurried in consternation through Cranbourne Alley, followed by Liston, bawling after him, "There he goes ! — that's the man who doesn't like tripe !" to the immense amusement of the numerous passengers, many of whom recognized the popular comedian, till the horrified bookseller took to his heels and ran, as if for his life, up Long Acre into Bow Street, pursued to his very doorstep by a pack of young ragamuffins, who took up the cry, "There he goes!—the man that don't like tripe!"

Our intimacy, which commenced with the production of "Charles XII.," continued throughout his life, the latter days of which were very deplorable. His sole occupation was sitting all day long at the window of his residence in St. George's Row, Hyde Park Corner (the house has just been pulled down), with his watch in his hand timing the omnibuses, and expressing the greatest distress and displeasure when one of them appeared to him to be late. It became a sort of monomania. His spirits had completely forsaken him. He never smiled or entered into conversation, and eventually sank into a lethargy from which he awoke no more in this world. I attended his funeral by invitation, walking with Charles Kemble, who was much affected by the loss of his old friend and fellow-comedian.

CHARLES KEMBLE.

Mr. Kemble had been appointed Examiner of Plays, on the decease of Mr. Colman, and had in consequence taken his leave of the stage during Mr. Osbaldiston's management of Covent Garden Theatre, December 23d, 1836, though he afterwards played some of his principal characters, by the express desire of her Majesty, for a few nights, during the occupancy of that theatre by Mr. and Mrs. Charles Matthews. On his retirement, the members of the Garrick invited him to a dinner at the Albion Hotel, Lord Francis Egerton (afterwards Earl of Ellesmere) in the chair. His lordship made a most eloquent and brilliant speech in proposing the toast of the evening. He spoke of the Kembles as "that illustrious family," and declared that, all Conservative as he was, he had been so excited by the oratorical power of Charles Kemble in the character of Antony, that at the close of his speech to the citizens over the body of Cæsar, he had frequently felt he could have rushed into the streets with the most democratic of mobs, and "sacked the houses of the senators." He was indeed an Antony that might have "raised the stones of Rome to rise and mutiny." The following song, written by John Hamilton Reynolds, and set to music by Balfe, was sung by the latter after the toast: —

1.

Farewell! our good wishes go with him to-day!
Rich in fame — rich in name — he has play'd out the play.
We now who surround him would fain make amends
For past years of enjoyment. We hail him as friends:
Though the sock and the buskin for aye be removed,
Still he serves in the cause of the Drama he loved.
Our chief, nobly born, genius crown'd, our zeal shares:
His coronet's hid by the laurel he wears.[1]
  Well! wealthy we have been, though fortune may frown,
  And they cannot but say that we have had the crown.

2.

Shall we never again see his spirit infuse
Life — life in the young gallant forms of the muse?
Through the lovers and heroes of Shakespeare he ran —
All the soul of the soldier — the heart of the man!
Shall we never in Cyprus his revels retrace?
See him stroll into Angiers with indolent grace?
Or greet him in bonnet at fair Dunsinane?
Or meet him in moon-lit Verona again?
  Well! wealthy we have been, though fortune may frown,
  And they cannot but say that we have had the crown.

3.

Let the curtain come down — let the scene pass away —
There's an Autumn, though Summer has squander'd its day!
We may sit by the fire, though we can't by the lamp,
And re-people the banquet — re-soldier the camp.
Oh! nothing can rob us of memory's gold;
And though he quits the gorgeous, and we may grow old,

[1] Lord Francis Egerton was distinguished for his literary abilities.

With our Shakespeare in hand, and bright forms in our brain,
We may dream up our Siddons and Kembles again.
Well! wealthy we have been, though fortune may frown,
And they cannot but say that we have had the crown.

Only those who have had the good fortune to witness those performances can appreciate the happy allusions in the second verse to the characters of Cassio, Falconbridge, Macduff, and Romeo, in which during my time I have never seen his equal.

Charles Kemble had been amongst the first to recognize the dawning genius of Macready, and had remaraked to John Kemble, "That young man will be a great actor one of these days." "Con quello viso Charles?" was the doubtful answer of that "noblest Roman of them all," who, pardonably enough, considered classical features indispensable to the effective representation of classical characters. Mr. Kemble became, in his later years, exceedingly deaf, but still continued to enjoy society, and contribute his full share to "the feast of reason, and the flow of soul."

SHERIDAN KNOWLES.

Of all the eccentric individuals I ever encountered, Sheridan Knowles was, I think, the greatest. Judge, gentle reader, if the following anecdotes may not justify my assertion. Walking one day, with a brother-dramatist, Mr. Bayle Bernard, in Regent's Quadrant, Knowles was accosted by a gentleman in these terms: — "You're a pretty fellow, Knowles! After fixing your own day and hour to dine with us, you never make your appearance, and from that time to this not a word have we heard from you!" "I couldn't help it, upon my honor," replied Knowles; "and I've been so busy ever since I haven't had a moment to write or call. How are you all at home?" "Oh, quite well, thank you; but come now, will you name another day, and keep your word?" "I will — sure I will." "Well, what day? Shall we say Thursday next?" Thursday? Yes, by all means — Thursday be it." "At six?" "At six. I'll be there punctually. My love to 'em all.' "Thank ye. Remember, now. Six next Thursday." "Al!

right, my dear fellow, I'll be with you." The friend departed; and Knowles, relinking his arm with that of Bayle Bernard, said, "Who's that chap?" not having the least idea of the name or residence of the man he had promised to dine with on the following Thursday, or the interesting "family at home," to whom he had sent his love. Upon one occasion when he was acting in the country he received an anxious letter from Mrs. Knowles, informing him that the money—£200, which he had promised to send up on a certain day, had never reached her. Knowles immediately wrote a furious letter to Sir Francis Freeling, at that time at the head of the Post-office, of which, of course, I cannot give the precise words, but beginning "Sir," and informing him that on such a day, at such an hour, he himself put a letter into the post-office at such a place, containing the sum of £200 in bank-notes, and that it had never been delivered to Mrs. Knowles; that it was a most unpardonable piece of negligence, if not worse, of the post-office authorities, and that he demanded an immediate inquiry into the matter, the delivery of the money to his wife, and an apology for the anxiety and trouble its detention had occasioned them. By return of post he received a most courteous letter from Sir Francis, beginning "Dear sir," as, although they were personal strangers to each other, he had received so much pleasure from Mr. Knowles' works, that he looked upon him as a valued friend, and continuing to say that he (Knowles) was perfectly correct in stating that on such a day and at such an hour he had posted a letter at —— containing bank-notes to the amount of £200, but that, unfortunately, he had omitted not only his signature inside, but *the address outside*, having actually sealed up the notes in an envelope containing only the words, "I send you the money," and posted it without a direction! The consequence was that it was opened at the chief office in London, and detained till some inquiry was made about it. Sir Francis concluded by assuring him that long before he would receive his answer the money would be placed in Mrs. Knowles' hands by a special messenger. Knowles wrote back, "My dear sir, you are right, and I was wrong. God bless you! I'll call upon you when I come to town."

One day also in the country he said to Abbot, with whom he had been acting there, "My dear fellow, I'm off to-morrow. Can I take any letters for you?" "You're very kind," answered Abbot; "but where are you going to?" "*I haven't made up my mind.*"

Seeing O. Smith, the popular melodramatic actor on the opposite side of the Strand, Knowles rushed across the road, seized him by the hand, and inquired eagerly after his health. Smith, who only knew him by sight, said, "I think, Mr. Knowles, you are mistaken; I am O. Smith." "My dear fellow," cried Knowles, "I beg you ten thousand pardons — I took you for your *namesake*, T. P. Cooke!"

An opera was produced at Covent Garden during my engagement, the story of which turned upon the love of a young count for a gipsy girl, whom he subsequently deserts for a lady of rank and fortune; and in the second act there was a fête in the gardens of the château in honor of the bride elect. Mr. Binge, who played the count, was seated in an arbor near to one of the wings witnessing a ballet. Knowles, who had been in front during the previous part of the opera, came behind the scenes; and, advancing as near as he could to Binge without being in sight of the audience, called to him in a loud whisper, "Binge!" Binge looked over his shoulder. "Well, what is it?" "Tel me. Do you marry the poor gypsy after all?" "Yes," answered Binge, impatiently, stretching his arm out behind him, and making signs with it for Knowles to keep back. Knowles caught his hand, pressed it fervently, and exclaimed "God bless you! You are a good fellow!" This I saw and heard myself as I was standing at the wing during the time.

LEIGH HUNT.

The production of "The Legend of Florence" brought me into personal communication with Leigh Hunt, which ripened into the most intimate friendship, terminating only with his death. Of all my literary acquaintances, dear Leigh Hunt was,

I think, the most delightful, as assuredly he was the most affectionate. Living within a short walk of us, his disengaged evenings were usually passed in Brompton Crescent, and most charming evenings he made them by the brightness, the originality, and loving-kindliness of his nature. Suffering severely from the *res angusti domus*, there was no repining, no bitterness, no censoriousness in his conversation. He bore his own privations with cheerful resignation, and unaffectedly rejoiced in the better fortune of others. He was greatly delighted with the success of his play, and began another, the scenes of which he brought to us as he wrote, and read as only he could read. He had the wildest ideas of dramatic effect, and calculated in the most utopian spirit upon the intelligence of the British public. As I often told him, if he read them himself, the magic of his voice, the marvelous intonation and variety of expression in his delivery, would probably enchain and enchant a general audience as it did us; but the hope of being so interpreted was not to be entertained for a moment. As an example of the playfulness of his fancy, take the following: I was on my way to the theatre one morning with Charles Mathews in his carriage. We had not spoken for some minutes, when, as we were passing a wholesale stationer's at the west end of the Strand, Mathews, in his whimsical way, suddenly said to me, "Planché, which would you rather be? Roake or Varty?" such being the names painted over the shop-windows. I laughed at the absurdity of the question, and declined hazarding an opinion, as I had not the advantage of knowing either of the persons mentioned. On my return home in the evening, for I usually dined at the theatre, I found Hunt at tea with my family, and told him the ridiculous question that had been put to me. "Now, do you know," he said, "I consider that anything but a ridiculous question. I should say it was an exceedingly serious one, and which might have very alarming — nay, fatal consequences under certain mental or physical conditions. You might have become impressed by the notion that it was absolutely necessary for you to come to some decison on the question, and so absorbed in its consideration that you could think of nothing else. All business, public or private, would be neglected. Perpetual pondering on one problem, which daily became more difficult of solution, would result in monomania. Your health undermined, your brain overwrought, in the last moments of fleeting existence, only a few seconds left you in which to make your selection, you might rashly utter 'Roake!' then, suddenly repenting, gasp out 'Var,' and die before you could say 'ty.'"

He had a most amusing habit of coining words. Having paid my poor invalid wife, what she considered a great compliment, she said, "Oh, Mr. Hunt, you make me really begin to fear that you are — pardon me the epithet — a humbug." "Good gracious!" he exclaimed, "that a man who has been imprisoned for speaking the truth should be accused of *humbugeism!*" — the softening of the *g* adding elegance to the novelty of the expression. He had familiar names — *noms d'amitié* — for us all, made to rhyme according to an Oriental custom. My two daughters, Kate and Matilda, were, of course, "Katty and Matty." My wife's name, Elizabeth, instead of Betty, became "Batty." Her sister, Fanny, was transmuted to "Fatty," which she indignantly objected to as personal. "And what is papa's name to be?" asked one of my girls. "Papa's? oh, James must obviously be 'Jatty,'" and so we remained to the end of the chapter.

TOMKINSON.

He was a wealthy man, and a liberal purchaser of pictures, having some pretensions to rank as a *connoisseur.* Extremely diminutive in person, the pomposity of his manner, the grandiloquence of his conversation, and the extravagance of his similes, formed the most amusing contrast to it imaginable. He was one of the delights of Young's existence. He would listen with the profoundest gravity to one of the little man's orations, and, at the end of it, snatch him up in his arms and carry him, struggling and kicking, round the room in the ecstasy of his admiration. A few flowers of rhetoric culled from the speeches of this remarkable individual will convince the reader that the eloquence was of no ordinary description, if it do not raise a reasonable doubt of the veracity of my report of it. Having bought a painting by one of the old masters — I forget the painter and the subject — he asked Mr. Mathews (the elder), who was fond of pictures, to call and see it. Ushering him, with much solemnity, into the room it had been hung in, and undrawing a green curtain by which it was covered, he silently quitted the room, leaving his visitor to contemplate the picture for some minutes. On rejoining him and receiving his congratulations on having made so desirable an aquisition to his collection, Tomkinson said, "Sir! since ever you were born, — so long as you shall live, — never shall you see — such a picture as this!"

Calling one day on the Countess of Essex, she happened, in the course of conversation, to mention, casually, that she had not seen the new bridge at Southwark. "What!" exclaimed Tomkinson, with a start, "you have not seen Southwark Bridge! It is a marvelous work! To give you an idea of its magnificent proportions, you shall take St. Paul's Cathedral, you shall place it on the river, it shall float through the centre arch of Southwark Bridge, it shall never touch it! You shall take the monument, you shall lay it at full length across the river, it shall float through the centre arch of Southwark Bridge, it shall never touch it!" The language is absurd enough; but the emphasis with which it was delivered, the serious expression of his features, the apparently perfect unconsciousness of any exaggeration in his similes, it is impossible for words to describe, or to convey a notion of the effect upon his auditors. I don't remember that I ever saw him smile. I am satisfied I never heard him laugh; but the difficulty to avoid laughing at him has sometimes caused me considerable inconvenience.

Albert Smith.

In the "Ascent of Mount Parnassus," which was a species of *revue*, I introduced a scene representing the room at the Egyptian Hall fitted up for Smith's entertainment aforesaid, and in which the popular entertainer himself was personated by Mr. Caulfield, of the Haymarket company. I had previously asked and received Smith's permission to take this liberty with him, which was most good-naturedly accorded by that genial artist, with whom I had been long on terms of intimacy, and who felt assured that he had nothing to fear from any use I should make of his name or his property.

He entered indeed into the fun of the thing with such spirit that he determined to act the scene himself some night without apprising Buckstone of his intention. Accordingly one evening, having privately intimated his intention to Mrs. Fitzwilliam, his own performance terminating at ten, affording him just time enough to reach the Haymarket before the scene was discovered, and no change being required in his dress, on the cue being given, Smith appeared "in his habit as he lived," to the astonishment and mystification of Buckstone — who alone had been carefully kept in ignorance of the matter — and the immense amusement of the whole company assembled at the wings to witness the effect. Smith was immediately recognized by the audience, who received him with repeated cheers, and in obedience to a unanimous call, he made his bow to them at the end of the scene, addressing a few pleasant words to them in explanation, and retired amidst hearty laughter and applause both before and behind the curtain.

Missing Moore.

On the first occasion of my dining in company with Mr. Rogers, at the Duchess-Countess of Sutherland's, he asked Mr. Luttrell and me to meet Moore, who had promised to breakfast with him the next morning. I went of course, and so did Luttrell; but there was no Tom Moore. A note arrived from him to say he was obliged to breakfast at Holland House. Again and again similar disappointments took place. One day I was chatting with Haynes Bayly in the balcony of the Athenæum, when he suddenly said, "Here comes Tom Moore." "Where?" I exclaimed eagerly, as I had never set eyes on him; but before he could point him out to me, he had passed under the balcony in which we were standing, and was no longer in sight. On expressing my vexation, Bayly said, "Oh, never mind, he's coming in here. Let us go down-stairs, and I will introduce you." Down-stairs we hastened, but there was no Tom Moore. On inquiry, the porter informed us that Mr Moore had simply asked for his letters, and, being told there were none, had not entered the club, but gone down the steps into St. James's Park. During the last season of my engagement at the Haymarket — 1847 — returning home to dinner, I met Mr. Carter Hall, who asked me what I was going to do that evening. On my replying, "Nothing particular," he said, "Well, as you are disengaged, Tom Moore is coming to us, and we shall be happy if you will meet him." "I should be only too delighted, but I fear it's impossible." "What do you mean?" I told him briefly how invariably I had been disappointed, and that I really felt it was not to be. He laughed, and assured me that I should be fortunate this time, for that Moore was going to dine quietly and early with a friend, who had promised faithfully to bring him at eight o'clock; but, he added, "Mind you are punctual, for Moore is far from well, and will not stay above an hour." I had just come from the theatre, and knew there was nothing, barring accidents, which could necessitate my presence that evening, so gladly accepted Mr. Hall's invitation. It was no party — only two or three friends and a quiet cup of tea. We should have Moore all to ourselves. How I rejoiced that I had met Mr. Hall! I hurried home, dressed, and had just finished dinner, when a servant came round from Farren's house in Brompton Square, with a note desiring to see me at the theatre as soon after eight as possible on most particular business. Farren was stage manager. Mr. Webster was out of town. I could not venture to neglect the summons, as I could form no guess of what the business might be. It was past seven o'clock, and Farren, who had to play in the first piece, was on the stage at that moment. He had not been at the theatre in the morning, so had not had an opportunity of speaking to me. There was no help for it; go up to town I must. But Moore was to be at "the Rosery" at eight precisely, and would not stay long. At least I should see and speak to him, if only for a minute I was at Mr. Hall's at ten minutes to eight. Eight o clock struck but no Moore; a quarter past eight, but no Moore. It was agony point. I left the house under a promise from Mr. Hall that, if Moore did come, he would detain him as long as possible. I had a vehicle in waiting, and told the coachman to drive as fast as he dared to the Haymarket, rushed up to Farren's room, who was undressing, and found that "the particular business" might have been communicated in the note he had sent me, and attended to at my leisure. I was out of the theatre again in five minutes, and back at the Rosery before nine, to hear that Moore had arrived immediately after I left, and had but that instant departed. As I felt, it was not to be! I am not aware that he ever visited London again. At any rate, I never had the happiness even to behold him.

MR. AND MRS. BARTLEY.

With Mr. and Mrs. George Bartley I had only a professional acquaintance. The lady had been accepted by the public as a leading tragédienne, and her husband was a sensible, unaffected actor, without any pretension to genius, but thoroughly dependable to the extent of his ability. He was also a courteous, discreet gentleman, well calculated to fill the position he so long sustained, under various lessees, of stage manager. Of the intelligence of a British public his opinion was not flattering. "Sir," he would say to me, "you must first tell them you are going to do so and so; you must then tell them you are doing it, and then that you have done it; and then, by G—d" (with a slap on his thigh), "*perhaps* they will understand you!" British public, on your honor, as ladies and gentlemen, is this true? Without "indorsing the bill," I will only say that his advice was most valuable to young writers. Perspicuity is a primary qualification in the plot of a play, and its absence cannot be compensated for by either language or incident. Mr. and Mrs. Bartley visited the United States — I forget in what particular year — but shortly after they were fairly in blue water, one of the crew became mutinous, and received a very severe cut on the head from, I believe, the captain, in the presence of the passengers. Mrs. Bartley, who was beginning to suffer from the *mal de mer*, was much shocked and alarmed, became very ill, and retreated immediately to her cabin, from which she did not emerge again till they were almost in sight of port. The first day that she ventured on deck the man that she had seen cut down was at the wheel. Approaching him with kindly interest, she inquired, "How is your head now?" and received for answer, "West and by north, ma'am!"

When Bartley first joined the Covent Garden company, Fawcett, an excellent actor, was stage-manager, and in possession, of course, of all the best parts. One day he sent for Bartley, and said, "George, I'm going to give you a chance. Hamlet is put up for next week, and you shall play the 'First Gravedigger.' I've plenty to do, and it is but fair to give you a turn.' Bartley expressed his gratitude. Fawcett shook hands with him and walked away, muttering to himself, but loud enough for Bartley to hear him, "There's a wind at night comes up that cursed grave-trap enough to cut one's vitals out!"

Charles Farley.

Charles Farley, who attained the venerable age of eighty-seven, is described in a theatrical obituary as a "pantomime-arranger." This is doing him scant justice. He was not only a good melodramatic actor, but sustained very creditably a line of character parts in the plays of Shakespeare and the best of our old English comedies — Roderigo, in "Othello," Cloten, in "Cymbeline," Osric, in "Hamlet," Cacofogo, in "Rule a Wife and have a Wife," and many others; notably, although utterly ignorant of French, Canton, in "The Clandestine Marriage." So little did he know of the language of our lively neighbors, that he is reported to have waited day after day at the doors of one of the theatres in Paris in order to witness the first performance of a new grand spectacle, entitled, as he imagined, "Relache," mistaking the bills with that word only in large letters which he saw posted up there, to indicate the production of some important novelty. During the visit of the allied sovereigns to Europe, Farley strolled one afternoon into the house of the eminent printsellers, Colnaghi & Co., Pall Mall East, to whom he, and all the theatrical profession indeed, were deeply indebted for the great and gratuitous assistance so liberally rendered to them by those gentlemen in matters of costume and scenery. "What a pity you were not here a little sooner, Mr. Farley," said Mr. Dominic Colnaghi to him, as he entered. "The Emperor Alexander was standing on this very spot not a quarter of an hour ago, looking at that portrait of Napoleon"—a very fine one then on view there. "Indeed!" said Farley eagerly; "and what observation did he make on it?" "He said, 'C'est très-ressemblant.'" "Ah!" rejoined Farley, with a deep sigh and a mysterious shake of the head, "he might *well* say that!" My friend Dominic was too much of a gentleman to inquire what interpretation his interrogator had given to the important words which had escaped the lips of the Emperor of all the Russias.

MADAME VESTRIS.

A singular instance occurred of the way in which that "wonderful woman" jumped with true feminine felicity, at conclusions for which she could not herself account, and which to others appeared preposterous. I dined with her and Mathews nearly every day, in their room in the theatre, George Bartley, the acting manager, making occasionally a fourth. One day when I was alone with them, and long before any calculation could be fairly made of the ultimate result of the season, Madame Vestris said, abruptly, after a short silence, "Charles! we shall not have this theatre next year." "What do you mean?" he and I exclaimed simultaneously. "Simply what I say." "But what reason," inquired Mathews, "can you possibly have for thinking so?" "No particular reason; but you'll see." "Have you heard any rumor to that effect," I asked. "No; but we shall not have the theatre." "But who on earth will have it then?" we said, laughing at the idea; for we could imagine no possible competitor likely to pay so high a rent. "Charles Kemble," was her answer. "He will think that his daughter's talent and popularity will be quite sufficient, and we shall be turned out of the theatre. But, she continued, seeing us still incredulous, "three things may happen: Miss Kemble may be ill; Miss Kemble may not get another opera like 'Norma;' and Miss Kemble may marry." Every one of these predictions was fulfilled. The rent not being fully paid up according to the conditions of her lease, it was declared forfeited; and Mr. Charles Kemble took the theatre himself upon his own shoulders. Just before the season commenced, Miss Kemble *was* taken ill, and the opening of the theatre had to be postponed in consequence. The opera prepared for her did not prove attractive; and very shortly afterwards she became the wife of Mr. Edward John Sartoris, now M. P. for Caermarthenshire. The theatre closed prematurely, and after an abortive attempt of Henry Wallack, and a brief and desperate struggle of Bunn, ceased to be a temple of the national drama.

Death of Theodore Hook.

On the 24th of August, 1842, I lost my ever-kind friend, Theodore Hook. His two last notes to me are without date, but I well remember the circumstances under which they were written. I had a general invitation from him for Sundays, which I rarely availed myself of, as we generally had a friend or two to dinner ourselves on that only day in the week professional persons — medical men excepted — can count upon with security, and a few of our pleasant neighbors would occasionally drop in in the evening; but I heard that Hook had been ill, and wrote him word that I would run down to see him on the afternoon of the following Sunday. I received this reply: —

"Fulham
(Blowing a gale of wind).

"Don't come here next Sunday, for I shan't be at home. Do come Sunday week; and if my house stands through the gale of wind which is now shaking it, I shall be delighted. Come at *one*, and (I don't mean a rhyme) have lunch*eon* Yours truly,

T. E. H."

I went, of course, and found him pretty nearly himself again — full of fun and anecdote, — but I remarked with regret that he ate nothing, but drank tumbler after tumbler of claret. His most intimate and attached friend, Mr. Broderip, the magistrate — "the Beak," as Hook always introduced him — who was present, told me that solid food rarely passed his lips, and that he feared the digestive organs were fatally impaired.

On being pressed to eat a portion at least of a cutlet, he merely shook his head, and said, "Apropos of cutlets, I once called upon an old lady, who pressed me so urgently to stay and dine with her that, as I had no engagement, I could not refuse. On sitting down, the servant uncovered a dish which contained two mutton chops, and my old friend said, 'Mr. Hook, you see your dinner.' 'Thank you, ma'am,' said I; 'but *where's yours?*'"

Having written to him from St. Leonard's-on-Sea, on some private matters which had annoyed me, he wound up his reply in these words: —

"I have been *very* ill, and am as you may perceive, scarcely able to hold my pen. I wish *I* was at St. Leonard's-on-Sea to enjoy the fresh breezes, and then I would tell you *personally*, as I now write you, that I am vexed at what you communicated, and that I am truly yours, THEODORE E. HOOK.

"(Hand shaky.)"

JULIAN CHARLES YOUNG.

CHARLES MAYNE YOUNG'S FATHER.

HIS father was a London surgeon of considerable eminence. The late Sir Aston Key, no mean authority, told me that he had never seen his equal as a demonstrator of anatomy; and that, as an operator, he believed him to have been second only to John Hunter. It is painful for the biographer to write disparagingly of a grandfather whom he never knew; yet truth compels him to state that, from the concurrent testimony of persons indifferent, as well as of those best qualified to form an opinion, he was selfish and self-sufficient, profligate by habit, irascible in temper, imperious in domestic rule, and utterly callous to the claims of blood and affection. In person he was handsome, and in manner impressive, though in deportment haughtier than became a professional man. When he wished to please, he found no difficulty in doing so; for his voice was so melodious, his manners so insinuating, and his diction so graceful, that ordinary observers, imposed upon by these adventitious accessories, were apt to overlook his errors, and accept him at his own valuation. His parts were unquestionably far above mediocrity, and his rhetorical powers of a high order. An exemplification of that fact occurs to me; for the knowledge of which I am indebted to the late Mr. Shuter.

Two ruffians were one night discovered in the act of depositing a corpse at the door of Thomas Young's anatomical museum. They were instantly apprehended and committed for trial.

Young, by whom they had been employed, knew they could not pay for counsel's aid, and therefore came forward in their defense, avowing himself to have been the instigator of the offense, and they but his instruments. He argued that, though they might have infringed the letter of the law, they had done violence neither to its spirit nor to the animus of the law-maker. That there had been no sacrilegious intention on their part, and that the *malfaisance* complained of on his had been committed in the interests of science, and with the object of saving human life! The effect of his appeal on the judge and jury, enhanced as it was by his animated action and delivery, was so great, that he not only succeeded in obtaining the acquittal of the prisoners, but in extorting from the judge the following compliment in open court: "Mr. Young, few here are ignorant of your high reputation as a surgeon; but after the extraordinary display of forensic ability we have just witnessed, you must permit me to add, that if you had bent the powers of your mind to the study and practice of the law, there are no heights in the legal profession to which you might not have aspired."

Edmund Kean and Mother Carey.

During the Christmas vacation, Thomas Young was in the habit of giving frequent dinners to his friends and acquaintance, at which his son Charles was allowed to appear as soon as dessert was put upon the table. On one of those occasions (when, by the by, one of his lions, Prince Le Boo, was present), as Charles was descending the stairs to the dining-room, in his smartest clothes, he saw a slatternly woman seated on one of the chairs in the hall, with a boy standing by her side, dressed in fantastic garb, with the blackest and most penetrating eyes he had ever beheld in human head. His first impression was that the two were strolling gypsies from Bartholomew Fair, who had come for medical advice.

He was soon undeceived; for he had no sooner taken his place by his father's side, and had heard the servant whisper their presence in the hall, than, to his surprise, the master, instead of manifesting displeasure, smirked and smiled, and with an air of self-complacent patronage, desired his butler to bring in "the boy." On his entry he was taken by the hand, patted on the head, and requested to favor the company with a specimen of his histrionic ability. With a self-possession marvelous in one so young, he stood forth, knitted his brow, hunched up one shoulder-blade, and with sardonic grin and husky voice, spouted forth Gloster's opening soliloquy in Richard III. He then recited selections from some of our minor British poets, both grave and gay; danced a hornpipe; sang songs, both comic and pathetic; and, for fully an hour, displayed such versatility, as to elicit vociferous applause from his auditory, and substantial evidence of its sincerity by a shower of crown pieces and shillings — a napkin having been opened and spread upon the floor for their reception. The accumulated treasures having been poured into the gaping pockets of the lad's trowsers, with a smile of gratified vanity and grateful acknowledgment, he withdrew, rejoined his tatterdemalion friend in the hall, and left the house rejoicing. The door was no sooner closed than every one present desired to know the name of the youthful prodigy who had so astonished them. The host replied, that "This was not the first time he had had him to amuse his friends; that he knew nothing of the lad's history or antecedents; but that his name was Edmund Kean; and that of the woman who seemed to have the charge of him, and was his supposititious mother, Carey."

Gaspar Grimani.

Gaspar Grimani was a man of singular ability and erudition. As a classical scholar he took no mean rank. He was master of seven modern languages; and his attainments in mathematics and astronomy were considerable. On the latter science he wrote a work in several volumes, which he was never able to publish. His eldest brother being heir to the title and estates, his parents dedicated Gaspar to the service of the Roman Catholic Church, without at all consulting his feelings in the matter. Shortly after he had been ordained, but before he had been made a priest, a curious adventure befell him, which exercised a marked influence over his future life. He was riding alone, on an unfrequented road, in the neighborhood of a large dense forest. On abruptly turning a corner he saw a sight which would have made many put spurs to their horse's sides, and gallop off; but Grimani was made of different metal. He beheld the figure of a man prostate, wounded, bleeding to death, and surrounded by a group of angry brigands, whose captain he had been, but whom they had risen against and murdered. The moment the unhappy wretch, whose life was ebbing fast, descried Gaspar Grimani, and saw by his religious garb that he was in holy orders, he called to him and implored him, for the love of God, to come to him and "confess" him. One of the men, seeing him about to dismount from his horse with the purpose of doing so, peremptorily bade him "halt;" swearing that, if he moved another yard, he would put a bullet through him. Gaspar gently remonstrated with him, but in vain. Once more the fast-expiring man piteously appealed to him, as he valued his own soul, to come and save his. A man of impulse, and heedless of consequences, Grimani sprang from his horse, rushed up to the miscreant who had menaced him, wrenched his pistol from out his belt, and kneeling by the wounded sufferer, supported him with one arm, while with the other he presented the pistol at the group around him, and with loud and resolute voice commanded them to "stand back." Impressed by his fearlessness, and awed by his manner, they instinctively obeyed him, and retired to a considerable distance while the dying mar made his confession. Grimani, after having prayed with him and given him absolution, received him in his arms a corpse. The band drew near. Grimani rose as they did so, and, without evincing the slightest particle of fear, at once returned the pistol to its owner, while he stood calmly with folded arms, awaiting his fate. To his surprise, the brigand who had threatened to shoot him approached him reverently and thus addressed him:—"Per Bacco! you are the bravest man we ever saw! We admire you! We like you! We are astonished at your courage! We have a proposition to make to you. If you will stay with us and be our captain, we will gladly serve under you; and we will soon help to put more money in your pocket than you will ever earn as a priest." Grimani smiled, thanked them for the honor they had done him in making the offer, declined it, and rode away without receiving the slightest molestation at their hands.

YOUNG AND THE ELEPHANT.

In July, 1810, the largest elephant ever seen in England was advertised as "just arrived." As soon as Henry Harris, the manager of Covent Garden Theatre, had heard of it, he determined, if possible, to obtain it; for it struck him that if it were to be introduced in the new pantomime of "Harlequin Padmenaba," which he was about to produce at great cost, it would add greatly to its attraction. Under this impression, and before the proprietor of Exeter Change had seen it, he purchased it for the sum of 900 guineas. Mrs. Henry Johnston was to ride it; and Miss Parker, the Columbine, was to play up to it. Young happened to be one morning at the box-office adjoining Covent Garden Theatre, when his ears were assailed by a strange and unusual uproar within the walls. On asking one of the carpenters the cause of it, he was told "it was something going wrong with the elephant: he could not exactly tell what." I am not aware what may be the usage nowadays; but then, whenever a new piece had been announced for presentation on a given night, and there was but scant time for its preparation, a rehearsal would take place after the night's regular performance was over, and the audience had been dismissed. One such there had been the night before my father's curiosity had been roused. As it had been arranged that Mrs. Henry Johnston, seated in a howdah on the elephant's back, should pass over a bridge in the centre of a numerous group of followers, it was thought expedient that the unwieldy monster's tractability should be tested. On stepping up to the bridge, which was slight and temporary, the sagacious brute drew back his forefeet and refused to budge. It is well known as a fact in natural history that the elephant, aware of its unusual bulk, will never trust its weight on any object which is unequal to its support. The stage manager, seeing how resolutely the animal resisted every attempt made to compel or induce it to go over the bridge in question, proposed that they should stay proceedings till next day, when he might be in a better mood. It was during the repetition of the experiment that my father, having heard the extraordinary sounds, determined to go upon the stage, and see if he could ascertain the cause of them.

The first sight that met his eyes kindled his indignation. There stood the huge animal, with downcast eyes and flapping ears, meekly submitting to blow after blow from a sharp iron goad, which his keeper was driving ferociously into the fleshy part of his neck at the root of the ear. The floor on which he stood was converted into a pool of blood. One of the proprietors, impatient at what he regarded as senseless obstinacy, kept urging the driver to proceed to still severer extremities, when Charles Young, who was a great lover of animals, expostulated with him, went up to the poor, patient sufferer, and patted and caressed him; and when the driver was about to wield his instrument again with even still more vigor, he caught him by the wrist as in a vice, and stayed his hand from further violence. While an angry altercation was going on between Young and the man of color, who was his driver, Captain Hay, of the *Ashel* who had brought over Chuny in his ship, and had petted him greatly on the voyage, came in, and begged to know what was the matter. Before a word of explanation could be given, the much-wronged creature spoke for himself; for, as soon as he perceived the entrance of his patron, he waddled up to him, and, with a look of gentle appeal, caught hold of his hand with his proboscis, plunged it into his bleeding wound. and then thrust it before his eyes. The gesture seemed to say, as plainly as if it had been enforced by speech, "See how these cruel men treat Chuny. Can *you* approve of it?" The hearts of the hardest present were sensibly touched by what they saw; and among them that of the gentleman who had been so energetic in promoting its harsh treatment. It was under a far better impulse that he ran out into the street, purchased a few apples at a stall, and offered them to him. Chuny eyed him askance, took them, threw them beneath his feet, and, when he had crushed them to pulp, spurned them from him. Young, who had gone into Covent Garden on the same errand as the gentleman who had preceded him, shortly after reëntered, and also held out to him some fruit, when, to the astonishment of the bystanders, the elephant ate every morsel, and, after, twined his trunk, with studied gentleness, around Young's waist; marking by his action that, though he had resented a wrong, he did not forget a kindness.

It was in the year 1814 that Harris parted with Chuny to Cross, the proprietor of the menagerie at Exeter Change. One of the purchaser's first acts, was to send Charles Young a life ticket of admission to his exhibition; and it was one of his innocent little vanities, when passing through the Strand with any friend, to drop in on Chuny, pay him a visit in his den, and show the intimate relations which existed between them. The tragic end of the poor creature must be within the recollection of many of my readers. From some cause unknown, he went mad; and it took 152 shots, discharged by a detachment of the Guards, to dispatch him.

Mrs. Siddons as Volumnia.

In 1812, Kemble revived and adapted, with a splendor, in those days unparalleled, the play of "Julius Cæsar." No piece was ever more effectively cast: Brutus had for its representative, John Kemble; Cassius, Young; Anthony, Charles Kemble; Casca, Terry; First Citizen, Simmons; and Portia, Mrs. Siddons. I have never spoken with any one fortunate enough to have seen that play rendered, as it then was, who has not admitted it to have been the greatest intellectual recreation he ever enjoyed.

It was really difficult to believe that one had not been transported while in a state of unconsciousness, from the purlieus of Bow Street and the vicinity of Covent Garden Market, to the glories of the Capitol, and the very heart of the Julian

Forum ; so complete, in all its parts, was the illusion of the scene. When but six years old, I saw the play on the first night of its representation ; and I was allowed to see it again in 1817, with the same cast, minus Mrs. Siddons. And, although I was then but eleven, the impression left upon my mind has never been effaced. If it appear a thing incredible, that any play, however well put on the stage, however gorgeous its accessories, and however spirited the acting, should have left definite and durable traces on the brain of a child of such tender years, it must be mentioned that he had not only inherited a turn for the stage, but had read and re-read the play in question over and over again, had committed its chief speeches to memory, had rehearsed them by heart, and often represented the characters before small but select audiences, composed of all the squabs, bolsters, and pillows available in the house. The consequence was, that when I saw "Julius Cæsar" for the second time, I attended to the stage-business, and more particularly to the by-play, with an intentness and inquiring interest, which it amuses me, even now, to recall. Owing to my reproductions, in the privacy of my little bedroom, of the effects I had seen and heard on the boards of the great theatre, I was tolerably qualified, in my own opinion at least, to distinguish between the comparative merits of each actor. And there was, perhaps, nothing which elicited more of my boyish admiration, than the fidelity with which the players of prominent parts indirectly indicated the peculiar idiosyncrasies of each (and this too before they had opened their lips) by their very mien and movement. Ordinary actors, on first making their entrance in the second scene of the first act, march in procession towards the course, with all the precision of the Grenadier Guards, stepping in time to the martial music which accompanies them. And, even on the part of leading actors, I have noted a tameness of deportment (as stilted as if they were automata) until speech has stirred them into action.

In the play I am writing of, as then enacted, one would have imagined that the invariable white toga, beautiful as it is when properly worn and tastefully adjusted, would have rendered it difficult, at first, for any but frequenters of the theatre to distinguish, in the large number of the *dramatis personæ* on the stage, John Kemble from Daniel Terry, or Charles Young from Charles Kemble. Whereas, I feel persuaded that any intelligent observer, though he had never entered the walls of a theatre before, if he had studied the play in his closet, would have had no difficulty in recognizing in the calm, cold, self-contained stoical dignity of John Kemble's *walk*, the very ideal of Marcus Brutus ; or in the pale, wan, austere, "lean and hungry look" of Young, and in his quick and nervous *pace*, the irritability and restless impetuosity of Caius Cassius ; or, in the handsome, joyous face, and graceful tread of Charles Kemble, — his pliant body bending forward in courtly adulation of "Great Cæsar," — Mark Antony himself ; while Terry's sour, sarcastic countenance would not more aptly portray "quick-mettled" Casca, than his abrupt and hasty *stamp* upon the ground, when Brutus asked him "What had chanced that Cæsar was so sad ?" In support of my theory of the mute eloquence of gait and movement, Charles Young was wont to speak in terms of almost wanton admiration, of a bold point he saw Mrs. Siddons once make, while playing the comparatively inferior part of Volumnia for her brother's benefit.

In the second scene of the second act of "Coriolanus," after the victory of the battle of Corioli, an ovation in honor of the victor was introduced with great and imposing effect by John Kemble. On reference to the stage directions of my father's interleaved copy, I find that no fewer than 240 persons marched, in stately procession, across the stage. In addition to the recognized *dramatis personæ*, thirty-five in number, there were vestals, and lictors with their fasces, and soldiers with the spolia opima, and sword-bearers, and standard-bearers, and cup-bearers, and senators, and silver eagle-bearers, with the S. P. Q. R. upon them, and trumpeters, and drummers, and priests, and dancing-girls, etc., etc.

Now, in this procession, and as one of the central figures in it, Mrs. Siddons had to walk. Had she been content to follow in the beaten track of those who had gone before her, she would have marched across the stage, from right to left, with the solemn, stately, almost funereal, step conventional. But, at the time, as she often did, she forgot her own identity. She was no longer Sarah Siddons, tied down to the directions of the prompter's book; she broke through old traditions — she recollected that, for the nonce she was Volumnia, the proud mother of a proud son and conquering hero. So that, when it was time for her to come on, instead of dropping each foot at equi-distance in its place, with mechanical exactitude, and in cadence subservient to the orchestra; deaf to the guidance of her woman's ear, but sensitive to the throbbings of her haughty mother's heart, with flashing eye and proudest smile, and head erect, and hands pressed firmly on her bosom, as if to repress by manual force its triumphant swellings, she towered above all around, and rolled, and almost reeled across the stage; her very soul, as it were, dilating, and rioting in its exultation; until her action lost all grace, and, yet, became so true to nature, so picturesque, and so descriptive, that pit and gallery sprang to their feet, electrified by the transcendent execution of the conception.

The Gait proclaims the Man.

Shakespeare makes Polonius tell his son Laertes, that "the *apparel* oft proclaims the man." But a greater than Shakespeare — Solomon — tells us "that man's attire and *gait* show what he is." And true it is, that self-sufficient men, bashful men, energetic, phlegmatic, choleric, sanguine, and melancholy men, may each and all be known by their attire and "gait." Of the force and justice of this axiom, I am tempted to give an appropriate, though a ludicrous confirmation. Theodore Hook was one day standing on Ludgate Hill, in conversation with Dubois, a well-known wag of the Stock Exchange, and one or two other kindred spirits; when their attention was called to an aldermanic-looking person, "with fair round belly with good capon lined," strutting along like a peacock, with double chin in air, his chest puffed out, and a stride of portentous self-importance. Hook, with his characteristic audacity, immediately crossed over the street, went up to him, took off his hat deferentially,

> "And in a bondman's key,
> With bated breath and whispering humbleness,"

thus saluted him: "I really beg your pardon, Sir, for the liberty I take in stopping you. But I should feel very much obliged to you, and so would some friends of mine over the way, if you would kindly gratify a curiosity, which we find irrepressible. We have been observing you, as *you walked*, with very lively admiration; and we cannot divine who you can be? *Arn't you somebody very particular?*" Unjustifiably impudent, as this question was, at all events, it shows that the interrogator's inference of the man's character was deduced from his "gait." Even from an anecdote as trivial as this we may learn that, if it be the conscientious actor's aim to show "the very age and body of the time his form and pressure," he cannot too microscopically analyze and imitate the slightest peculiarities which "mark the man."

MLLE. DUCHESNOIS.

Dined with Fabre, and after went to the Théâtre Français to see Mlle. Duchesnois in Mérope. She is supremely ugly; and yet she does not spare the spectator's eyes, but gives them as full a view of her features as she can. Through all the range of her feelings she seems to have no consciousness of her great misfortune; but relies implicitly on the effect of play of countenance on the feelings of her audience. I suppose she is right, for they seemed as little alive to her hideous aspect as she was herself. In spite of this, it would be unjust not to admit that she feels earnestly herself. But — but — she did not touch *me*.

She seems to possess more mind, and stronger feeling, too, than Mlle. Georges; but she has the fault which pervades all French tragic acting — the sentiment is never *approfondi*. Greatly as I am charmed with the actors of genteel comedy in Paris, I think the tragic actors much inferior to our own in the assumption of individual character. They seem all to move in one groove. Their gestures and tones are all stereotyped. They never lead one on to sympathize with the sorrows they simulate, or with the heroism they feign. With a fond disposition to like them, I shall return home, not at all put out of countenance by what I have witnessed as yet."

Kemble's Farewell.

In 1817 I went with Mr. Isaac Pocock, the author of "The Miller and his Men," to see John Philip Kemble bid farewell. Young had not only an admiration for Kemble as an actor, but felt gratitude to him as a man for having reflected honor on the profession by his moral conduct in it. The last time they played together, which was in "Julius Cæsar," Kemble, after the play, entered Young's dressing-room, and presented him with several properties which he had worn in favorite characters, and begged him to keep them in memory of their having fought together, alluding to the battle near Sardis, in which, as Brutus and Cassius, they had been just engaged. "Well," he said, "we've often had high words together on the stage, but never off." On Young saying something to him, which touched him, he suddenly caught hold of his hand, wrung it in his, and then hurried from the room, saying: —

> "For this present
> I would not, so with love I might entreat you
> *Be any further moved.*"

Young and Kean.

The year 1822 was an important one for Young. At this time, his long-standing engagement with Covent Garden having expired, the managers proposed to renew it, on conditions to which he refused to accede. For many years the combined attractions of John and Charles Kemble, Mrs. Siddons, Miss O'Neil, Charles Young, and William Macready, had rendered Covent Garden the favorite resort of the lovers of the legitimate drama. To so low an ebb indeed was the exchequer of the rival house reduced, that its committee gravely entertained the idea of closing, till "the tide in their affairs" should turn and propel them on to better fortune, when Edmund Kean's sudden and unparalleled success revived their hopes and refilled their coffers. Of course, in proportion, as the star of one house was in the ascendant, that of the other began to wane. A great part, therefore, of the receipts of Covent Garden were diverted from their ordinary channel, and, in consequence, its managers, on purely financial grounds and in self-defense, felt constrained to reduce the salaries of the principal actors on their staff. It was in the prosecution of this intention that they proposed to reduce Young's salary from £25 a week to £20, and from three months' vacation for provincial tours to two. If one cannot blame the managers for consulting their own interests, neither can one wonder that the actor, in the prime of life, and in the zenith of his fame, should have refused to accept diminished remuneration for his labor. This questionable economy proved eventually as detrimental to its authors as it was beneficial to its subject; for no sooner was it known that Charles Young's connection with Covent Garden was at an end than the manager of Drury Lane waited on him and offered him £50 a night for nine months (three nights a week); three months' leave for country work, and a clear benefit, provided that he would consent to play with Kean, in certain stipulated pieces, exchanging parts with him on alternate nights. Thus Kean was to play Othello, and Young Iago; and the next night Young Othello, Kean Iago. The same rule was to hold good with regard to every piece in which their joint talents were to be exercised. One hundred and fifty pounds per week was a wonderful rise from twenty-five; and proved a bait too alluring to resist. Bills were posted all over London, advertising the early appearance on the same boards of the two men who had long been regarded as the representatives of two opposite schools of art. The wide-spread excitement produced, few but the *habitués* of the theatre in those times could believe. Places were secured at the box-office five and six weeks beforehand, and the comparative merits of the two histrionic athletes were canvassed at fashionable tables with as much vivacity and warmth of temper as the far more important political questions of the hour. Kean was the Coryphæus of a new school, Young of the old. Kean was supposed to have had the mantle of George Frederick Cooke descend upon him, Young was looked on as the disciple of Kemble. Kean's forte was known to be the vigorous delineation of the stronger passions — jealousy, malignity, revenge. Young's *specialité* was allowed to be dignity, pathos, and declamation.

On the very first night of their appearance in the same play I was present; on the very last night of their playing together I was present; and in every piece in which they acted together I have seen them. On each and every one of these occasions I should find it difficult to determine which carried off the palm. The writer of the last published life of Edmund Kean has been pleased to write in terms of measureless contempt of Charles Young's powers as an artist. He has a perfect right to his opinion; but I doubt if his hero, had he been alive, would have indorsed it, or admitted either the justice or the good taste of his criticism. And I venture to think so for this reason. Both the rival candidates for histrionic fame were engaged on terms of perfect equality. Each received exactly the same salary, each was in turn to play the same parts: and had the manager thought there was such vast disparity between the qualifications of the two candidates, he would never have given both the same terms. If Kean had considered himself so far superior to Young in public estimation, he would have been indignant at his receiving the same salary as himself, and would have expected his name to be printed in the bills in larger characters than his rival's. To show that Kean did not think as meanly of Young as his secretary-biographer seems to have done, I may mention that on the first night of their playing together, while Young was in his dressing-room receiving congratulations on his success from "troops of friends," Kean was storming about in search of Price, the manager, and vowing that he would not give up Othello the next night to Young. On Price's telling him that he was bound by the terms of his agreement to do so, he exclaimed, in violent anger, "I don't care! if he plays after me the same part I have just played, I will throw up my engagement, and you may seek your redress in a court of law." On Price's trying to pacify him, and asking him what had caused him to think so differently in the evening from what he had done in the morning, he said, "I had never seen Young act. Every one about me for several years has told me he could not hold a farthing rushlight to me; but he can! He *is* an actor; and though I flatter myself he could not act Othello as I do, yet what chance should I have in Iago after him, with his personal advantages and his d——d musical voice? I don't believe he could play Jaffier as well as I can, but fancy me in Pierre after him; I tell you what," said he, "Young is not only an actor, such as I did not dream him to have been, but he is a gentleman. Go to him, then, from me, and say that, if he will allow me to retain Othello, and to keep to Jaffier, if I succeed in it, I shall esteem it as a personal obligation conferred upon me. Tell him he has just made as great a hit in Iago as I ever did in Othello."

Young was anxious to oblige Price, knowing how seriously refusal on his part would affect the interests of the treasury, and unhesitatingly complied with Kean's request.

My impression as to the comparative powers of Kean and Young may fairly enough be regarded with suspicion. My judgment will be supposed to be biased by filial partiality. But I never was a blind admirer of my father's theatrical talent. It is, therefore, in no narrow spirit of partisanship, but under deliberate and impartial conviction that I shall try to distinguish between them, and award to each his due. Each had certain physical requisites which especially qualified him for his vocation. Young had a small, keen, brown, penetrating eye, overshadowed by a strongly-defined and bushy eyebrow. Kean's eye was infinitely finer; it was fuller, blacker, and more intense. When kindled by real passion off the stage, or by simulated passion on, it gleamed with such scorching lustre as literally to make those who stood beneath its rays quail. In this feature, beyond all question, he had an immense superiority over Young. In figure, stature, and deportment, Young had the advantage over Kean; for he had height, which Kean had not; and, though Young's limbs were not particularly well moulded, he moved them gracefully; and his head, and throat, and bust, were classically moulded. Kean in his gait shuffled. Young trod the boards with freedom. Young's countenance was equally well adapted for the expression of pathos or of pride; thus, in such parts as Hamlet, Beverley, The Stranger, Daran, Pierre, Zanga, and Cassius, he looked the men he represented. Kean's variable and expressive countenance, and even the insignificance of his person, rendered him the very type of a Shylock, a Richard, or a Sir Giles Overreach. Even his voice, which was harsh and husky (except in low and pathetic passages such as "the farewell" in "Othello," in which it was very touching), so far from detracting from its impressiveness, rather added to it. Young's voice, on the other hand, was full bodied, rich, powerful, and capable of every variety of modulation, and therefore in declamatory power he was greatly superior to Kean, and Kemble too. Beautiful in face and person as Kemble was, and great as he was as an actor, his asthma put him at a signal disadvantage with my father in speeches where volume of voice and the rapid delivery of long sentences was needed. The great effects which Kean produced upon his audience were the spontaneous effusions of real genius. Young's happiest hits were the result of natural sensibility, quickness of apprehension, and study. Kean dazzled his audience by coruscations of fancy, and the vivid light which he shed on passages of which the meaning was obscure. Young hardly ever astonished; but, with the unprejudiced, rarely failed to please. Kean's acting, as a rule, was unequal, negligent, and slipshod. He seemed to be husbanding his powers for a point, or for an outburst of impassioned feeling. Young's conceptions were good and truthful, and were harmoniously sustained. I have heard my father say that the passages on which Kean had bestowed most pains, and which were chastely and beautifully delivered, he never got a hand for; while his delivery of those which, to use his own phrase, caused "the house to rise to him," were in bad taste and meretricious. Had he been content to follow the leadings of his better judgment, he would have scorned to pander to the ignorant appetites of the groundlings; and he would have been more than repaid by earning golden opinions from the more judicious few. In declaring my own opinion I have no desire to inoculate others with it. But I should be disingenuous if I did not avow, in the teeth of all that has been said and written, that I hold Kean to have been rather a surprising actor than a legitimate one. I humbly conceive that an actor of the highest excellence, though an artist, should conceal his art (*ars est celare artem*), adhere rigidly to nature, and never try to improve upon it. Now, Kean, not satisfied with looking, thinking, and feeling, as his original would have looked, and thought, and felt, was wont to superadd points of character which he thought would render his impersonation more effective. John Kemble never took such liberties, and still less Mrs. Siddons. She never indulged in imagination at the expense of truth. So anxious was she to adhere to accuracy, that it is well known that when she had to play Constance in "King John" she would speak to no one, but would seat herself between the wings and listen to the machinations of John and Philip, the better to realize her wrongs, and vent, with greater force and fidelity, her sense of them. I am far from denying that Kean had genius; but it was fitful, wayward, and ill-regulated; and he stooped to unworthy means to obtain applause. Let me try to make my meaning more intelligible. Braham was not merely a splendid vocalist; but he was a scientific musician. No man understood better, or more thoroughly appreciated in others, purity of style; yet no man oftener violated the canons of good taste. For this reason I cannot call him a *legitimate* singer. I have heard him sing the best sacred music at the house of friends whom he knew to be refined and fastidious musicians, and then his rendering of Handel has been glorious and worthy of his theme. I have heard him, at an oratorio at the theatre, the very next night, sing the same airs to a miscellaneous audience, and so overlay the original composition with florid interpolations as entirely to distract the listener's attention from the simplicity and solemnity of the theme. This violation of propriety was attributable to the fact of his having observed, that, a display of flexible vocalization always brought down thunder from the gods in the gallery; and therefore he was tempted by the greed of clap-trap applause to sacrifice his own convictions of propriety to the demands of the vulgar and unenlightened. It was the same depraved taste that young amateurs, captivated by the vibrato passages of Rubini, in which, by the by he never indulged without a purpose, would insert them into every song they sang, though there was nothing in the words to justify their introduction. In like manner, when Kean discovered that his imitation of the hysterical sob under powerful agitation caused fine ladies to faint, and Byron to weep, from nervous sympathy, he was perpetually indulging in it, not only when it was inappropriate, but where its manifestation became absolutely ludicrous. No man in his sober hours knew better than Kean, that in condescending to such small trickery he was prostituting his art to an ignoble vanity; for one night when he had been playing before a very intelligent audience, and had been indulging in the propensity referred to, and had been lustily hissed in consqeuence, he whispered to Ralph Wewittzer, as he retreated behind the scenes, "By Jove, old fellow! they've found me out. It won't do any more. I must drop my hysterics!"

Anecdotes of Young.

He was always very glad to hear good preaching; and when residing at Brighton, in old age, was a constant attendant on the ministry of Mr. Sortain. Mr. Bernal Osborne told me that, one Sunday morning, he was shown into the same pew with my father, whom he knew. He was struck with his devotional manner during the prayers, and by his wrapt attention during the sermon. But he found himself unable to maintain his gravity when, as the preacher paused to take breath after a long and eloquent outburst, the habits of the actor's former life betrayed themselves, and he uttered, in a deep undertone, the old familiar "Bravo."

He was sitting at dinner next a lady of rank and considerable ability, who was rather prone to entangle her neighbors at table in discussions on subjects in which she was well "up," when she suddenly appealed from the gentleman on her right to my father, who was on her left, and asked him if he would be kind enough to tell her the date of the Second Punic War. He, who had not the remotest idea whether it was 218 before Christ, or 200 after, and who was too honest to screen his ignorance under the plea of forgetfulness, turned to her and said, in his most tragic tones, "Madam, I don't know anything about the Punic War; and, what is more, I never did. My inability to answer your question has wrung from me the same confession which I once heard made by a Lancashire farmer, with an air of great pride, when appealed to by a party of his friends in a commercial room: 'I tell ye what, in spite of all your bragging, I'll wedger (wager) I'm th' ignorantest man i' coompany.' "

He was once dining at the house of a well-known nobleman, when a fashionable scion of the aristocracy, as if bent on insulting him, began to inveigh, in terms of more than ordinary rancor, on the degradations of the stage, and to insist pertinaciously, on the invariably vicious lives of actresses. Charles Young admitted that there was, unhappily, too much truth in his charges, but humbly submitted that they were too sweeping, and required qualification. "They are all alike!" was the retort. "Unhappily," replied my father, "a harshly-judging world, which winks at, and countenances, by its presence, successful vice in high places, has nothing but the cold shoulder and the harsh epithet for many whom destitution has driven, first, to despair, and then to evil courses." He then cited the honored names of the late Countess of Derby, Countess of Craven, Countess of Essex, Lady Thurlow, and Lady Beecher, as instances of stainless characters, who had passed through the furnace of temptation and come forth scathless. One lady, whose life and conduct had been from her childhood, as an open book, to Young, was then assailed by this gentleman, in the most unscrupulous manner. He boasted of his own familiarity with her, in terms so coarse that the indignant player rose from the table, uttering these words before he left the room: "If, sir, you will prove the truth of your assertion, I will tender you, in the presence of these same gentlemen, the most abject apology on which they can insist; if you do not, whenever I hear your name I will brand it as that of a calumniator and braggart." Bowing, then, politely to his host, he left the room, expecting that the matter would not end there. However, he never heard more from the gentleman in question.

YOUNG AND THE MAGDALEN.

On one of the very foggy nights of November, as Charles Young was stepping out of the stage door of Covent Garden Theatre, on his way home (in such weather, he preferred braving the perils of the *trottoir* on foot to those of the *pavé* in a hackney coach), he heard the link-boy, whose aid on such nights was indispensable, apply abusive epithets to one of the many Circes who used to hang on the skirts of the great theatres, and saw him push her rudely aside into the gutter. Young angrily remonstrated with him on his unmanly violence, and turned to look at the object of his ill-usage. She bore herself so meekly, and cast so sad and deprecating a look at him, that he called her to his side, snatched the link from the boy, and bade him follow, while he spoke to her. The direct and artless way in which she replied to his questions, the diffidence of her manners, and the plaintive accents of her voice, encouraged him to hope that she was not yet so hardened in vice as to be irreclaimable; that, in short, she had been the reluctant victim of circumstances rather than a volunteer in the ways of sin. He gave her half a crown and his card, at the same time (with his address), and invited her to come to him the next morning at ten o'clock. She courtesied her acknowledgments, and forthwith vanished in the fog. The link-boy resumed his torch and his office, and, casting a familiar grin behind him, preceded his employer, and pioneered him safely home.

At the hour appointed on the following morning the young woman made her appearance. The particulars of the interview I never heard pass from my father's lips; in fact, the poor Magdalen's errors were never once alluded to by him to any one. From what I know of her story as told me forty years ago by a friend of her own, she was in the first instance *blameless;* for she was no consenting party to her own undoing. Outraged by a villain, whose statement it was her father's interest to prefer to hers (he was the squire of the village in which she had been born, and was her father's landlord), she was disowned, thrust from the door, and flung penniless upon the streets.

As soon as Young, after rigid inquiry, had verified her statements, he offered to insure her against penury, if she would promise to retire to some secluded spot and try to employ her remaining days usefully and virtuously. For two-and-thirty years — in short, until the day of her death — her annuity was paid to her quarterly, without fail. She settled in a neat little cot in Bakewell, in Derbyshire, where she led not only a most respectable but a most useful life; for, out of her own slender pittance, she always found something to spare for those still poorer than herself; and wherever sickness or sorrow entered, in that house was she a willing and a welcome visitant. So prudently did she administer the funds at her disposal, that she not only died owing no man anything, but left upwards of twenty pounds behind her to defray her funeral expenses. The last act of this poor Magdalen's life was to raise her emaciated hands and invoke a blessing on her benefactor's head.

A Scotch Prayer.

Among the very few papers which my father left behind him I found the following. I think the prayer quoted sufficiently characteristic to justify insertion.

"There is no class of persons more truly devout than the

shepherds of Scotland. Among them the exercise of family worship is never neglected. It is always gone about with decorum; but, formality being a thing despised by them, there are no compositions so truly original, occasionally for rude eloquence, and not unfrequently for a plain and somewhat unbecoming familiarity.

"One of the most notable men for this sort of homely fireside eloquence was Adam Scott, of Upper Dalgleish. I had an uncle who herded with him, and from him I had many quotations from Adam Scott's prayers. Here is a short sample.

"'We parteeclarly thank Thee for thy great gudeness to Meg; and that it ever cam into your head to tak ony thought o' sic a useless bow-wow as her [alluding to a little girl of his who had been miraculously saved from drowning]. For Thy mercy's sake — for the sake o' Thy puir sinfu' creeturs now addressing Thee in their ain shilly-shally way; and, for the sake o' mair than we daur weel name to Thee, hae mercy on our Rob. Ye ken Yoursel', he's a wild mischievous callant, and thinks nae mair o' committing sin than a dog does o' licking a dish. But put Thy hook intil his nose, and Thy bridle intil his gab, and gar him come back to Thee, wi' a jerk, that he'll no forget the langest day he has to live. Dinna forget puir Jamie, who's far awa frae us the night. Keep Thy arm o' power about him, and, ech Sirs, I wish ye wad endow him wi' a little spunk and smeddum to act for his sell; for if Ye dinna, he'll be but a bauchle i' this warld, and a backsitter i' the next. Thou hast added ane to our family. [N. B. — One of his sons had just married against his approbation.] So has been Thy will. It wad never hae been mine. But, if it is of Thee, do Thou bless the connection. But, if the fule hath done it out o' carnal desire, against a' reason and credit, may the cauld rain o' adversity settle in his habitation.'"

A French Letter.

The next letter will tell its own tale. It has not the date of the year in which it was written; but the original, which was sent to a friend of my father's, was given him by the proper owner as a curiosity.

"C—— D——s PRIORY, Aug 27
till Sept 10 that I shall go at Lady E—— F.

MY DEAR E——.—I am shameful to have not had the pleasure to entertain you since you have with disdain abandon London; but the respect to which I am indebted for your eldest sister had oblige me to think of her Ladyship before you. i hope that you have a better weather during your excursions on the lacs than that we have here; for almost every day the tunder is rolling upon our head with noise that should faint you, being as coward as a turkey; but what is more tiresome is the lamentations of peoples, which seeing the rains fall all the days, predict us with famine, plage, and civil wars, by the scarcity of bread, but it is a great error, for the harvest look very well. Be not surpriz'd i write so perfectly well in English, but since i am here, i speak and hear speaking all the day English; and during the nights if some rats or mouses trouble me, i tell them Go lon, and they obey, understanding perfectly my English. Sir G——e is suffering with a rheumatism. Lady H——e O—— who have the pretension to be a very good Physitien, but who is very ignorant, after that he have yesterday well breakfast, has given him a physic, and after he have dined she give him another, and she desire that he take a walk, *au clair de la lune*, in place of to be near good fire. No: a dog or cat would be more prudent. Before yesterday, the brother having eat and drank too much, and being tormented with a strong indigestion, my lady gave him 8 grains of James Powder. the unhappy brother was near to die, and one was obliged to send to a physitien at Shelford, who arriving, found him so well, that he judged it best to wait if the nature would save him or not; but happily, being a strong nature, he was restored. Lady H——e, the best of women is the worst of Physitien. She had killed some year ago a superb ox with James Powder; and, on another occasion, having received 24 turkeys very fatigued to have walked to foot a too long journey, she contrive to refresh them to give them some *huile de castor;* but 12 of that number died, and the rest did look melancholy, so long as they did live. i have receive at this moment a letter from Lady S——n. i put my thanks at her feet as the post go at 2 o'clock. i have not time to write to her ladyship, but i will comply soon with the liberty she gave me. Be sure that I have not forgot Lady S——n in my prayers, though not so good as i could wish indeed. Believe the faithful friendship that i feel for you, my dear sister-in-law, since that you were so much high than my finger. Write me often and my old wife. Believe me that i love a friendly letter more than a purse of guineas. Yours,

"Comte De C——z."

The Youngs at Abbotsford.

In the year 1821, being considered too old to remain longer with advantage at a private school, and too young for admission at Oxford, my father, who had been assured that my youth (I was fifteen) would not disqualify me for admission into the Scotch University of St. Andrew's, wrote to Walter Scott to ask him his opinion on the subject. He replied that, though he had a very high one, he would rather my father did not take any decisive step until he had seen his son-in-law Lockhart, who had greater familiarity with the place than any he could boast. To this end he proposed that we should go and stay a few days at Abbotsford. Before describing the visit, I may as well state the result of it. It was arranged that I should pass a three years' course at St. Andrew's; but as "the term" did not commence for three or four months, that I should spend the interim under the care of a Dr. Gillespie, a personal friend of Lockhart's, a joint contributor with him to "Blackwood's Magazine," an excellent scholar, and the son-in-law of Dr. John Hunter, the Professor of Humanity at St. Andrew's.

We left Edinburgh the day before we were expected at Abbotsford, in an open carriage, for Melrose. There we dined and slept. Shortly after eight o'clock next morning we proceeded by invitation, to breakfast at Abbotsford. As we drew near the house, which had been designated "a romance in stone and lime," the thought of soon beholding the Great

Magician in "his habit as he lived," caused my heart to throb high with joy — a joy not altogether unmixed with awe.

As we turned into the gate, and were being driven round towards the stables, my father jogged my elbow, and told me to look to the right. On doing so, I perceived, at a table in a window, a figure busily engaged in writing, which was none other than the Wizard's self. I saw his hand glibly gliding over the pages of his paper — the hand whose unwearied activity had dispensed pleasure to so many thousands — the hand whose daily perseverance had so excited the astonishment of its owner's opposite neighbor [1] when he lived in Castle Street, Edinburgh — the hand which, years after, when his daughter put the pen into it, refused its wonted office.

As soon as we had disincumbered ourselves of our luggage and our wrappers, we were ushered into a handsome dining-room, in which the breakfast equipage was set, and the loud-bubbling urn was emitting volumes of steam. The party gathered there together consisted of Lady Scott, Miss Scott, Charles Scott, and his friend Mr. Surtees.

It was not long before we heard the eager tread of a stamping heel resounding through the corridor, and in another second the door was flung open, and in limped Scott himself. Although eight-and-forty years have passed away since that memorable morning, the great man's person is as palpably present to me as it then was when in the flesh. His light blue, waggish eye, sheltered, almost screened, by its overhanging penthouse of straw-colored bushy brows, his scant, sandy-colored hair, the Shakespearian length of his upper lip, his towering Pisgah of a forehead, which gave elevation and dignity to a physiognomy otherwise deficient in both, his abrupt movements, the mingled humor, urbanity, and benevolence of his smile, all recur to me with startling reality. He was dressed in a green cut-away coat with brass buttons, drab vest, trowsers, and gaiters, with thick shoes on his feet, and a sturdy staff in his hand. He looked like a yeoman of the better class; but his manners bespoke the ease, self-posses-

[1] *Vide* Lockhart's *Life of Scott*.

sion, and courtesy of a high-bred gentleman. Nothing could exceed the winning cordiality of his welcome. After wringing my father's hand, he laid his own gently on my shoulders, and asked my Christian name. As soon as he heard it, he exclaimed with emphasis — "Why, whom is he called after?" "It is a fancy name in memoriam of his mother, compounded of her two names, Julia Ann." "Well! it is a capital name for a novel, I must say."

This circumstance would be too trivial to mention, were it not, that, in the very next novel which appeared "by the Author of Waverly," the hero's name was Julian. I allude, of course, to "Peveril of the Peak."

We sat down at once to breakfast; such a one as I had never seen before, and never have seen since. It reminded me of a certain one at Tillietudlam given by a certain Lady Margaret Bellenden. Besides tea and coffee and cocoa, there was oatmeal parritch, wheaten bread, and "bannocks o' barley meal," and rolls; and on the sideboard, venison pasty, ham, collared eel, kippered salmon, reindeer tongue, and a silver flagon of claret. Though the bill of fare was tempting, and the keen morning air through which we had driven might be supposed to have given an edge to my appetite, I was so excited by everything I saw around me, that it failed me altogether. I could but sit still and nervously crumble my bread, and listen to the sparkling conversation at the table.

Breakfast ended, Scott told us that "the lion must retire to his den till lunch-time, when he should be at large, though perfectly tame and submissive to orders. Meanwhile," said he, "I consign you, Young, to my lady's care, or, if you prefer it, to Charles's. You will find him an experienced master of the ceremonies; and if Julian would like it, I can lend him a gun, and he might bring us home a hare or two for dinner."

As I was no shot, I preferred accompanying my father round the house and grounds, under the guidance of our *cicerone*, who justified his father's commendations by the readiness with which he gave us chapter and verse for all the many curiosities within and without, and thus pleasantly wiled away the time till luncheon was announced. The nature of the conversation which took place during the dispatch of that meal I am unable to recall; although I have rather an uncomfortable recollection of a speech of Lady Scott's, which startled me by its apparent want of appreciation of her husband. I dare say it was said without any real meaning, but none the less it had a discordant sound which grated on my ears. My father had been admiring the proportions of the room and the fashion of its ceiling. She, observing his head uplifted, and his eyes directed towards it, exclaimed, in her droll Guernsey accent, "Ah! Mr. Young, you may look up at the bosses on the ceiling as long as you like; but you must not look down at my poor carpet, for I am ashamed of it. I must get Scott to write some more of his nonsense-books, and buy me a new one!"

As she was in the secret of the authorship of the novels, and was pledged, in common with all the family, to keep it inviolate, it is clear that, when she spoke of his nonsense-books, she must have referred to his poems, about which there was no disguise.

Luncheon concluded, it was proposed that we should ride, under Scott's guidance, to Dryburgh Abbey. As soon as he had seen us mounted on his two well-bred hacks, with an alacrity striking in a lame man, he flung his right leg over the back of his iron-gray cob, and summoning around him Maida, his deer-hound, Hamlet, his jet-black greyhound, and two Dandie Dinmont terriers, between all of whom and their master there evidently existed the freemasonry of a common attachment, he put spurs to his horse and started off at a sharp trot for our destination. He seemed to enjoy the exhilaration of fast riding; for he soon broke into a hand-gallop with all the high animal spirits of a boy just out of school. Now and then he would rein up his steed rather abruptly to point out to our notice objects of romantic or legendary interest; here, were sites memorable because of raids and forays committed on them by Border chiefs; there, our attention was called to changes effected in the outline and surface of the country, since my father's last visit, through improved agriculture. Then we listened to his hopeful auguries of the tale his fir plantations would tell when they should have attained to larger growth! When we arrived at Dryburgh, the stores of archæological lore connected with the abbey, which he poured forth with lavish volubility, astounded me; although I must own I was a far more appreciative listener when he told us his racy anecdotes of Lord Buchan's eccentricities and Henry Erskine's wit.

By the time we had reached home, after our delightful ride, the gong was sounding for dressing. On descending to the drawing-room, we found several friends and neighbors of Scott's assembled there. They were all strangers to me, and therefore it is no wonder that I should forget their names. The dinner, in point of profusion, was exactly what I might have expected from the foretaste I had had at luncheon and breakfast. The characteristic feature of the meal was its absence of all stiffness and restraint — indeed, its joyous hilarity; and yet the laws of *bienséance* were never violated. There was, however, one material drawback to my entire enjoyment of my dinner, in the droning notes of the bagpipe, which never intermitted till the cloth was about to be removed. I can well believe that, to a native Scot, the historical associations of the bagpipe may be most endearing; nor will I deny that, in certain states of the atmosphere, when sound is mellowed by distance, or when it is heard on a march by the hillside, or used as a stimulus to exhausted nerves in action, as was the case at Waterloo, or as a cordial for the drooping hearts of captives, as at Lucknow, it must have a music of its own which none else can equal. But, to unfamiliar and sensitive English ears, its buzzing din interrupting conversation, distracting attention, and irritating the temper, it certainly is a nuisance. Walter Scott was a Scotchman, and loved to keep up feudal habits, and therefore to him it was the very reverse. It was an established *usage de maison* that John of Skye, a grand fellow, in full Highland costume — a lineal descendant of Wallace, by the by — should, during the hour of dinner, parade up and down the front of the windows, and squeak and squeal away, until summoned to receive his reward. When the cheese had been removed, and the cloth brushed, a footman stood at the *right* of "the sheriff" (as his retainers loved to call him), and the piper at his *left*, still bonneted. The footman poured forth a bumper of Glenlivet and handed it to his master; he, in turn, passed it on to John of Skye. There was a smack of the lips, a stately bow to the company, and the Highlander was gone.

After the gentlemen were supposed to have had their quantum of wine, they withdrew to the armory for coffee, where the ladies joined them. In the centre of a small, dimly-lighted chamber, the walls of which were covered with morions, and claymores, and pistols, and carbines, and cuirasses, and antique shields and halberds, etc., etc., each piece containing a history in itself, sat the generous host himself in a high-backed chair. He would lead the conversation to the mystic and the supernatural, and tell us harrowing tales of glamour and second-sight and necromancy; and, when he thought he had filled the scene enough, and sufficiently chilled our marrows, he would call on Adam Ferguson for one of his Jacobite relics — such as "Hey, Johnny Cope, are ye wauking yet," or "The Laird o' Cockpen," or "Wha wad na fecht for Charlie?" — and these he sang with such point and zest, and such an undercurrent of implication, that you felt sure in what direction his own sympathies would have flowed had he been out in "the '45." When he had abdicated the chair, my father was called upon to occupy it, and he gave us from memory, the whole of "Tam o' Shanter." It seemed to be an invariable custom at Abbotsford, that every one admitted within its circle should utilize the gift within him, so as to contribute to the common stock of social amusement. As I have mentioned my father's recitation of "Tam o' Shanter," I may as well introduce here Lady Dacre's lines addressed to him after hearing him read them years before.

TO MR. YOUNG,

On his reading "Tam o' Shanter" with peculiar spirit.

The same rude winds wi' mighty sweep
Upheave the waters of the deep,
To dash them on ilk jutting steep
Their fury meets,
And cozie 'mang low flowrets creep,
Stealing their sweets.

And suns that rear the forest's pride,
To bear upo' the subject tide
Britannia's thunders far and wide,
Wi' milder ray
Will glint adown the copsewood side
On ilka spray.

So thou wi' learn'd and tunefu' tongue
Will pour, mellifluous, full and strong,
Great Shakespeare's bold, creative song
Wi' master skill
Resistless to the list'ning throng
Thou sway'st at will:

And Tam o' Shanter, roaring fou,
By thee embodied to our view,
The rustic bard would own sae true,
He scant could tell
Wha 'twas the living picture drew,
Thou, or himsell.

When we had retired to bed, my nerves were so much on the stretch, in consequence of all I had seen and heard, that I could not sleep till morning. As I lay pondering on the character and qualities of our host, I could not help thinking how much the circumstances which surround a man, conjoined, no doubt, with organization and temperament, help to mould the poet. Thus, for instance, if he take "man" for his theme, he will write best of that class of men with which he has mingled most; while, if he look to "nature" for his subject, he will paint her best in those of her forms with which he is most familiar. I think there can be no question, that the early life and bodily training of Scott had much to do with the formation of his mind, and with the character of his compositions. "A wild and woodland rover," of so much thew and muscle, spending so much of his youth in the open air, now dashing through the foaming flood after the otter, now stalking the roe-deer, "free to tread the heather where he would," could hardly fail to have the range of his sensibility to beauty enlarged and quickened by the romantic scenery around him: while the legendary tales and the historic associations with which the Highlands and the Lowlands teem, would impregnate his ardent fancy with a fecundity of imagery, which, while it explains his marvelous descriptive power, and the masculine vigor of his verse, also accounts for its utter absence of passion and of sentiment.

Nothing in Walter Scott struck me more than his ignorance of pictures, and his indifference to music. There was not one picture of sterling merit on his walls! A young lady in the house sang divinely; but her singing gave him no pleasure. He was much too honest to affect to be what he was not, or to have what he had not; thus he admitted "that he had a reasonable good ear for a jig," but confessed that "solos and sonatas gave him the spleen." The late Sir Robert Peel also hated music; and Rogers used to say, when speaking of Lord Holland, that "he had so little appreciation of art, that he firmly believed painting gave him no pleasure; while music gave him absolute pain." Byron, again, like Tasso, cared so little for architecture, that he lived nine months in Pisa before he cast an eye on the Baptistery; and Madame de Staël cared so little for the grandest scenery in the world, that though she lived so long at Copet, she never cared to see the glaciers. In the instances I have cited deficiencies in taste do not much surprise me; but it did disappoint me to find that one who had painted natural scenery with such artistic power and fidelity, and who had composed lays as tuneful as those of "The Last

Minstrel," could be insensible to the charms of the twin sisters, Music and Painting.

Each day that we remained at Abbotsford, fresh visitors came to dine, or sleep, or both, with two exceptions. Once we dined at six, and went to Melrose by moonlight to see the abbey. Every one who has read "The Lay" remembers the opening of the second Canto,

> "If thou would'st view fair Melrose aright,
> Go visit it by the pale moonlight."

Now, I have so often heard it confidently asserted that the writer of those lines never visited Melrose, himself, by moonlight, that, considering the lapse of years and the lapses of a treacherous memory, I am disposed to doubt the correctness of my own impressions. But that my father, Ferguson, and I, went one night after dinner, in Scott's sociable, to Melrose by moonlight I will swear, and, but for the many statements to the contrary, I would have sworn that I distinctly remembered Scott himself sitting opposite to me in a queer cap with a Lowland plaid crossed over his breast, and saying, after my father had repeated in the churchyard Gray's Elegy, "Bravo, Young;" but I so often find myself mistaken, where memory is concerned, that I doubt my own evidence. Until I am contradicted, however, I shall believe that another day we all went to Chiefswood and dined with Lockhart and his sweet wife. I was much struck with Lockhart's beauty. He was in the prime of life; the sorrows of after years had not grizzled his jet black curly locks; nor had time dimmed the lustre of his splendid eye. His deference and attention to his father-in-law, it was delightful to witness. After dinner I had another opportunity of observing Scott's insensibility to music, when detached from association. Two sisters sang duets in French, Italian, German, and Spanish, with equal address. One had a clear soprano voice, the other a rich contralto. Their vocalization was faultless, their expression that of real feeling. I was so bewitched with their singing, that I could not refrain from an occasional glance at Scott, to see if he were proof against such captivation. But the more they sang, and the better they sang, the more impenetrable did he appear. He sat, absent, abstracted, with lip drawn down and chin resting on his gold-headed crutch, his massy eyebrows contracted, and his countenance betokening "a sad civility." At last, Mrs. Lockhart, thinking she had sufficiently taxed the good-nature of her gifted friends, uncovered her harp, and began to play the air of "Charlie is my darling." The change which instantly passed o'er the spirit of the poet's dream was most striking. Pride of lineage, love of chivalry, strong leanings to the Stuart cause, were all visibly fermenting in the brain of the enthusiastic bard. His light blue eye kindled, the blood mantled in his cheek, his nostril quivered, his big chest heaved, until, unable longer to suppress the emotion evoked by his native melodies in favor of a ruined cause, he sprang from his chair, limped across the room, and, to the peril of those within his reach, brandishing his crutch, as if it had been a brand of steel, shouted forth with more of vigor than of melody, "And a' the folk cam running out to greet the Chevalier! Oh! Charlie is my darling," etc.

This honest, irrepressible outburst of natural feeling would have thrown his friend Tom Moore into convulsions; for he once told Lord and Lady Lansdowne, at Bowood, when I was present, that he had been invited, when in Edinburgh, by Blackwood, to one of his suppers at Ambrose's. On going there he found many he knew — Scott, Lockhart, Jeffery, Muir, John Wilson, James Ballantyne, and three or four ladies; and, among their number, two peeresses, who had, only that very day, begged for an invitation, in the hope of meeting Moore. Their presence being unexpected by the majority of the club, members had dropped in in their morning dress; while the two ladies "of high degree" were in full evening costume, or, as Moore described it, "in shoulders." When supper was half over, James Hogg, the Ettrick Shepherd, appeared. A chair had been designedly left vacant for him between the two aristocrats. His approach was discernible before his person was visible: for he came straight from a cattle fair, and was reeking with the unsavory odors of the sheep and pigs and oxen, in whose company he had been for hours. Nevertheless he soon made himself at home with the fair ladies on each side of him: somewhat too much so; for, supper over, the cloth with drawn, and the toddy introduced, the song going round, and his next door neighbors being too languid in their manner of joining in the chorus to please him, he turned first to the right hand, then to the left, and slapped both of them on their backs with such good will as to make their blade bones ring again; then, with the yell of an Ojibbeway Indian, he shouted forth, "Noo, then, leddies, follow me! 'Heigh tutti, tutti! Heigh tutti, tutti!'"

DR. CHALMERS.

In height and breadth, and in general configuration, he was not unlike Samuel Taylor Coleridge. I have, since I knew Coleridge, sometimes thought, that if Chalmers' head had been hidden from sight, I could easily have mistaken him for that remarkable man. His face was pallid and pasty; and, I rather think, showed slight traces of small-pox. His features were ordinary; his hair was scanty, and generally roughed, as if his fingers had been often passed through it; his brow was not high, but very broad and well developed.

His skull, phrenologically speaking, argued great mathematical power; but showed deficiency in the very qualities for which he was conspicuous, namely, benevolence and veneration.

There was one feature in his face which struck me as so very peculiar, and I may say, anomalous, that I have often wondered never to have heard or read any comment upon it from others; I allude to his eye. The eye by its mobility, its power of expressing the passions, and the spirit it imparts to the features, is usually considered as the index of the mind. Now, I never beheld so mute, impassive, inexpressive an eye as that of Chalmers. It was small, gray, cold, and fishy When, either in preaching from the pulpit or lecturing in the class-room, he was excited by his subject; when his heart grew hot within him, and the fire burned; when the brilliancy of his imagery and the power of his phraseology carried the feelings of his auditory away with all the impetuosity of a torrent; nay, when he seemed transported out of himself by the sublimity of his conceptions, and the intense reality of his convictions, so as to cause him to defy conventionalities, and set at naught the artifices of rhetoric, and make him swing his left arm about like the sails of a windmill; when every fibre of his body throbbed and quivered with emotion; when his listeners' mouths were wide open, and their breath suspended, the cheeks of some bedewed with tears, and the eyes of others scintillating with sympathy and admiration — *his* eye remained as tame and lustreless as if it had been but the pale reflex of a mind indifferent and half asleep!

Whether Chalmers preached *extempore* or *memoriter* when he was the minister of the Tron Church, Glasgow, or whether he preached from book when he was followed in crowds by the best intellects in London. I have no means of knowing; but I can declare, with confidence, that I never heard him at St. Andrew's — and I have heard him often — that he had not his manuscript in full before him. It is a well-known fact, that Presbyterians think that the duties of the pulpit are the most important which can devolve upon a minister; and that, with few exceptions, they have an invincible repugnance to a sermon conned over and composed in the study, on the ground of its lacking spontaneity and the apparent impress of the Spirit. Therefore it was always a subject of wonder to me how Chalmers managed to reconcile his hearers to his sermon-reading, which, in any other case, would unquestionably have been to them a stumbling-block and an offense.

I have a distinct recollection, one Sunday, when I was living at Cults, and when a stranger was officiating for Dr. Gillespie (who had been summoned to Edinburgh on business), observing that he had not proceeded five minutes with his "discourse," before there was a general commotion and stampedo. The exodus, at last, became so serious, that, conceiving something to be wrong, probably a fire in the manse, I caught the infection, and eagerly inquired of the first person

I encountered in the church-yard what was the matter, and was told, with an expression of sovereign scorn and disgust—"Losh keep ye, young man! Hae ye eyes and see not? Hae ye ears and hear not? *The man reads!*"

Dr. Haldane.

He was one of the most estimable of men; universally respected by all who knew him; and yet, in spite of a pleasing person, a genial manner, a good position, a good house, and a handsome competency, he was well advanced in life before he could make up his mind to marry. No misogynist was he! Womankind he loved, "not wisely but too well;" and yet when in their presence his self-possession forsook him, and he became a much oppressed and bashful man. Shortly before I left St. Andrew's, the nephew of his patron Lord Melville, who had been his inmate and companion for three years, also was about to leave. The loss of the society of one whose great ability had led all who knew him to expect he would one day fill high place in the councils of his sovereign, grieved him much. When it was reported that he had fitted up his house afresh, at the very time when appearances were of less consequence to him, it was generally supposed, and currently reported, that he was going to change his state. There is nc doubt the rumor was well founded; for, on a given day, at an hour unusually early for a call, the good Doctor was seen at the house of a certain lady, for whom he had long been supposed to have a predilection, in a bran-new coat, wiping his "weel pouthered head" with a clean white handkerchief, and betraying much excitement of manner, till the door was opened. As soon as he was shown "ben," and saw the fair one, whom he sought, calmly engaged in knitting stockings and not at all disturbed by his entrance, his courage, like that of Bob Acres in the "Rivals," began to ooze out at the tip of his fingers, and he sat himself down on the edge of his chair in such a state of pitiable confusion as to elicit the compassion of the lady in question. She could not understand what ailed him; but felt instinctively that the truest good-breeding would be to take no notice of his embarrassment, and lead the conversation herself. Thus, then, she opened fire: "Weel, Doctor, hae ye got through a' your papering and painting yet?" (A clearing of the throat preparatory to speech, but not a word uttered.) "I'm told your new carpets are just beautifu'." (A further clearing of the throat, and a vigorous effort to speak, terminating in a free use of his handkerchief.) "They say the pattern o' the dining-room chairs is something quite out o' the way. In short, that everything aboot the house is perfect." Here was a providential opening he was not such a goose as to overlook. He "screwed his courage to the sticking place," advanced his chair, sidled towards her, simpering the while, raised his eyes furtively to her face, and said, with a gentle inflection of his voice, which no ear but a willfully deaf one could have misinterpreted, "Na! Na! Miss J——n. It's no *quite* perfect. It canna be quite that so long as there's ae thing wanting!" "And what can that be?" said the imperturbable spinster. Utterly thrown on his beam-ends by her willful blindness to his meaning, the poor man beat a hasty retreat, drew back his chair from its dangerous proximity, caught up his hat, and, in tones of blighted hope, gasped forth his declaration in these words: "Eh! dear! Eh! Well 'am sure! The thing wanting is, a — a — a — sideboord!"

The Lost Ring.

Some few years ago, a gentleman, a bachelor, residing in lodgings on the first floor of a respectable but small house in this town, appeared before the bench of magistrates with a charge against the maid of his lodging of having robbed him of a ring.

It appeared that he occupied the front drawing-room on the first floor, and slept in the back; that, one night, having undressed by the drawing-room fire, and wound up his watch, he deposited it, with his chain, two seals, and a ring attached to it, on the chimney-piece, and jumped into bed in the next room. In the morning, on dressing himself and going to the chimney piece for his watch, he discovered that the ring, which he valued, was gone. As he was in the habit of sleeping with the folding doors between the rooms ajar, and was always a light sleeper, he felt confident that no one had entered the room since he had left it over-night, except the maid, who had come in early, as usual, to dust and sweep the room, and lay the table for breakfast. The servant was so neat in her person, so pretty, gentle, and well conducted, that he felt loath to tell her his suspicions ; but the moral certainty he entertained of her guilt, and the great value he set on the ring, determined him to conquer his scruples. On hearing herself charged with the theft, she started and stared, as if doubting the evidence of her ears ; indignantly denied the charge, burst into tears, and told her mistress that she would not remain another hour under her roof ; for that her lodger had taxed her with dishonesty. The landlady espoused the cause of her maid, and used such strong language against her accuser, that his blood, in turn, was roused ; and he resolved to bring the matter to a determinate issue before the magistrates. Pedder said he was on the bench ; and that, prepossessed as he and his coadjutors were by the girl's looks and manners, they felt quite unable to resist the weight of circumstantial evidence produced against her, and never had a moment's hesitation in committing her for trial at the next assizes.

Five or six weeks after she had been in jail the prosecutor went into Shaw's, the pastry-cook's, in the Old Steyne, for an ice. While he was pausing, deliberately, between each spoonful, the sun burst forth in all its strength, and darted one of its beams along the floor of the shop, bringing into light an object which glistened vividly between the joists of the flooring. He took out his penknife, inserted the point of it between the boards, and to his utter amazement, fished up his lost ring. He ran back to his lodgings, and, on referring to his diary, he found that, on the evening of the very night on which he had left his watch and its appendages on the chimney-piece, he had been at Shaw's having some refreshment;

and he conjectured that, as half the split ring from which his seals hung, had been, for some time, a good deal wrenched apart, it must have come into contact with the edge of the counter, and thus liberated the ring from its hold; that it had fallen on the ground, been trodden under the feet of some of the visitors to the shop, and in this way been wedged in between the boards of the flooring. Stung to the quick by self-reproach, at the thought of having tarnished the good name of an innocent girl, by false accusation, and of having exposed her to the unmerited sufferings of prison life, he instantly took a post-chaise and drove off to the jail in which she was confined, asked every particular about her from the governor, and found him enthusiastic in his admiration of her, and utterly incredulous of her guilt. "She's the gentlest, sweetest-tempered creature we have ever had within these walls; and nothing shall make me believe she is a thief," said he. "No more she is," was the eager answer. "She has been falsely charged by me, and I have come to make her every reparation in my power." In one brief word, he offered her his hand, and married her.

Coleridge and Wordsworth.

1828. *July* 6. Mrs. Aders, an old London friend of mine, who was in the habit of spending her summers at a chateau she had on the Rhine, hearing I was going for a twelve-month's tour on the Continent, begged me to visit her at Godesberg on my road south. I had read so much of the beauty of the place, and heard so much of the cultivated society she contrived to attract around her, that I was only too glad to avail myself of her invitation. When I had been under her roof for a fortnight, fearing to outstay my welcome, I announced my intention of leaving on the morrow. The declaration was received with flattering indignation. I was accused of being *ennuyé* with the place and the people in it. On my expatiating on the enjoyment I had had in my visit, I was challenged to prove the sincerity of my protestations by consenting to prolong my stay another fortnight. "You will not regret doing so," said my hostess, "for I expect those here to-morrow whom I am sure you would like to meet. Who they are I shall not tell you, till I introduce you to them." She then reiterated her invitation with such sincere cordiality, that I felt no longer any hesitation in accepting it.

In the evening of the following day, having overwalked myself in the morning, I retired early to my room, and had not been many minutes in bed before the cracking of postilions' whips, the rumbling of carriage wheels, the ringing of bells, the slamming of doors, and the other discordant noises common to a late arrival, told me that the expected visitors had come.

Next morning I was down, and in the breakfast-room betimes, awaiting with curiosity the entrance of the strangers. After a while, Mrs. Aders made her appearance, and told me they were so fatigued, that they had asked leave to have their breakfasts sent up to their bedchambers. Our meal concluded, I once more tried to ascertain the names of the new comers. But my hostess evaded the question, and withdrew to her boudoir; and I was compelled to adjourn to the saloon, that I might dispatch my letters before I was interrupted. I had scarcely entered the room, and was trying to improve a bad sketch I had made the day before, when an old gentleman entered, with a large quarto volume beneath his arm, whom I at once concluded to be one of the anonymous gentry about whose personality there had been so much mystery. As he entered, I rose and bowed. Whether he was conscious of my well-intentioned civility I cannot say, but at all events he did not return my salutation. He appeared preoccupied with his own cogitations. I began to conjecture what manner of man he was. His general appearance would have led me to suppose him a dissenting minister. His hair was long, white, and neglected; his complexion was florid, his features were square, his eyes watery and hazy, his brow broad and massive, his build uncouth, his deportment grave and abstracted. He wore a white starchless neckcloth tied in a limp bow, and was dressed in a shabby suit of dusky black. His breeches were unbuttoned at the knee, his sturdy limbs were encased in stockings of lavender-colored worsted, his feet were thrust into well-worn slippers, much trodden down at heel. In this ungainly attire he paced up and down, and down and up, and round and round a saloon sixty feet square, with head bent forward, and shoulders stooping, absently musing, and muttering to himself, and occasionally clutching to his side his ponderous tome, as if he feared it might be taken from him. I confess my young spirit chafed under the wearing quarter-deck monotony of his promenade, and, stung by the cool manner in which he ignored my presence, I was about to leave him in undisputed possession of the field, when I was diverted from my purpose by the entrance of another gentleman, whose kindly smile, and courteous recognition of my bow, encouraged me to keep my ground, and promised me some compensation for the slight put upon me by his precursor. He was dressed in a brown-holland blouse; he held in his left hand an alpenstock (on the top of which he had placed the broad-brimmed "wide-awake" he had just taken off), and in his right a sprig of apple-blossom overgrown with lichen. His cheeks were glowing with the effects of recent exercise. So noiseless had been his entry, that the peripatetic philosopher, whose back was turned to him at first, was unaware of his presence. But no sooner did he discover it than he shuffled up to him, grasped him by both hands, and backed him bodily into a neighboring arm-chair. Having secured him safely there, he "made assurance doubly sure," by hanging over him, so as to bar his escape, while he delivered his testimony on the fallacy of certain of Bishop Berkeley's propositions, in detecting which, he said, he had opened up a rich vein of original reflection. Not content with cursory criticism, he plunged profoundly into a metaphysical lecture, which, but for the opportune intrusion of our fair hostess and her young lady friend, might have lasted until dinner-time. It was then, for the first time, I learned who the party consisted of; and I was introduced to Samuel Taylor Coleridge, William Wordsworth, and his daughter Dora.

The reported presence of two such men as Coleridge and Wordsworth soon attracted to Mrs. Ader's house all the illuminati of Bonn — Niebuhr, Becker, Augustus Schlegel, and many others. It is matter of lamentation to me, now, to think that I have not preserved any traces of the conversations at which I was privileged to be present. But, alas! my ignorance of German, and my inaptitude for metaphysics, debarred me from much information that, but for those accidents, I might have obtained. I recall nothing but a few fragmentary remarks, which, for a wonder, I *could* understand. Schlegel was the only one of those I have named who spoke English, so that his were the only remarks I recollect, and they hardly worth repetition. I fancy I see him now, twitching his brown scratch wig, and twisting a lock of artificial hair into a curl, and going to the glass to see how it became him. He talked admirably, yet not pleasingly, for whatever the topic, and by whosever lips it was started, he soon contrived to make himself the central object of interest. The perfect self-satisfaction with which he told of his involuntary successes with the fair sex, was both amusing and pitiable. He said that when he lived with Madame de Staël at Copet, he supplied her with all the philosophical materials for her "L'Allemagne." Coleridge told him that there never had been such a translation of any work in any language as his of Shakespeare. Schlegel returned the compliment, scratched *his* back in turn, and declared that Coleridge's translation of Schiller's "Wallenstein," was unrivaled for its fidelity to its original and the beauty of its diction. Both of them praised Cary's "Dante" highly. Schlegel praised Scott's poetry. Coleridge decried it, stating that no poet ever lived, of equal eminence, whose writings furnished so few quotable passages. Schlegel then praised Byron. Coleridge immediately tried to depreciate him. "Ah," said he, "Byron is a meteor. Wordsworth, there" (pointing to him) "is a fixed star. During the first *furore* of Byron's reputation, the sale of his works was unparalleled, while that of Wordsworth's was insignificant, and now each succeeding year, in proportion as the circulation of

Byron's works has fallen off, the issue of Wordsworth's poems has steadily increased."

I observed that, as a rule, Wordsworth allowed Coleridge to have all the talk to himself; but once or twice Coleridge would succeed in entangling Wordsworth in a discussion on some abstract metaphysical question: when I would sit by, reverently attending, and trying hard to look intelligent, though I did not feel so; for at such times a leaden stupor weighed down my faculties. I seemed as if I had been transported by two malignant genii into an atmosphere too rarefied for me to live in. I was soaring, as it were, against my will, 'twixt heaven and the lower parts of the earth. Sometimes I was in pure ether — much oftener *in the clouds*. When, however, these potent spirits descended to a lower level, and deigned to treat of history or politics, theology or belles lettres, I breathed again; and, imbibing fresh ideas from them, felt invigorated.

I must say I never saw any manifestation of small jealousy between Coleridge and Wordsworth; which, considering the vanity possessed by each, I thought uncommonly to the credit of both. I am sure they entertained a thorough respect for each other's intellectual endowments.

Coleridge appeared to me a living refutation of Bacon's axiom, "that a full man is never a ready man, nor the ready man the full one:" for he was both a full man and a ready man.

Wordsworth was a single-minded man; with less imagination than Coleridge, but with a more harmonious judgment, and better balanced principles. Coleridge, conscious of his transcendant powers, rioted in a license of tongue which no man could tame.

Wordsworth, though he could discourse most eloquent music, was never unwilling to sit still in Coleridge's presence, yet could be as happy in prattling with a child as in communing with a sage.

If Wordsworth condescended to converse with me, he spoke to me as if I were his equal in mind, and made me pleased and proud in consequence. If Coleridge held me by the button, for lack of fitter audience, he had a talent for making me feel *his* wisdom and my own stupidity: so that I was miserable and humiliated by the sense of it.

I remember reading, once, in a life of Plato, that if ever Aristotle were absent from his master's lectures, Plato would say to his other scholars, "Intellect is not here to-day;" and if Coleridge could have divined the confusion of my mind, when he was trying to indoctrinate me with his own extravagant speculations, he would probably have tapped my skull and applied the same words to me, though in a less flattering sense.

While he confined himself to his "judgments, analytic and synthetic," I had a glimmering conception of his meaning; but when he gave tongue on "*a priori* knowledge and *a posteriori* knowledge," and spake of "modality," and of the "paralogism of pure reason," my feeble brain reeled, and I gasped for escape from the imaginary and chimerical to the material and the practical.

I had occasional walks with Coleridge in the garden, and many with Wordsworth over the fields. The former was an indifferent pedestrian, the latter a practiced one. I revert with great delight to a long expedition I one day made with Wordsworth alone. He had heard of the ruins of an old Cistercian abbey, Heisterbach, on the side of the Rhine opposite to that on which we were staying. He asked me, playfully, to join him, in these words: —

> "Go with us into the abbey — there;
> And let us there, at large, discourse our fortunes."
>
> *Shakespeare.*

Hitherto I had only seen Wordsworth in the presence of Coleridge; and had imagined him, constitutionally, contemplative and taciturn. To-day I discovered that his reticence was self-imposed, out of consideration for the inordinate loquacity of his brother poet.

Coleridge always speechified or preached.

"His argument
Was all too heavy to admit *much talk*."

Wordsworth chatted naturally and fluently out of the fullness of his heart, and not from a wish to display his eloquence. As I listened to him in this happy walk, I could not but apply to him one of Hooker's wise saws, "He who speaketh no more than edifieth is undeservedly reprehended for much speaking."

Idolatry of nature seemed with Wordsworth both a passion and a principle. She seemed a deity enshrined within his heart. Coleridge studied her rather as a mighty storehouse for poetical imagery than from innate love of her, for her own sweet sake. If once embarked in lecturing, no landscape, however grand, detained his notice for a second: whereas, let Wordsworth have been ever so absorbed in argument, he would drop it without hesitation to feast his eyes on some combination of new scenery. The union of the great and the small, so wonderfully ordered by the Creator, and so wondrously exemplified on the banks of the great German river, had little attraction for the author of "The Ancient Mariner." The grander features of a landscape he took in at a glance; and he would, with signal power of adaptation, dispose them into a magic world of his own. The rolling mist, as it hung suspended over the valley, and partially revealed the jagged tower and crag of Drachenfels, the river shooting out of sight the burden on its bosom with the velocity and force of an arrow; the presence of elemental power, as exhibited in the thunderstorm, the waterfall, or the avalanche, were stimulus enough to stir the pulses of his teeming brain, and set his imagination afloat with colossal speculations of hereafter. With him terrestrial objects soon expanded into immensity, and were quickly elevated above the stars. The more Rasselas-like mind of the recluse of the Lakes, on the other hand, who "loved the life removed," would direct itself to the painstaking investigation of nature's smallest secrets, prompt him to halt by the wayside bank, and dilate with exquisite sensibility and microscopic power of analysis on the construction of the humblest grasses, or on the modest seclusion of some virgin wild-flower nestling in the bosom, or diffidently peering from out the privacy of a shady nook composed of plumes and verdant ferns. In that same stroll to Heisterbach, he pointed out to me such beauty of design in objects I had used to trample under foot, that I felt as if almost every spot on which I trod was holy ground, and that I had rudely desecrated it. His eyes would fill with tears and his voice falter as he dwelt on the benevolent adaptation of means to ends discernible by reverential observation. Nor did his reflections die out in mawkish sentiment; they lay "too deep for tears," and, as they crowded thickly on him, his gentle spirit, subdued by the sense of the Divine goodness towards his creature, became attuned to better thoughts; the love of nature inspired his heart with a gratitude to nature's God, and found its most suitable expression in numbers.

The melody of Coleridge's verse had led me, as in the case of Scott, to credit him with the possession of the very soul of song; and yet, either from defective ear or from the intractability of his vocal organs, his pronunciation of any language but his own was barbarous; and his inability to follow the simplest melody quite ludicrous. The German tongue he knew *au fond.* He had learned it grammatically, critically, and scientifically, at Göttingen: yet so unintelligible was he when he tried to speak it, that I heard Schlegel say to him one evening, "Mein lieber Herr, would you speak English? I understand it: but your German I cannot follow." Whether he had ever been before enlightened on his malpronunciation of German, I know not; but he was quite conscious that his pronunciation of French was execrable, for I heard him avow as much. He was a man of violent prejudices, and had conceived an insuperable aversion for the *grande nation*, of which he was not slow to boast. "I hate," he would say, "the hollowness of French principles: I hate the republicanism of French politics: I hate the hostility of the French people to revealed religion: I hate the artificiality of French cooking: I hate the acidity of French wines: I hate the flimsiness of the French language: — my very organs of speech are so anti-Gallican that they refuse to pronounce intelligibly their insipid tongue."

He would inveigh with equal acrimony against the unreality and immorality of the French character of both sexes, especially of the women; and in justification, I suppose, of his unmeasured invective, he told me that he was one day sitting *tête-à-tête* with Madame de Staël in London, when her man-servant entered the room and asked her if she would receive Lady Davey. She raised her eyebrows and shrugged her shoulders, and appeared to shudder with nausea, as she turned to him and said, "Ah! ma foi! oh! mon cher ami! ayez pitié de moi! Mais quoi faire? Cette villaine femme. Comme je le deteste! Elle est, vraiment, insupportable!" And then, on her entry, flung her arms around her, kissed her on both cheeks, pressed her to her bosom, and told her that she was more than enchanted to behold her.

Query. Have our neighbors across the water a monopoly of such conventional duplicity? or has honest John Bull his own proper share of it?

I have heard Coleridge say, more than once, that no mind was thoroughly well organized that was deficient in the sense of humor: yet I hardly ever saw any great exhibition of it in himself. The only instance I can recall, in which he said anything calculated to elicit a smile, during the two or three weeks I was with him, was when he, Wordsworth and I, were floating down the Rhine together in a boat we had hired conjointly. The day was remarkably sultry; we had all three taken a considerable walk before our dinner; and what with fatigue, heat, and the exhaustion consequent on garrulity, Coleridge complained grievously of thirst. When he heard there was no house near at hand, and saw a leathern flask slung over my shoulder, he asked me what it contained. On my telling him it was Hock Heimar, he shook his head, and swore he would as soon take vinegar. After a while, however, finding his thirst increasing, he exclaimed, "I find I must conquer my dislike — eat humble pie, and beg for a draught." He had no sooner rinsed his mouth with the obnoxious fluid, than he spat it out, and vented his disgust in the following impromptu: —

"In Spain, that land of monks and apes,
The thing called wine doth come from *grapes;*
But, on the noble river Rhine,
The thing called *gripes* doth come from wine."

It must not be assumed that the reciprocal admiration entertained by the two poets for each other's gifts made them blind to each other's infirmities. Wordsworth, in speaking of Coleridge, would admit, though most regretfully, the moral flaws in his character: for instance, his addiction to opium, his ungrateful conduct to Southey, and his neglect of his parental and conjugal obligations. Coleridge, on the other hand, forward as he was in defending Wordsworth from literary assailants, had evident pleasure in exposing his parsimony in the same breath in which he vaunted the purity and piety of his nature.

After the trio had left Godesberg, and were returning homewards *viâ* Amsterdam and Rotterdam, they paid a visit to Haarlem. Mrs. Aders received a letter from Coleridge, dated from that place, in which he told her that they had not arrived many minutes at their hotel before one of the principal waiters of the establishment entered the room, and asked them if they would like to accompany a few persons in the house to hear the celebrated organ played, as a party was then in the act of forming.

"Oh," said Wordsworth, "we meant to hear the organ! but why, Coleridge, should we go with strangers?" "I beg your pardon," interrupted the waiter, who understood and spoke English well, "but it is not every one who is willing to pay twelve guilders (£1); and as the organist will never play privately for less, it is customary for persons to go in parties and share the expense between them." "Ah, then I think I will not go: I am tired," said Wordsworth. "Then you and I will go together, Dora," answered Coleridge. Off they went, arm in arm, leaving Wordsworth behind them, reclining on a couch. They had not been long in the Church of St. Bavon, listening to the different stops which the organist was trying to display to the greatest advantage -- the solo stops, the bell stops, the trumpet stop, the vox humana stop — before Coleridge was made sensible of the unwelcome intrusion of a strong current of air throughout the building. He turned his head to see the cause; and, to his amusement, descried his gentle friend, noiselessly closing the door, and furtively making his way behind one of the pillars, from whence he could hear without being seen, and thus escape payment. Before the organist had concluded his labors, Wordsworth had quietly withdrawn. On the return of his friend and his daughter, he asked them how they had enjoyed their visit to St. Bavon, but said nothing of his own!

When Wordsworth was in London, during the height of the season, he was aware it would be expected, after his appointment to the laureateship, that he should present himself at one of the *levées* of the sovereign. As his means had never been large, it was rather a proof of wise economy, than of meanness, that he should have shrunk from the idea of buying a costly court-suit for one day's wear. In this dilemma Rogers came to his rescue, and told him that, as he should never go to court again, he was welcome to make what use he could of his clothes, bag-wig, sword, buckles, etc. By the help of a little tailoring he was enabled to avail himself of Rogers' kindness, and attend the *levée*. When it was over, he called in St. James's Place, and accompanied Rogers to Miss Coutts's. As they were walking together up the footway (under the gardens of the Arlington Street houses) which leads into Piccadilly, and is directly opposite to Stratton Street, Wordsworth's attention was arrested by the prepossessing looks of a little girl, who was sitting on the grass alone. He stopped and talked to her, and asked her of her parents, her home, whether she went to school, etc., and being well pleased with the ingenuous answers that she gave him, he put one hand on her head, and with the other dived down into the recesses of his coat-pocket, and drew forth a little copy of his minor poems, telling her to look at him well, and note his person; to be sure also to observe well the time of day, and the spot; and to recollect that that little book had been given to her by the author, the celebrated William Wordsworth!

N. B. The narrator of this story was Rogers himself.

I hope that no one will infer from my inserting these two anecdotes of Wordsworth, that, because I am not his unqualified eulogist, I therefore wish to throw ridicule or discredit on so great and good a man. I know the stories to be true, and, if true, they should be told; for such details serve to elucidate character; and what man so strong that has not his weak side? There is no greater monster than a faultless man. Personal partiality has often tempted biographers, who have meant to be honest, to yield to a *suppressio veri*, from fear of doing injustice to their subject. Now I conceive that none but a purblind hero-worshipper would deny that the real wrong is knowingly to allow a mistaken impression of a character to go forth uncorrected. There are shades as well as lights in the idiosyncracy of every man on earth.

I regard Wordsworth as having been so essentially eminent and virtuous, that no man can better afford to have the truth spoken of him.

When Coleridge, Wordsworth, and his daughter, had left Godesberg, I felt that I had no longer excuse for lingering in quarters where I had already tarried but too long, and therefore I proceeded to visit some friends at Frankfort. After a few days' stay there I went on to Heidelberg, with the object of studying German.

With the exceeding beauty of the spot I was enchanted, although the manners of the students disgusted me. I had seen something of them in Bonn, but in Heidelberg they out-Heroded Herod. When Coleridge heard that I was going to Heidelberg, he said, "If I were not pledged to the dear Wordsworths, I would go with you, for I long to see Tiedemann, the great anatomist; and with that arch-heretic Paulus, I want to measure swords — I mean in argument. And by the by, talking of measuring swords, let me give you a piece of advice, which, as coming from one who has himself been a student at a German university, you should not despise. You will, ten to one, be wantonly insulted by some of the students, who will challenge you on the slightest pretext. Instantly accept, but name pistols as your weapons." I did not forget this advice, which was well-timed, for I had not been long in Heidelberg before I was struck with the offensive rudeness of the students, who, with their fancifully embroidered frocks, and bare throats, and long hair, and long pipes, and swaggering strut, seemed to infest the main street with the express object of provoking a quarrel with passers by, challenging them, and thus at their expense "renowning." I owe it to Coleridge's advice that I did not get into a serious scrape. A young man, without the slightest provocation, deliberately jostled me off the *trottoir* into the middle of the street, and then charged me with having been the assailant. He was so insolent and so voluble, that, being unable to speak his language, I knocked him down. He sprang up, and challenged me to meet him at the Heischgasse, the inn for duels. With an indifference which, God knows, I did not feel, I bowed to him, and told him in French I would meet him at the appointed place and bring my pistols with me at eight on the morrow." He then called me a coward, said he only fought with the weapon established by German usage, the rapier; and, to my unbounded satisfaction, retired. Luckily no other students were by, or they might have made us proceed to extremities.

DR. HÜHLE.

While in Heidelberg, I used to take daily lessons in German, from a certain Dr. Hühle, who had been for some years the minister of the German Lutheran chapel in the Strand. Although, personally, of irreproachable reputation, his discourses had been so distasteful and unprofitable to his congregation, that, not knowing how otherwise to get rid of him, they clubbed together to purchase him an annuity. They then deputed some of the more influential of their members to wait on him and assure him of a fact (hem !) of which he seemed to be strangely unconscious — namely, that his health was rapidly declining, owing to his exertions in their behalf. They begged him to retire, before it was too late, to his birthplace in Germany, where, breathing his native air, they hoped he would end his declining years in that tranquility which he had so nobly earned, and to which they hoped their little offering might, in some degree, contribute. On that pittance he retired to Heidelberg, where, with the help of teaching English, he managed to eke out a sufficient livelihood for his slender wants.

He was, without exception, the dirtiest and dingiest man I ever set eyes upon. He lodged at a tanner's ; and I sometimes found it no easy matter, in mounting his stairs, to pick my way through the blood-stained skins which were spread upon them to dry, and which had just been purchased from the butcher. On my first visit to him, I was saucy enough to ask him how he came to select such a house for his quarters. "Surely," said I, "however odorous you find the smell of the tanyard, the smell of the reeking skins of newly-slaughtered beasts must be very disagreeable ?" "Nod at all, Saar. I took dese lodgings on brinciple ! Know you not vat your myriad-minded poet says ? Ven Hamlet asks de Clown by de grave shide, 'How long vill a man lie i' de earth ere he rot ?' — de Clown say, 'Iv he be not rotten before he die, he'll last eight or nine years. A tanner vill last you nine years.' And vy ? Because, for de same reason vich kept flesh-butchers from catching de cholera ven all else in deir neighborhood had it."

I said he was the dirtiest man I ever saw. I may safely add, he was the vainest ! I found him, on a particular occasion, seated in a filthy old dressing-gown, with a pipe in his mouth, enveloped in a cloud of tobacco-smoke, overlooking, sorting, and making selections from a large pile of sermons and manuscripts. I said to him, "Have you never published any of your many compositions ?" Looking over his pipe at me, with an air of great importance, he thus addressed me : — "Saar ! You are not de erste persone who have asked me dat question mit surbrise. Der Herr von Nöhden, die Librarium of die Breeches Mooseum at London, von day said to me ver plain —

Mein goote freund, vy do you not bublish ?' I shook mein head. 'Oh,' said dat great man, 'you musht bublish ! You musht indeed ! I vill speak out ! You musht evacooate your brain, or, by —— ! you vill burshht ! '"

THEODORE HOOK.

My father was on a visit the other day to Mr. Johnnes Knight's at Welwyn. Among other *beaux esprits* Theodore Hook was there. In the course of the evening he was asked to improvise for the amusement of the company. "With all my heart," said he, "if you will only give me a subject which will fire my muse. Remember how often I have played Punch, and how many subjects I have turned into song for you before. Therefore be lenient, and give me something new, but easy."

After thinking over several subjects, it was at last suggested that he should take for his theme the very village in which they were all assembled — Welwyn.

Without one minute's pause for reflection, he ran his fingers over the key-board of the pianoforte, and sang the following lines impromptu : —

IMPROMPTU ON WELWYN, BY THEODORE HOOK.

1.

"You ask me where, in peaceful grot,
I'd choose to fix my dwelling?
I'll tell you ; for I've found the spot ;
And mortals call it Welwyn.

2.

"Its shade a quietude imparts,
All other shades excelling ;
The county where it stands is Herts,
And hearts are lost at Welwyn.

3.

"I feel my own throw off its load
When passing by the Bell Inn!
And why?— Because I know the road
Will lead me on to Welwyn.

4.

"And when arrived beneath those trees,
Secure from storm or felling,
The charms of Beauty, Friendship, Ease,
All welcome me at Welwyn.

5.

"In other times, ere mute his tongue,
His 'Thoughts' there Young sat telling;
Now I, although I am not Young,
Give all my thoughts to Welwyn.

6.

"And when my sorrows or my grief
I wish to be repelling,
I always pray for such relief
As kindness gives at Welwyn.

7.

'Shall I implore those heathen dons
On high Olympus dwelling?
No, faith! I'll write to Mrs. Johnnes
To ask me down to Welwyn."

Murder will Out.

My father told a story to-day which he heard from James Welch, a solicitor of Wells, too good to forget.

A mile or two from some town in Somersetshire there was a manufactory — I think, of cloth — the treasurer and cashier of which lived some distance from it in a cottage of his own. He was known to pass to and fro every Saturday with a large sum of money in specie on his person, with which to pay the workmen their weekly wages.

A man in the neighborhood, pressed by want, under a sudden impulse, determined, as a means of extricating himself from his difficulties, to waylay and rob him.

As there had been no premeditation or malice aforethought in the case, he had not provided himself with any offensive weapon. He wrenched, therefore, a strong rail out of some palings which skirted the roadside. Before he could extract a long nail by which the rail had been fastened to the boarding, the very man he was waiting for came by. He followed him stealthily, and beat out his brains. His victim dispatched, he was alarmed by the distant tramp of horses' feet, and was barely able to drag the body into the nearest ditch, and cover it over with dried leaves and rubbish, when two horsemen came in sight. As there was no time for him to possess himself of the spoil, he decamped as fast as he could to a farm-yard about a mile off, where he knew the hay harvest was not yet concluded. Seeing no better place of retreat, he climbed up, by the help of a ladder, to the top of one of the large ricks which had been left to settle before being thatched, and burrowed his way into it backwards, leaving out enough of his head to admit of his breathing. He had no alternative but to spend the night there, meaning, at early dawn, after rifling the body left in the ditch, to make for some point near the coast. Thirty years after, when he had confessed his guilt, he described, with terrific force, the unutterable horror of that night, haunted, as he was, with remorse, and in momentary dread of detection ; buried up to his chin in fermenting, newly-made hay, and menaced, for an hour or two, by flights of angry, hungry crows, which, shortly after his arrival in his quarters (attracted by the smell of blood), had swooped down upon him, and kept hovering about, cawing and screaming, and wheeling and whirling, round and round, within a foot of his face, and only deterred from pecking at his eyes by the sudden movement of his head, and an occasional gruff whoop, which daunted them. About four in the morning he extricated himself from his feverish hot-bed, and retraced his steps towards the ditch in which his victim and his treasure were secreted. The murdered body was undisturbed. He ransacked the large pockets of the coat, which were heavily laden with gold and silver. He found, also, a belt filled with bank-notes strapped round his waist, and under his waistcoat. With these he fled — on — on — till he reached the sea-port for which he was making. On his arrival he jumped into the first packet which was starting for America. In due time, and without any untoward accident, he arrived at the place for which he was bound — set up a school there, and soon acquired a first-rate reputation as a teacher. At the end of thirty years of uninterrupted success, during which he amassed an independence, he thought he might safely return and settle in his native country. I think the first county to which he repaired was Yorkshire. He had not been long there before he felt irrepressible yearnings to revisit his birthplace, a spot fraught with miserable reminiscences, yet endeared to him by the associations of early days, ere blood-guiltiness had poisoned his existence. Satisfied that, from the cessation of intercourse with friends for thirty years, the effects of time on his person, the wear and tear of an arduous profession, and the change produced by his altered dress and manners, he might defy detection, he repaired to the village in which he had once dwelt.

As a precaution against risk, he thought it prudent to shun frequented thoroughfares, and to approach the cottage he had once called "home" by a by-path across the fields. In following the road he had selected, he had to pass through the village churchyard. On entering it, he was much struck by the vast improvements effected since his absence. Old crumbling walls had been razed to the ground ; neat iron railings had been substituted in their place ; villas of pretension now reared their chimneys where there had been only barns, hovels, and cow-sheds ; the church itself had been restored, and its yard extended and beautified.

As he sat on a tombstone, smoking his pipe, and ruminating on the strange metamorphoses of thirty years, he noticed that the sexton was busy digging a grave. He drew nigh, and, finding him to be a stranger, entered freely into conversation with him. While thus engaged, the grave-digger threw up several human bones, of which the listless visitor took but little heed. Presently he jerked from his shovel, at his very feet, a human skull. That did not disturb him, though it was remarked by the sexton that he suddenly ceased talking. Bitter memories sat heavy on his soul. All at once his eyes began to open, and then became transfixed: his cheeks grew deadly pale, his body trembled, from the crown of his head to the sole of his foot. And why? An inanimate skull could have no terrors for him. It could tell no tales! no! But there was that protruding from the back of the skull which kindled the dormant fires of conscience within him, as if they had been fires of hell. A nail! He stood petrified and breathless; "Cold fearful drops stood on his trembling flesh," and, as his gaze became more riveted, he beheld — horror of horrors! — the skull turn slowly round, without any visible agency, and direct its empty sockets upon him. He shrieked out, in irrepressible agony of spirit, "Guilty! guilty! O God!" and fell insensible to the earth. When his faculties were restored, he told those whom the sexton had summoned from the parsonage to his help, that "this was none other than the Lord's doing." He made an ample confession before the authorities, was tried, convicted, and executed.

The seemingly miraculous incident, the moving of the skull, was explained on natural grounds. A dormouse, revived by the outer air, had woke up from his slumbers, and, in running from one side of his resting-place to the other, had caused the movement which had so disturbed and harrowed the conscience of the guilty one.

Sir Thomas Lawrence's Advice.

Went to Sir Thomas Lawrence's with Tomkison. On our way, after, to the Royal Academy, Tomkison told me that he took Sir Thomas, not long ago, to see some paintings of a very promising young artist, in whom he felt interest. Lawrence said many encouraging things to the young man, which he received with becoming modesty. As he was leaving, the youthful aspirant to fame said to Sir Thomas, — "You have been kind enough to praise what you have seen! Would you give me some piece of advice which may help me in my pursuits for the future?" "I do not know that I have anything to say, except this," said Sir Thomas: "You have round your room two or three rough, clever, but coarse, Flemish sketches. Were I you, as a young man desirous to rise in my profession, I would not allow my eye to become familiarized with any but the highest forms of art. If you cannot afford to buy good oil-paintings of the first class, buy good engravings of great pictures; or, have nothing at all upon your walls. You allow, in intercourse with your fellows, that 'evil communications corrupt good manners.' So it is with pictures. If you allow your mind to become familiar with what in art is vulgar in conception, however free and dashing the handling, and however excellent the feeling for color, your taste will, insensibly, become depraved. Whereas, if you habituate your eye only to look on what is pure and grand, or refined and lovely, your taste will, insensibly, become elevated. An artist of well-earned reputation, who owed his position in his profession entirely to his own genius, and who had never seen any of the works of the greatest painters, went with me to see one of the grandest collections on the continent. It was arranged according to the different schools. It began with the German — the Albert Durers, the Quentin Matsys, and Holbeins. It then proceeded with the Flemish and Dutch — the Vandycks, the Breughels, the Ostades, the Teniers, the Gerard Dows, the Rysdaels and the Rubenses. He was so enchanted with the vigor of pencil, the audacity of invention, the mastery of form, and the superb feeling for color which characterized the works of Rubens, that I had difficulty in dragging him away from them. We then visited the Spanish school, with its Murillos and Velasquez, etc.; the Bolognese school, with its Guercinos and Caraccis, and Carlo Dolces and Guidos; then the Venetian school, with its Tintorettos, and Giorgiones, and Paul Veroneses, and Titians; and, lastly, the Umbrian, with its Peruginos, Francias, Michael Angelos, and Raphaels. When the custodian came to tell us it was the hour for the gallery to close, my friend's taste had been so educated by what he had seen, and his appreciation for art had been so developed, that, after contemplating the heavenly and chastened expression of the highest Italian types, on his repassing the Rubenses, which a few hours before had so delighted him, he positively shuddered at their grossness, and hastened away from them as if he were in a low neighborhood."

Constable the Artist.

I sat a long time with Constable the artist, and watched him paint. He is a most gentle and amiable man. His works will have greater justice done them by posterity, when they have become mellowed and toned down by time. His theories of art are original and instructive. I was surprised to see the free and frequent use he makes of his palette-knife in painting; often, where he wants to impart force and breadth to his subject, preferring it to his brush. He told me that, if he lived in the country, and could afford it, he would never paint a landscape anywhere but in the open air. He told me that he believed most artists sketched their subjects out of doors, and finished them in; and that he could always distinguish the parts of a picture which had been painted *al fresco* from those which had been elaborated in the studio.

My uncle, George Young, mentioned to me a beautiful instance of Constable's imperturbable sweetness of temper. He called on him one day, and was received by him in his front room. After half an hour's chat, the artist proposed to repair to the back, to show him a large picture on which he was engaged. On walking up to his easel, he found that one of his little boys, in his absence, had dashed the handle of the hearth-broom through the canvas, and made so large a rent in it as to render its restoration impossible. He called the child up to him, and asked him gently if he had done it. When the boy admitted his delinquency, he took him on his knee, and rebuked him in these unmeasured terms: — "Oh, my dear pet! See what we have done! Dear, dear! What shall we do to mend it? I can't think — can *you?*"

YOUNG PRESENTED AT COURT.

I was this day, for the first, and I sincerely hope the last, time presented at the *levée* at St. James's. It was no "vaulting ambition" on my part which caused me to "o'erleap myself," but a royal summons. The fact is, Sir Horace Seymour, one of William the Fourth's equerries, had called on me and told me that the King had said to him, "I hear you have got a new clergyman as chaplain in Gerald Wellesley's place. Why has he never been to pay his duty to me?" Sir Horace told his Majesty he was sure I had kept away from diffidence. "Nonsense! Tell him Hampton Court Chapel is a Royal one; and, as he is now its minister, I expect to see him here at my next *levée*."

After this, I had no alternative but to submit — and go.

Sir George Seymour was kind enough to take me in his carriage, and Sir Horace to present me. Before going into the large waiting-room, where all the presentees were waiting for the doors to be thrown open, I expressed my fears to Sir Horace that I should be guilty of some solecism in good manners, from my utter ignorance of court usages. He ridiculed my nervousness, and promised to stand by me and pilot me through the quicksands and shoals by which I conceived I must be surrounded in such a place. "Follow in the wake of others, and imitate their example. Bow lower than you would to any one else; and, when you have kissed hands, mind you don't turn your back," were the simple instructions given me. My turn came in due time, and in spite of all the cautions I had had, the very instant I had kissed hands I turned my back upon the sovereign and hurried off. I had no sooner thus committed myself, and was mourning my delinquency, than Sir Horace came hurrying after me, and laughingly caught hold of my shoulders, saying, "Take heart; your retreat has been covered by a Surrey baronet, who, on seeing the royal hand outstretched, instead of reverently kissing it, caught hold of it and wrung it lustily."

Still further to comfort me in my despondency, he told me, that, a few days previously, at a former *levée*, a city alderman, more familiar with a yard measure than a sword, in backing from the presence, got the martial weapon so entangled between his legs, that he was tripped up by it and thrown prostrate on the floor. As he lay floundering there, the Sailor King, in utter defiance of all the established rules of regal reserve and dignity, whispered, with infinite glee, to those around him, "By Jove, the fellow has caught a crab," and then burst into a hearty peal of laughter.

PAGANINI.

I heard Paganini. The *furore* there has been about this man has bordered on fatuity. The prices paid for seats to see and hear him have been fabulous.

On the principle, I presume, of "omne ignotum pro magnifico" the great violinist has shut himself up in close confinement since his arrival in this country, and refused to receive any one but his *entrepreneur* and his dentist. In both cases the relaxation of his rule was a matter of necessity, and not of choice. With the gentleman who had engaged him he could not avoid making certain preliminary engagements for his *début*. Still less could he dispense with the help of the dentist; for, as nature had failed him in her supplies, art was called in to aid him. Sorely discomfited, on arriving in London, by the state of his teeth, and hearing that among the brethren of the profession, Cartwright was *facile princeps*, he sent for him; and after having such teeth as he had filed and scraped, he asked him if he could undertake to supply him with such as he had not by the following Thursday. The commission was unhesitatingly accepted, and faithfully executed. On Paganini's asking Cartwright what he owed for the service he had rendered him, the dentist assured him that he felt honored by having had it in his power to administer to the comfort of such a man; and that the only remuneration he could think of claiming at his hands would be his giving him the pleasure of his company at dinner the next day.

After such extraordinary liberality, Paganini felt that he had no alternative but to accept the invitation so gracefully given. It happened that ten minutes after the great lion of the hour had left the door in Burlington Street, the Duke of Devonshire entered it, by appointment, to have his teeth looked at. Cartwright asked his noble patient in the course of his manipulations if he had yet been fortunate enough to hear Paganini. The Duke said that he had tried to get him at Devonshire House, but had been unable to induce him to go, his reason for refusal being that it would not suit him to play in private till after his appearance in public. "Well," said Cartwright, "there is no rule that has not its exception, and I shall be very much surprised, my Lord Duke, if I do not hear him to-morrow." "How so?" exclaimed his Grace. "Because he dines here; and I feel sure will bring his instrument with him." "Good gracious," said the Duke, "I wish you would ask me to meet him." Of course Cartwright immediately did so. The Duke told every one he called on in the afternoon that he was going to meet the great lion next day, and where. By a curious coincidence the Duke of ——, and the Duke of ——, and the Duke of ——, and the Duke of ——, instantly discovered that their teeth were much out of order; and the next morning between ten o'clock and one, four dukes had been under Cartwright's hands, and received invitations to his table for the same day. The consequence was, that when Paganini arrived at seven P. M. to dinner, in a hackney-coach, expecting to meet a professional friend or two of his host, he found himself sitting down with the most aristocratic party he had ever met in his life, and among them the very magnate whom he had refused to honor with his fiddle.

SMITH'S PUNS.

Dined with Mr. Jesse. Met, as one always does, a most agreeable party at his house. None among them shone more brilliantly than James Smith, one of the joint authors of "Rejected Addresses." His talk — for conversation it was not — was very racy and witty, and his memory nothing short of marvelous. He quoted pages of Pope and Goldsmith; and sang some of his facetious songs to his own accompaniment. Jesse gave me a curious instance of his ready wit. When he was preparing for the press his "Gleanings in Natural History," James Smith one day unexpectedly burst in upon him. The moment he saw him, he said, "My dear Smith, you have come in the very nick of time, as my good genius, to extricate me from a difficulty. You must know that to each of my chapters I have put an appropriate heading: I mean by that, that each chapter has prefixed to it a quotation from some well-known author, suited to the subject treated of — with one exception. I have been cudgeling my brains for a motto for my chapter on 'Crows and Rooks,' and cannot think of one. Can you?" "Certainly," said he, with felicitous promptitude, "Here is one from Shakespeare for you!

"'The cause (caws), my soul, the cause (caws).'"

After dinner we were talking of divers incongruities in language, genders, and grammar as a science. I had the effrontery to say that it had always struck me that grammars might be very much simplified in their construction; and that there was one error common to the grammars of the one or two languages with which I had any familiarity which I should like to see corrected — namely, the giving the rule before the definition; that this was putting the cart before the horse; and I fancied that, if a number of instances were given first, from which the scholar saw that "an adjective agreed with its subjective in gender, number, and case," he would deduce the rule almost for himself: whereas, according to the present system, the pupil must accept the rule as arbitrarily defined, without understanding it, until the definitions made it clear. There was so much quotation from Horne Tooke, and Harris, and Priestly, and Lord Monboddo, that I began to feel I was getting out of my depth, and therefore made a diversion by remarking the singular fact that though the sun in most languages was masculine, in German it was feminine; and the moon, usually feminine, masculine. "By the by," said I, "if I recollect rightly, in Latin, the names of rivers are generally masculine." "I forget," said James Smith, "but that can't be the invariable rule in English, for the two great American rivers must be feminine — Miss-souri and Miss-sisippi."

Count Danniskiold.

The Count is a Dane of high rank, an accomplished man, and one of the most elegant dancers in Europe. He speaks English admirably, and rarely makes a blunder. However, he made an amusing one last night. He was being bantered on having paid marked attention to one of the Miss C——'s, a young lady in the neighborhood, reputed rich, but rather plain. On some one saying, "You can't admire her looks, Count!" he replied, in a deprecating tone, "Come, come — you are a leetle hard upon me. She may not be beautiful, but, I must say, I tink she has a sweet expression in some of her eyes."

The Pillar of Gold.

Shortly after taking up my residence at Hampton Court, I went to call on Mrs. Boehm, at her apartments in the palace. She was the widow of a very wealthy West Indian merchant, who had retired from business, and had purchased the estate of Ottershaw. Their benevolence to the poor, their reputation for hospitality, and their proximity to Oatlands, soon recommended them to the notice of the Duke and Duchess of York, who conceived regard for them, and introduced them into the very highest circles.

On being shown into the vacant drawing-room, and after admiring a very large full-length portrait of a handsome lady playing the harp, which I afterwards heard was meant for Mrs. Boehm's self in younger days, I observed an ornament in the centre of her table, remarkable rather for its material value than for any originality in its design. It was a pillar of solid gold; I should think of some twelve inches in height, with a square base, if I recollect aright. I was stooping to decipher the inscription, when its owner herself entered. Perceiving how I was engaged, she begged me to suspend any further investigation until she had told me its history.

"You must understand, Mr. Young, that the object you were looking at was presented to me by his Royal Highness the Prince Regent in commemoration of an event of great historical importance which occurred under my roof when I lived in St. James's Square. I allude to no less a fact than the first news of the success of our arms at Waterloo."

On my manifesting some curiosity to hear the details of a scene of such rare and exceptional interest, the good lady, nothing loth, with an air of pride at the recollection of departed glories, mingled with mortification at their collapse, proceeded with her narrative.

"Ah! Mr. Young, very few of his Majesty's subjects ever had a more superb assembly collected together than I had on the night of the 21st of June, 1815. That dreadful night! Mr. Boehm had spared no cost to render it the most brilliant party of the season; but all to no purpose. Never did a party, promising so much, terminate so disastrously! All our trouble, anxiety, and expense were utterly thrown away in consequence of — what shall I say? Well, I must say it — the unseasonable declaration of the Waterloo victory! Of course, one was very glad to think one had beaten those horrid French, and all that sort of thing; but still, I always shall think it would have been far better if Henry Percy had waited quietly till the morning, instead of bursting in upon us, as he did, in such indecent haste; and even if he had told the Prince alone, it would have been better; for I have no doubt his Royal Highness would have shown consideration enough for my feelings not to publish the news till the next morning."

She then went on to give me a formidable list of the distinguished persons who had reflected the lustre of their presence on her party; laying special stress on the names of two or three Princes of the Blood Royal. In her somewhat discursive account, she stated that, while in the act of receiving her visitors to the dinner which preceded the ball, as she was standing by the Prince Regent, the groom of the chambers, in a loud and pompous voice, shouted forth, "Their Royal Highnesses the Duke of Sussex and Prince Augustus of Sussex!" — (since better known by the humbler title of Sir Augustus d'Este). On hearing this announcement, the Regent, with eyes flashing and color heightened, turned his back on his brother of Sussex, and said to the Duke of York, who was standing next to him, "Frederick, tell Adolphus from me, that if he ever allows that young man to assume that title again, he and I do not speak to each other."

"After dinner was over, and the ladies had gone up-stairs, and the gentlemen had joined them, the ball guests began to arrive. They came with unusual punctuality, out of deference to the Regent's presence. After a proper interval, I walked up to the Prince, and asked if it was his Royal Highness's pleasure that the ball should open. The first quadrille was in the act of forming, and the Prince was walking up to the dais on which his seat was placed, when I saw every one without the slightest sense of decorum rushing to the windows, which had been left wide open because of the excessive sultriness of the weather. The music ceased and the dance was stopped; for we heard nothing but the vociferous shouts of an enormous mob, who had just entered the Square, and were running by the side of a post-chaise and four, out of whose windows were hanging three nasty French eagles. In a second the door of the carriage was flung open, and, without waiting for the steps to be let down, out sprang Henry Percy — such a dusty figure! — with a flag in each hand, pushing aside every one who happened to be in his way, darting up stairs, into the ball-room, stepping hastily up to the Regent, dropping on one knee, laying the flags at his feet, and pronouncing the words, 'Victory, Sir! Victory!' The Prince Regent, greatly overcome, went into an adjoining room to read the dispatches; after a while he returned, said a few sad words to us, sent for his carriage, and left the house. The Royal brothers soon followed suit; and in less than twenty minutes there was not a soul left in the ball-room but poor dear Mr. Boehm and myself. Such a scene of excitement, anxiety, and confusion never was witnessed before or since, I do believe! Even the band had gone, not only without uttering a word of apology, but even without taking a mouthful to eat. The splendid supper which had been provided for our guests stood in the dining-room untouched. Ladies of the highest rank, who had not ordered their carriages till four o'clock A. M., rushed away, like maniacs, in their muslins and satin shoes, across the Square ; some accompanied by gentlemen, others without escort of any kind ; all impatient to learn the fate of those dear to them ; many jumping into the first stray hackney-coach they fell in with, and hurrying on to the Foreign Office or Horse Guards, eager to get a sight of the List of Killed and Wounded."

Sir Horace Seymour.

In height, he was six feet four inches, and, like Poins, "a proper fellow of his hands." His mein was princely ; and his smile so gracious, and his reputation for daring so established, that he rarely entered a drawing-room without fluttering the pulses of that sex who are even more sensitive to bravery than to beauty. With George IV. he was an extraordinary favorite. He entertained such an admiration for his handsome looks and figure, that, whenever he designed any alteration in the uniform of his regiments — which was very often — he always had the patterns fitted to his figure. And he had such an exalted estimate of his courage, and so little reliance on his own, that he delighted to have him near his person. He would submit to negligences, ignorances, over-sights, and shortcomings from him which he would not have tolerated from one of his own brothers.

On one occasion, for instance, either at the Cottage at Virginia Water or at the Pavilion (I forget which), Seymour, in waltzing, knocked over a magnificent China jar of great price. To the astonishment of all present, instead of the Regent's giving way to wrath, he merely put his hand gently on the offender's shoulder, smiled, and said with infinite good humor, "My dear Horace, what a careless fellow you are!" He tried hard, on the eve of his coronation, to induce Mr. Dymoke, through the intercession of Lord Willoughby d'Eresby, to waive his rights as champion, in favor of his *protégé;* but to no purpose.

The late Marquis of Anglesey, who had had abundant opportunities of witnessing Horace Seymour's feats of personal prowess (for he had been his body aide-de-camp at Waterloo), declared one day at dinner, at Admiral Bowater's, that, in the final pursuit at Waterloo, at least, after the last great charge, he saw him, in imitation of the French (whose swordmanship, by the by, he has often extolled to me), charge "at point" and pink out of their saddles, by sheer force of arm and length of sword, six or seven cuirassiers, one after the other.

The Marquis of Anglesey, then Earl of Uxbridge, at a particular crisis in the battle of Waterloo, seeing the Cumberland regiment of Hanoverian hussars considerably in the rear on the Brussels road, ordered them forward, and posted them in a position as little exposed as possible. "But, as soon as the shot began to fly about them a little, the colonel and his whole regiment took themselves out of the field. Lord Uxbridge," says Siborne, "ordered Captain Horace Seymour (as he then was) to go to the colonel, and insist on his return. Colonel Hake told him he had no confidence in his men, who were mere volunteers, and that their horses were their own. The regiment continued moving to the rear, notwithstanding Captain Seymour's repeating the order to halt, and asking the second in command to save the honor and character of the corps by placing himself at its head, and fronting the men. Finding his remonstrances produced no effect, he laid hold of the bridle of the colonel's horse, and commented on his conduct in terms such as no man of honor could have been expected to listen to unmoved. This officer, however, appeared perfectly callous to any sense of shame, and far more disposed to submit to these attacks upon his honor, than he had been to receive those of the enemy upon his person and his regiment. Upon rejoining the Earl of Uxbridge, and relating what had passed, Captain Seymour was again directed to proceed to the commanding officer, and to desire that, if he persevered in refusing to resume his position in the line, he would at least form the regiment across the high-road out of fire. But even this order was disregarded, and the corps went altogether to the rear, spreading alarm and confusion all the way to Brussels."

Mr. Siborne is considered such high authority, that I suppose his statement may be relied upon; though I have heard from a member of the family that Seymour caught hold of the recreant colonel by the collar, threw him out of his saddle, and offered to lead the men into action himself: but that they had been so infected by the cowardice of their colonel, that they instantly turned tail and gallopped off to Brussels *ventre à terre.*

It is a rather singular coincidence that Sir Horace should have been the first to see Picton fall, and the first to hear from Lord Uxbridge's lips of the shot which rendered the amputation of his leg necessary. In stating the first of these circumstances, Siborne mentions that Picton's death, "which was instantaneous, was first observed by the Earl of Uxbridge's aide-de-camp, Captain Horace Seymour, whom he was at the moment desiring to rally the Highlanders. Captain Seymour, whose own horse was just then falling, immediately called the attention of Picton's aide-de-camp, Captain Tyler, to the fact of the general having been wounded; and in the next moment the hero's lifeless corpse was, with the assistance of a private soldier of the nearest regiment, borne off from his charger by that officer."

With regard to the circumstances attending Lord Uxbridge's wound, I find my recollection of Sir Horace's account of it to me again at variance with that of Siborne's statement. In saying this, however, I must repeat that my memory has always been a very bad one; and that, therefore, the representation of one, who has taken conscientious pains in verifying facts, as Siborne has done, is not to be impugned.

My impression is, that Sir Horace told me it was late in the evening, after the Prussians had come up, and when he was riding off the field in company with Lord Uxbridge, that his companion said to him, "I'm hit!" "Oh! surely," said Seymour, "it is fancy." "No: I am hit, and by a spent ball. Get off your horse, and judge for yourself." Sir Horace then dismounted, and Lord Uxbridge guided his finger to the spot. "Feel — feel," said he; and as Seymour did so, his finger went into a small hole, in which, he said, he could distinctly feel bits of bone grating against each other like so many small shells.

With help, he lifted him from his saddle, and forthwith conveyed him to the neighboring village of Waterloo, where his leg was amputated. During the operation Lord Uxbridge indulged in jokes at his own expense; saying, he should lose ground in the esteem of the ladies by the loss of his leg; "for," said he, "as legs go, it was not a bad one."

In one of my many rides with Sir Horace, I asked him if the pictures of Lord Uxbridge, with his drawn sword, charging at the head of his cavalry, and leading them into action, were to be considered as truthful, and to be taken *au pied de la lettre.* "Yes," said he. "But was it right for one in such a responsible position to put himself forward as he did?" "Perhaps not," he replied, "strictly speaking. It was wrong. But the fact was he put himself into unnecessary peril; not, I fear, so much from a desire to animate his followers by his example, as because he sought death, being at that time weary of life; he was so miserable in his domestic relations. I will give you a proof of it. At one moment when it was pouring with rain, he tore off his oil-skin from his busby, that his rank in the service, defined by the ornament in front of the cap, might make him the more conspicuous a mark. Just before the great charge of —— [I think he said the Life Guards at Genappe], he cried out to me with a fierce recklessness of tone, 'Now, Horace, which of us will be in among them first?' He dug his spurs into his horse's sides, and took the lead of us all." Whether this was the charge of which Sir Andrew Barnard used to speak, I cannot say. But he declared that, in one charge, he saw Sir Horace dash into the very centre of a dense body of cavalry, and, by the weight of his horse, the length of his sword, and the strength of his arm, cleave his way clean through them. On turning round to see where he was, he found himself alone in the enemy's lines. Of course he thought the game was all up with him. But, favored by the smoke in which he was enveloped, he turned his horse's head; and, resolved to sell his life dearly, charged through them back again from behind. The enemy's troops, seeing one man alone among them, at first were puzzled to know whether he were friend or foe; and, impressed by his handsome uniform, his stature and bearing, instinctively fell back, and made a lane for him to pass through. While taking advantage of their doubts or their courtesy — whichever it may have been — he descried his friend D—— standing by some guns, a prisoner. It was the work of a second for Seymour, flinging back his left leg, and crying out "Quick, quick! jump! I've a stirrup to spare," to catch hold of D—— by the breech, throw him across the pommel of his saddle, as if he had been a sack of corn, and gallop off with him. Both escaped, as if by miracle, for many shots were fired after them, as soon as the French discovered their mistake.

I heard Sir George Seymour tell the following story of his brother's bravery when I was once staying with him at Lord Yarborough's, at Appuldurcombe: —

"On one of the four days, the 15th, 16th, 17th, or 18th, I cannot say which, there was, as if by common consent, as thorough a suspension of hostilities as if there had been an armistice. A stream ran between the opposing forces, to which the troops on either side eagerly repaired, for the purpose of slaking their raging thirst; and those who had recently been engaged in deadly combat were good-humoredly chaffing each other, when a gigantic soldier came forward from out the French ranks, and challenged any man in the English to meet him in single combat. 'Do you hear that, Horace,' said one of a group of cavalry officers who were collected together. 'Yes, I hear it!' said he, with clenched teeth. In another second he leaped his horse across the brook, dashed in among the French ranks, and in the sight of both armies fought with and slew the boastful Goliath."

This dauntless Paladin, where his affections were involved,

could be as gentle as a woman. When first I made his acquaintance, he had but recently lost his beautiful wife. No man ever suffered under such bereavement more poignantly. For many weeks he was nearly beside himself. At her burial, his violence was uncontrollable. He flung himself wildly on her coffin, and it took six strong men to drag him out of her grave. Long after her death he refused to see any but the members of his own family and myself. Although in his earlier days he had a reputation for gallantry, which was not confined to the battle-field, he became, after marriage, the most loyal and devoted of husbands. If any surviving members of his family should chance to cast their eyes on these pages, I hope, in consideration of the lapse of nearly forty years, they will forgive me if I mention a little illustration of the tenderness of this *beau sabreur*. He, one day, thrust into my hand one of his boy's lesson books, on which there was indented a nail mark of their mother's, which defined the limit of a task prescribed. I never shall forget the passion with which he kissed it, and then rushed to his bedroom to vent in solitude the anguish of his heart.

JOHN WILSON CROKER.

John Wilson Croker was a faithful public servant, and a passionate partisan. For one-and-twenty years he sat at the Admiralty Board, its influential and indefatigable secretary. For five-and-twenty years he was an active member of the senate; prompt and effective in debate; a master of detail; one of the pillars of the Tory party. For forty years he filled a prominent position, if not an elevated one, in the world of letters in which, if he had the reputation of meting hard measure to others, it was certainly measured to him again. Perhaps few men, who lived within the last half century, contrived to provoke a greater amount of personal hostility than Croker. He was a man of vast and versatile ability, of singular astuteness, of great powers of application, of a high sense of duty; but possessed an asperity of temperament which caused him to take a pessimist view of everything which came within his keen but narrow scrutiny.

Against the consistency of his political career I doubt if anything could be advanced by his bitterest antagonists;

> "He was constant as the Northern Star,
> Of whose true, fixt, and resting quality
> There was no fellow in the firmament"

of St. Stephen's. During a transition period, when even such men as the Iron Duke were forced to sacrifice their convictions, and bend to the pressure of imperious necessity, Croker stood firm as a rock. Believing, as he honestly did, that reform, if carried, would be the inevitable precurser of revolution, he adhered doggedly to the old traditional policy to which he had been attached; and opposed, with might and main, the doctrines of progress, which he felt persuaded would tend to the subversion of the monarchy, and the undermining of our most venerable institutions — especially the Church. I remember, in speaking of the perils of the Establishment, his saying,

> "C'est un vieux batiment, si on y touche, il crulera."

The virulence with which he assailed political opponents, and the merciless energy with which he slashed and tomahawked the writings both of friends and foes in the pages of the "Quarterly," begot an accumulation of antipathy to him which would have crushed a man of ordinary sensibility; but made only a transitory impression on his hardy and impenetrable nature.

The majority of the present generation, who have derived their impression of him either from Mr. Disraeli's able but sarcastic delineation of him under the character of Rigby, or else from the reports of those who have writhed under the lash of his incisive invective — will naturally think of him as one of the least lovable of men. But, however he may have abused his critical acumen to the pain and prejudice of others, in private life he exhibited qualities deserving of respect and admiration. To the poor and friendless he was generous: when not blinded by party feeling, he was conscientious; in the face of perpetual opposition, he was courageous. He was a tender husband, and an indulgent father. He had stuff enough in him for the making of a great statesman, though he hardly ever attained to that rank in public estimation. It is a notorious fact, that during the debates on the reform question, he took the wind out of Peel's sails. The fact was, that shortly before the bill came into committee, Croker had been confined to his bed for many days by serious indisposition. During that time, as he lay on his back, he studied the contents of every schedule, dissected them with anatomical precision, and sniffed out every unsavory clause that could be objected to. The consequence was, that when he had arisen from his bed, and found himself again on the floor of the House of Commons, he displayed such intimate knowledge of his subject, that Peel, who, from the multiplicity of his avocations, had not had leisure to devote the same study to the question, gladly gave to him the *pas*, and allowed him not only to bear the burden and the heat, but to win the honors of the battle. He so signalized himself on this occasion by his adroitness, that he astonished the most rancorous of his opponents, and greatly enhanced his reputation with the leaders of his party. From that time Peel never neglected to consult him on every great question that came before him. I told him that I had heard as much, and asked him if it were true. "Yes," said he, "he always asks my advice, and never takes it." From that time the Duke of Wellington gave him more and more of his confidence; and on his coming to power, offered him high place in his administration; but his health had been so shattered by the extraordinary excitement and exertion which he had undergone during the Reform agitation, that his wife exacted a promise from him that he would never accept office, or sit in a reformed House of Commons. His dread of the consequences to the country through the admission of the Reform Bill was quite genuine, though, as the event has proved, greatly exaggerated.

I heard him tell Theodore Hook and the late Mr. Jesse, at his own table, that he had warned Lord Palmerston, the very last day he saw him in the House of Commons, of the probable fruits which he might expect to reap from the seed he had sown: in plain words, the consequences of what he designated as his unpatriotic conduct in having aided in the passing of the Reform Bill through Parliament. "Well, Palmerston, you have raised the whirlwind, but you will never live to ride on it, nor direct the storm which will follow. I leave this house forever, a sadder, if not a wiser, man! All I pray for is a few brief years of political peace before I lay my head on my pillow and give up the ghost. You will go on your way exulting for a while; but probably will be, one day, impeached, and have to lay your head upon the block." False prophet as he has proved, his predictions were sincere.

I was one day dining with him at his house at Moulsey, when he dilated at great length, and with much gloom, on the disasters he had augured for England to King William the Fourth. "When William the Fourth," he said, "was Duke of Clarence and Lord High Admiral, I was, of course, as Secretary to the Admiralty, brought into frequent and intimate relations with him. I found him invariably frank and straightforward. He did not resent my being so too. You may remember — for it is matter of notoriety — that I opposed him tooth and nail when he amused himself at the public expense by squandering such heavy sums as he did on salutes, etc., etc. One day, after he had succeeded to the throne, he sent for me, telling me that he wished to talk over the bill with me. I was greatly struck by the magnanimity with which he permitted me to speak my mind. Think of my having dared to say as follows: 'Sire, when you yielded your high sanction to this bill, you admitted the justice of numerical representation in preference to representation according to property and intelligence. With all due deference to your Majesty, this was a lamentable error. In making this unreasonable concession to your subjects, you have played the part of the old Charlies, the very men who, salaried as they were to be the guardians of the public peace, and the conservators of public property, used to let in the thieves. Thus has your Majesty, the natural guardian of the constitution, and the conservator of monarchical principles, by opening the door to a vicious principle, let in the thieves. I see you smile, Sire. You may not live to see the consequences of your own acts, but they are none the less inevitable. If I strike a defenseless woman on the breast, I may see no signs of my own cruelty for years ; but in course of time my blow produces cancer, and she dies. And I conceive that when you affixed your sign manual to the Reform Bill, you, unwittingly no doubt, struck so deadly a blow against the breast of poor Britannia, that, ere long, it will engender a political cancer which will gradually eat out the very vitals of our beautiful constitution, republicanize our most venerable institutions, and upset the throne itself into the mud ! ' "

I suspect few people now alive are aware of the commencement of Croker's career in London. Horace Smith, James's brother, and one of the joint authors of "Rejected Addresses," told me that he, his brother, and Cumberland, formed the staff of the "Morning Post" when Colonel Mellish was its sole proprietor. On a certain quarter-day, when he was in the habit of meeting them at the office and paying them their salary, he took occasion to pass on them unqualified commendation for the great ability they had brought to bear upon his journal. He assured them that the circulation of the paper had quadrupled since their connection with it; "but — but — that he was, nevertheless, under the necessity of dispensing with their pens for the future." The two Smiths were so utterly unprepared for such a declaration, that they were tongue-tied. Not so the testy Cumberland, who took care to make himself as clearly understood as if he had been the veritable sir Fretful Plagiary.

"What," he asked his employer, "the D——l do you mean? In the same breath in which you laud your servants to the skies, and express your sense of obligation to them, you discharge them even without the usual month's warning!"

Mellish, quite unmoved, replied: "You must know, good Sirs, that I care for my paper, not for its principles, but as an investment; and it stands to reason, that the heavier my outgoings, the less my profits. I do, as I have said, value your merits highly; but not as highly as you charge me for them.

Now, in future, I can command the services of one man, who will do the work of three for the wage of one."

"The deuce you can," said Cumberland. "He must be a phœnix. Where, pray, may this omniscient genius be met with?"

"In the next room! I will send him to you."

As he left, a young man entered, with a well-developed skull, a searching eye, and a dauntless address.

"So, sir," screamed out Cumberland, "you must have an uncommon good opinion of yourself! You consider yourself, I am told, three times as able as any one of us; for you undertake to do an amount of work, single-handed, which we have found enough for us all." "I am not afraid," said the young man, with imperturbable *sang froid*, "of doing all that is required of me." They all three then warned him of the tact, discretion, and knowledge of books and men required; of the difficulties by which he must expect to find an enterprise of such magnitude beset, etc., etc. They began then to sound his depth; but on politics, belles lettres, political economy, even the drama, they found him far from shallow. Cumberland, transported out of himself by his modest assurance, snatched up his hat, smashed it on his head, rammed snuff incontinently up his nose, and then rushed by Mellish who was in the adjoining room, swearing and saying as he left, "Confound the potato. He's so tough, there's no peeling him!" The tough potato was John Wilson Croker.

Effect of Military Music.

A young man, of good family and considerable expectations, was appointed to the diplomatic staff of our ambassador at Petersburg. On his first appearance at dinner on the day of his arrival, the principal topic of conversation was the forthcoming *fête* of the year, about to be celebrated, if I am not mistaken, in the Church of St. Isaac.

The ambassador, turning affably to the young stranger, congratulated him on his good fortune in having arrived in time for the celebration. "I doubt," said he, "if in any other court in Europe you can see a more august ceremonial than that at which you will be present next week. By the by, don't forget that there is a seat set apart for you in my box as one of my staff."

The young man bowed respectfully, but with an air of indifference.

The following day, having had an interview with his chief concerning the contents of certain papers and letters which he had been desired to copy, on retiring he thus addressed him: —

"My Lord, you were kind enough yesterday to promise me what most persons in my position would deem a great treat, namely, a seat in your box, from which to witness this festival of which every one is talking. Will you think me very odd if I ask permission to absent myself on the occasion?"

Ambassador. "I should, indeed! What possible reason can you assign for such caprice?"

Attaché. "There will, I conceive, be military music. If so, — I must be frank with your Lordship, at the risk of provoking your ridicule, or even of incurring your displeasure, — I cannot be present. I have the strongest possible objection to all military music."

Ambassador. "Oh, you object on religious grounds to martial music in the house of God, do you?"

Attaché. "My Lord, however inappropriate I may think military music in the house of God, my unwillingness to be present there arises from lower and more selfish motives. You will smile, my Lord, when I tell you that I have an insuperable antipathy to the sound of a drum. I have lived so retired a life on my father's estate in the country, that I had never heard it but once in my life, and that was the other day, after a night spent in Paris on my road hither. I had fully intended staying there some days, but while in bed at the Hotel Bristol I heard the tramp of a regiment of soldiers marching down the Rue Castiglione to the sound of military music. I rushed to the window to see them, when suddenly I heard the *rappel.* Owing, I presume, to some nervous sensibility peculiar to my organization, I felt a torture so excruciating that I despair of describing it. I staggered to my bed, a faintness came over me, and my respiration became so seriously affected that I thought I must have died on the spot. I rang the bell violently for help, and after taking some sal-volatile and brandy, recovered sufficiently to pack up my things, ask for my bill, pay it, and hasten hither as fast as I could. You can now make allowance for my weakness in wishing to escape the recurrence of a similar infliction a second time."

The noble Lord laughed heartily at what he heard, and declared that if he allowed him to yield to such weakness he should consider he was helping to make him a confirmed hypochondriac. "My dear fellow," he went on to say, "did you ever tell your parents of this silly infirmity of yours?" "No, my Lord." "Then I am sure they will applaud me for not countenancing such folly; therefore I tell you distinctly I shall expect you to accompany me to the function." The young man felt it his duty to bow to his chief's decision, and therefore determined at all hazards to go. As the great day drew nigh, he told his *confrères* of the serious apprehensions by which he was beset; but got no more consideration from them than from their principal. At last the dreaded day arrived. The procession formed. Seats in the cathedral were set apart for ministers of state, the nobility, and the *corps diplomatique.* As the latter defiled by, the youngest *attaché*, according to the laws of precedence, took the last and lowest seat. When every one had been placed, space was kept by the military for the procession, which was composed of ecclesiastics of different grades, princes, prelates, and officers of distinction. Suddenly, outside the western gate was heard the clang of cymbals, the blast of trumpets, and the rub-a-dub of the great drum. On hearing it the ambassador, with a smile of ironical significance, looked past his followers to see the effect produced on his sensitive *protégé.* He was on the floor of the box — dead! On a post-mortem examination, it appeared that the shock to his finely-strung nervous system had caused a rupture of one of the valves of the heart.

Anecdotes of the French Police.

Dr. B—— was calling on my uncle to-day in Brighton. The subject of conversation on the *tapis* was the lamentable defects of our police regulations compared with those of Paris. Dr. B—— said that he considered he owed his life to the system of espionage prevalent in that town; and told the following tale in proof of it: —

Dr. B—— was a retired physician, who, having realized a handsome competency, dedicated much of his leisure to the cultivation of science. While engaged in a botanical tour through Switzerland, he received intelligence from Paris of the sudden death of one of his most valued friends. A letter from his widow informed him that he had been appointed, by her deceased husband, co-guardian and trustee with her to her son and daughter. She expressed an earnest hope that, as soon as he conveniently could, he would join her in Paris, and give her the benefit of his counsel under very trying circumstances. Thus appealed to, he conceived he had no alternative but to set out for Paris without further delay. On applying at the Messagerie, at Geneva, for a place in the diligence, he found every one both in the *intérieur* and in the *coupé* bespoken, so that he had no choice but to sit with the *conducteur* in the *banquette*, whose good-will he soon won by his affability and freedom from *hauteur*. The journey was accomplished without any impediment until, as they were approaching the *barrière* at the entry into Paris, the *conducteur*, breaking off in the midst of a lively conversation he was having with Dr. B——, and directing his voice to the "insides," hallooed out, "Messieurs et Mesdames, préparez vos passeports." Dr. B——, in obedience to this summons, thrust his hand first into the breast pocket of his great-coat, and then into the hind pockets of his frock, in search of his passport; but, to his consternation, could find it nowhere. What had become of it he never was able to discover. He thought it might have dropped out of his great-coat when he had flung it carelessly over the roof of the vehicle; but, whatever the cause of the misfortune, the effect was to involve him in a dilemma which might have jeopardized his liberty. In his distress he thought it best to tell the *conducteur* what had befallen him, and throw himself on his good-nature. On being appealed to, he told him that the only chance by which he could hope to escape the notice of the official at the *barrière* would be by having recourse to the following ruse: "Lie down," said he, "at the bottom of the *banquette*, under the leathern apron which has hitherto covered our knees; and while I step down from my seat on the left side, and the *gen-d'arme* is occupied in collecting passports from the passengers in the *intérieur*, creep out from under your covert on the right side, and mingle unhesitatingly with the crowd. I will engage the attention of the receiver of the passports till you are out of sight. He will not suspect me of conniving to deceive him — first, because I have never yet shown a disposition to do so; secondly, because he would never think me such a fool as to run the risk of discharge and imprisonment for the sake of serving a total stranger."

Dr. B—— adopted the friendly suggestion, and found it successful. As soon as the diligence had cleared the *barrière*, he jumped up again into his seat without any comment from the driver, who concluded that the *conducteur* would never have sanctioned his descent from his place unless he had previously surrendered his passport. On reaching his destination Dr. B—— rewarded the guard munificently for his services, and promised never to betray him.

After he had taken possession of his bed-room at his hotel he had a hasty dinner, and then made the best of his way to the residence of his late friend's widow. He found her and her daughter plunged in deep distress, though greatly comforted by his arrival. The mother, after furnishing him with details of her husband's last moments, disclosed to him the fruitful cause of her anxieties. The chief of them arose from her apprehensions as to the future of her only son — a young man barely one-and-twenty, not deficient in good qualities, but likely to be seduced into evil courses through infirmity of purpose. She described him as having become negligent of his sister at the very time when she most needed his sympathy, and as having grown impatient of maternal control. His deterioration of character she attributed to the influence of certain young men of high rank and low *morale*, who had acquired undue ascendancy over him, and had inoculated him with a passion for play. She implored her co-trustee to exercise every influence he could bring to bear upon her wayward boy, to wean him from so ruinous and degrading a propensity. Dr. B——, conscious of the delicacy and difficulty of the task imposed upon him, consented to undertake it on one condition only, namely, that she would not attempt to oppose the tactics he might choose to adopt, however incomprehensible they might seem, but confide in his discretion and good faith. To this proposition she assented, begging him at the same time to dine with her next day, so that he might have an opportunity of reviving acquaintance with the young man, whom he had not seen for some years.

The youth himself, aware of the high place Dr. B—— had filled in his father's esteem, and of the relation in which they now stood to each other — namely, that of ward and guardian, — anticipated no great satisfaction from the meeting. His reserve, however, rapidly melted away under the genial warmth of his mentor's cordiality. When his mother and sister had left the dinner table, the Doctor entered into conversation with his young friend with a vivacity that fascinated him. He proposed that they should go the next night to the opera, and afterwards look in at Frascati's, the great gambling-house of those days. As soon as the Doctor's back was turned, the mother was surprised to hear her son launch forth loudly in his praise, declaring that he was a "trump," and that he no longer wondered at his father's partiality for him. Dr. B——, having little reliance on the permanent effect of moral lectures delivered by an old man to a young one of vicious tendencies, preferred to gain his confidence by affecting community of tastes, and pretending afterwards to be penetrated with remorse, trying by argument to induce him to join him in the abandonment of a habit, the disastrous consequences of which he took care to paint in appalling colors. With the object of achieving so praiseworthy an end he was content, if necessary, to sacrifice fifty or sixty napoleons.

The following night, after the opera, they sallied forth for the gambling-table. Dr. B—— rushed up to it with well feigned avidity, and staked his money freely, persuaded in his own mind that from his utter ignorance of games of chance he must soon be a loser. To his amazement he met with an uninterrupted flow of good fortune, so that when he rose at three A. M. from the table, to his own disconcertment and the envy of his companion, his trowser and coat pockets were so full of louis d'or that it was only by holding them together he kept them from rolling out upon the floor. When invited, rather peremptorily by the *croupier*, to remain, and give his adversaries their revenge, he pleaded the hour in excuse for not doing so, promising, however, to return the next evening.

He bade his young friend "good-night," jumped into a fiacre, drove to his quarters, hurried to his room, and without giving a thought to the amount of his ill-gotten gains, poured them into the drawer of his toilet table and plunged into bed.

The next morning before he had risen he heard a tap at the door, followed by the entrance of two *gens-d'armes*. They marched up to the side of his bed, while one of them, referring occasionally to a note-book, thus addressed him: —

"Your name, Monsieur, is Dr. B——. On the 10th of this month you slept at ——. On the 11th you slept at La Cygne, in Lucerne. On the 13th you slept at the Hotel Sécheron. On the 14th you left Geneva in the *banquette* of the diligence, which started at —— o'clock. You were last seen eating your breakfast with the other coach passengers at the roadside inn at Les Rouses, on the Jura; but from that place we have lost sight of you. We know, however, that three days ago you entered this town without a passport, and we are at a loss to conceive how, in spite of the strictness of our police regulations, you succeeded in doing so. Luckily for you we know your antecedents. We know that you have been travelling with no political object, but simply for your own pleasure. We know that you dined with Madame —— and her son and daughter, in the Champs Elysées, two nights ago. We know that last night, in company with the son of your old friend, you visited first the opera, and then Frascati's, and that you won largely. Now we are authorized by our minister to say, that if you will deal unreservedly with us, and will tell us by what dexterous manœuvre you managed to pass the *barrière* without a passport, you shall not only be supplied with a fresh one *en règle*, but shall be insured protection while you remain in this city. You will readily perceive that we make these inquiries without any idea of punishing you for your infraction of the law, but with the object of warding off a repetition of the same trick at the hands of less scrupulous gentry than yourself."

Without compromising the conductor who had so generously befriended him, he then told them the whole truth, declaring his conviction that the audacity of the act was the chief cause of its success.

The men, satisfied of the truth of his representation, then went on to say, "Now, sir, you have been open with us; we in turn, will be open with you. You are in danger. Did you observe last night a German gentleman — a very stout one — with one or two decorations on his breast? He had won less than you had, but he refused to continue play, and consequently after you had left he was shot dead as he was going down the stairs. We warn you return without fail to-night to Frascati's, and lose back every sous you have won, or your life is not worth four-and-twenty hours' purchase."

In consequence of these alarming intimations, Dr. B—— told his young friend what had happened, and begging him to keep out of harm's way, adjourned at night to Frascati's in no very enviable frame of mind.

He played with studied, determined recklessness. No spendthrift ever wished more earnestly to win than he did to lose; but the more daring his ventures the more startling were his winnings. About the small hours of the morning, to his immeasurable satisfaction, the wheel of fortune turned against him: still his losses bore no proportion to his gains. Morning was breaking; he was unwilling to stay, yet afraid to go. At last he screwed up his courage to the sticking-place and hurried out of the room, but so full was his mind of the fate of the German baron the previous night, and of the warnings of the police, that instead of walking down the stairs he slid down the banisters, thinking by that undignified mode of descent he should present a more difficult mark for any murderer who might be lying in ambush for him. Whether it was thought prudent to reserve punishment for him to another night he knew not; but, to his ineffable delight, the instant he alighted in the hall he was met by a tall, cocked-hatted functionary, in whom he recognized one of his bedroom visitors, who handed him into a *cabriolet*, which was at the door, and escorted him to his hotel without uttering a word.

I am sorry that a story promising so well, should have no more sensational *dénouement;* but Dr. B—— told it us merely to prove the high state of efficiency of the Parisian police at that time. He felt so satisfied that he owed his life to their timely warning, and to the never-flagging vigilance with which they followed him about the streets, that he went to the head of the police-force and begged to be allowed to deposit in his hands a considerable sum of money in token of his sense of their attention. He was sternly and flatly refused, and reminded that the entire organization of the force was for the protection of person and property; and told, that if the system of rewards for the mere execution of duty was once permitted, the demoralization of the body would infallibly ensue.

Wellington's Copenhagen.

In the year, 1833 while living in Hampshire, no one showed my wife and myself more constant hospitality than the late Right Honorable Henry Pierrepont, the father of the present Lady Charles Wellesley. In his youth he had been the intimate associate of Lord Alvanley, Beau Brummell, and Henry, afterwards Lord de Roos. This little select clique was known as par excellence "the Dandies," who were not more distinguished for their taste in dress than for their powers of wit and repartee. On one of our many delightful visits to Conholt, Mr. Pierrepont had but just returned from Strathfieldsaye as we arrived. He had been there to meet the judges, whom the Duke was accustomed to receive annually, previously to the opening of the assizes. After dinner, Mr. Pierrepont was asked by the Duke of Beaufort, who, with the Duchess, was in the house, if he had had an agreeable visit. "Particularly so," was the answer. "The Duke was in great force, and, for him, unusually communicative. The two judges and myself having arrived before the rest of the guests, who lived nearer Strathfieldsaye than we did, the Duke asked us if we were disposed to take a walk, see the paddocks, and get an appetite for dinner. We all three gladly assented to the proposition. As we were stumping along, talking of Assheton Smith's stud and hounds, one of the judges asked the Duke if we might see Copenhagen, his celebrated charger. 'God bless you,' replied the Duke, 'he has been long dead; and half the fine ladies of my acquaintance have got bracelets or lockets made from his mane or tail.' 'Pray, Duke, apart from his being so closely associated with your Grace in the glories of Waterloo, was he a very remarkable — I mean, a particularly clever horse?'"

"*Duke.* 'Many faster horses, no doubt; many handsomer: but for bottom and endurance never saw his fellow. I'll give you a proof of it. On the 17th, early in the day, I had a horse shot under me. Few know it; but it was so. Before ten o'clock I got on Copenhagen's back. There was so much to do and to see to, that neither he nor I were still for many minutes together. I never drew a bit, and he never had a morsel in his mouth till eight P. M., when Fitzroy Somerset came to tell me dinner was ready in the little neighboring village — Waterloo. The poor beast I saw myself stabled and fed. I told my groom to give him no hay, but after a few go downs of chilled water, as much corn and beans as he had a mind for, impressing on him the necessity of his strewing them well over the manger first. Somerset and I dispatched a hasty meal; and as soon as we had done so, I sent off Somerset on an errand. This I did, I confess, on purpose that I might get him out of the way, for I knew that if he had had the slightest inkling of what I was up to, he would have done his best to dissuade me from my purpose, and want to accompany me.

"'The fact was, I wanted to see Blucher, that I might learn from his own lips at what hour it was probable he would be able to join forces with us next day. Therefore, the moment Fitzroy's back was turned, I ordered Copenhagen to be re-saddled, and told my man to get his own horse and accompany me to Wavre, where I had reason to believe old "Forwards" was encamped. Now, Wavre being some twelve miles from Waterloo, I was not a little disgusted, on getting there, to find that the old fellow's tent was two miles still farther off.

"'However, I saw him, got the information I wanted from him, and made the best of my way homewards. Bad, however, was the best; for by Jove, it was so dark that I fell into a deepish dyke by the roadside; and if it had not been for my orderly's assistance, I doubt if I should ever have got out. Thank God, there was no harm done, either to horse or man!

"'Well, on reaching headquarters, and thinking how bravely my old horse had carried me all day, I could not help going up to his head to tell him so by a few caresses. But, hang me, if, when I was giving him a slap of approbation on his hind-quarters, he did not fling out one of his hind legs with as much vigor as if he had been in stable for a couple of days! Remember, gentlemen, he had been out with me on his back, for upwards of ten hours, and had carried me eight-and-twenty miles besides. I call that bottom! ey?'"

In this simple and unpretending manner did the great man vaunt the merits of his horse, and forget altogether the infinitely greater fatigue (for his was mental as well as bodily) which he had himself undergone.

Wellington and the Bagman.

For full a quarter of an hour, during one of the greatest crises of the battle of Waterloo, when the great Duke had work enough on his hands to have employed a staff of double the dimensions of that allotted to him; and when he had in addition to his regular aides-de-camp, volunteer ones, in the persons of the then Duke of Richmond, Lord William Lennox (a youth not sixteen), and Lord Bathurst (then Lord Apsley), all flying about the field for him with messages oral or written, he found himself alone — and alone at the very moment that he most needed help. While traversing the horizon with his telescope, he had descried the commencement of a movement, on the part of Sir James Kempt's brigade, which he foresaw, if not promptly countermanded, would be likely to operate fatally on the successful issue of the battle. He had no one at his elbow by whom he could make the desired communication with the gallant brigadier. In this trying dilemma he turned himself round in his saddle and beheld, some hundred yards behind him, a single horseman, so quaintly attired as almost to excite a smile on his countenance. He wore a green cut-away coat (known in those days as a duck-hunter), drab vest, drab breeches, and mahogany-tinted top-boots. He bestrode a black short-jointed Flemish cob. He carried an English hunting-whip in his hand; and had on his head a civilian's hat, with a colonel's feather stuck in it.

The instant the Duke caught sight of him he beckoned him to him, and in his curt, pithy manner asked him who he was? what he was there for? how he had passed the lines? etc., etc. His answer was concise and direct enough. But I prefer to tell it as it was told to me by one who, in 1819, four years after the battle, had heard all the particulars from the lips of both parties concerned.

He told the Duke that he was a commercial gentleman — in other words, a bagman — travelling for a great wholesale Birmingham button manufactory; that he had been engaged in showing "specimens" to a retail house in Brussels, when his ears were assailed by the reverberation of heavy ordnance, and having had an intense desire all his life to see a battle, he begged eave to suspend his negotiation, abruptly left the shop, rushed to a horse-jobber, hired from him the best animal he could find, up to his weight, and made the best of his way to the scene of action. On coming at a turn of the road on a particular wood, he found two regiments, with piled arms, bivouacking.[1] On attempting to pass, he was challenged by one of the sentries, and roughly ordered to "be off." While the bagman was trying to propitiate him, and other soldiers, looking on, were disputing the propriety of yielding to his solicitation, one of the officers, who heard the altercation, went up and asked what was the matter. The stranger begged that he might be allowed to explain his position; and in doing so, pleaded so strenuously, yet respectfully, for leave "to see the fun," that the officer in question determined, if practicable, to grant his request. Before doing so, however, he warned him of the probable risk to his own person. "Oh," said he, "I will brave the risks, if only I may gratify my curiosity." Turning to a corporal who was standing near him, he asked him "what were his orders." "Nothing under a colonel's feather to pass, captain." "Well," said the good-natured officer, "we will soon settle that matter. Send out a man or two, and let them search among the bodies of the dead for a colonel's feather." In a few minutes one was found, brought, and inserted into our Birmingham friend's hat; and the sanction he craved was granted.

The bagman, carefully noting the lie of the ground, and guided by his natural intelligence, pushed on towards the only elevated spot he could perceive. As he beheld the clouds of

[1] I had the honor of telling this story to the late Lord Raglan (when Lord Fitzroy Somerset). He had never heard it, and, at first, could hardly believe it, *as* he had never heard it; but afterwards, from inquiries he made, and from the person's name which I gave him as my authority, he said "he had no doubt it was true." On my expressing to his lordship that I could not fancy, when troops were so much needed, that there could have been two regiments near at hand, and yet not called into play, he said, "Oh, yes; there were two regiments, and one was the 54th, which formed part of the force kept in reserve for the protection of the road to Brussels and they never were engaged on the field."

smoke and the lurid sky, and sniffed the scent of powder and of carnage as he got nearer and nearer, and heard the clash of steel and the stunning roar of artillery, he became wildly excited, and "eager for the fray," put spurs to his horse and galloped like a madman on and on, till suddenly he saw before him, on the summit of the hillock for which he was making, a figure, the very sight of which sobered his impetuosity, caused him instinctively to draw in his bridle-rein, take breath, and halt, as if petrified, in his course. The figure that met his eyes was seated on horseback rigid as a statue! The cocked-hat, the military cloak, with its short cape, drooping in long folds from his shoulders, the arms raised and extended, the hands holding in their grip a field-telescope, with which an eagle-glance was busily scanning the fiery hosts below and beyond, told him he was within ear-shot of the foremost man in Europe. As he took out from his coat-pocket his handkerchief, and nervously wiped his heated brow, an indefinable sense of awe set his pulses throbbing. He felt guilty. He felt a trespasser. He felt he was where he had no right to be. He was thinking whether he had not better beat a retreat, and retire to some spot where he would be screened from observation, when the object of his dread turned round and asked him his business there. The Duke was pleased with his answers, and determined to turn his metal and sense to good account.

"You are a funny chap! Why, you ought to have been a soldier! Would you like to serve your country, if I gave you the opportunity?"

"Yes, my lord."

"Would you take a message of importance for me, if I sent you with one?"

Touching his hat in the approved military fashion — "If I were trusted by you, my lord, I should think it the proudest day of my life."

The Duke, who at that time was no duke, but Lord Wellington, put into the man's hand his field-glass, and directed him where to look. "Those troops you see yonder are the Enniskillens ; those beyond are the Royals. There, you see those gray horses, they are the Scots Greys. They are commanded by Lord Edward Somerset. There, again, is the 42d. Between (pointing to certain spots) such-and-such a regiment lies Sir James Kempt's brigade, the 28th, the 32d, the 79th Highlanders, and the 95th Rifles. I have no materials for writing[1] by me, so mind you are very accurate in delivering my message." He then, having intrusted to him a brief, emphatic order (which he made him repeat, that there might be no mistake), he ended the interview with these words : "Tell him, by G—, if he perseveres in carrying out what he has begun to do, the game will be all up with us ! "

" I dare say you have often joined in a fox-hunt in England ? "

" Often, my lord."

"Well, in the hunting-field you don't think much of a man who is always 'skirting.' But I sha'n't think much of you in the battle-field, at least as my aide-de-camp, if you do *not* skirt. Your business is to execute my orders with as little risk to yourself as may be ; because, if you put yourself in danger, you imperil the safe delivery of my message, and so jeopardize the success of the fight. Mind, then, don't go near the smoke ; but pound away on that nag of yours until you reach the rear of Kempt's troops. Then tell the first man you can get speech with that you come from me, and must be taken to the general, and it will be all right."

The orders were barely delivered before the stranger was off at the top of his horse's speed to execute them. The Duke watched his progress with marked interest and approval for some little time ; when, presently, his approbation gave way to apprehension, and apprehension to indignation, as he observed his messenger doing the very thing he had specially warned him against — namely, dash through the very thick of the smoke

[1] I heard the Duke say once that he used to hang from one of the button-holes of his waistcoat a number of slips of parchment on which he wrote his orders, in size and shape something resembling the parchment labels used for travelling in these railway days ; but they were all by that time exhausted by the multiplicity of messages he had had to send out.

with all the fearlessness of an old cavalry officer. While the Duke was riding up and down, uneasily ruminating on the chances of his message ever reaching its destination, he was joined, first, by Sir Alexander Gordon; then by Sir Augustus Frazer; and then by Sir Horace Seymour, bearing a message from Lord Anglesey. As soon as they had all come up, within a minute or two of each other, the Duke said, "I have been wanting one of you gentlemen sadly. In your absence I have been so hard pressed for an aide-de-camp, that I have had to appoint a new one in the person of a Brummagem bagman.' He then told them of the mission on which he had sent him. Each proffered his services. The Duke declined them. "Perhaps I may want one of you," said he; "we'll wait a few minutes. I'm disposed to have faith in Brummagem. He's no fool!" He then dismounted from his horse, passed his horse's bridle into Seymour's hand, took from his dispatch-box, which was on the ground, the "Sun" newspaper, opened it to its full extent, spread it over his face, leaned his head on a sack of forage, and in another instant was asleep.[1] All three aides-de-camp stood silent by. At the expiration of five or six minutes' interval, he sprang up on his feet, opened his field-glass, and cried out, in a tone of unusual vivacity, "By Jove! It is all right. Kempt has changed his tactics. He has got my message; for he is doing precisely as I directed him. Well done, Buttons!"

The Duke, one evening after dinner, told my informant that he considered the counteraction of Kempt's original movement almost the pivot on which the fortunes of the battle turned; and certainly next in importance to the closing of the gates of Hougoumont by Sir John McDonnell, Captain Wyndham, Ensigns Gooch and Harvey; and last, not least, Sergeant Graham of the Coldstreams. Indeed, so indebted did the Duke feel to the hero of our tale for the intelligence and intrepidity he had displayed, that the instant the Prussians had

[1] It is a notable coincidence that both Napoleon and Wellington had the same enviable faculty of commanding sleep at will, and of being refreshed by a very few minutes' slumber.

come up, and he had ordered our harassed troops, who had sustained the chief brunt of the French attack, to lie down and rest, and leave the pursuit to the last comers, he had him cried, first on the field, then in the village of Waterloo, then at Brussels, and last of all, at Paris — but to no purpose.

For many years the Duke never could gain tidings of him, until one day, at dinner at his own table, happening to mention the circumstances, and express his regret at never having been able to learn anything of him since the event, one of his guests told him that he knew the man, and had heard him allude to the part he had played, very cursorily, and without boastfulness. The Duke instantly took down the man's address, wrote to him, and within a week obtained for him a commissionership of Customs in the west of England, in recognition of his services.

Wellington not surprised.

After dinner, the conversation turned on the vexed question, as to whether the Duke of Wellington had been taken by surprise at Waterloo, or not. After a lively and rather warm discussion, antagonistic opinions being advanced on each side with equal confidence, I turned round to Sir Henry Webster, who was coolly peeling an orange, and taking no part in the controversy, and asked him if he had not been at Waterloo. "Ah," said he, smiling, and raising his voice at the same time, "I have been amused at the speculations of some of you gentlemen, when here sits one who knows as much about the facts which you have been arguing as any man in the world. I beg distinctly to declare, that the Duke of Wellington was not taken by surprise. The real state of the case was this: the Duke knew perfectly well that the possession of Brussels would be of primary importance to Napoleon, on account of the moral, military, and political advantages to be gained from it. He knew, therefore, that Napoleon would make for it. The Duke's game was to anticipate him, and make Brussels his own head-quarters. He knew, also, that it was more than likely that Napoleon, by forced marches, would try to engage with the British forces before their strength had been increased by the addition of more of the allied troops. On the 15th, Napoleon had marched on Charleroi, and, at dawn, had unexpectedly fallen on the Prussians, and compelled them to fall back. Intelligence of the advance of the French was dispatched at once to the Duke. At three o'clock, while the Duke was eating an early dinner, the Prince of Orange galloped up to his hotel to tell him that the French were advancing by the valley of the Sambre on Brussels. He received the intelligence with his usual calmness. At five o'clock he had matured his plan of operations, and had his orders to the chief commanding officers ready, written on cards, intending them to be distributed, after supper, at the Duchess of Richmond's ball.

"Now, you may not perhaps know, gentlemen, that I was the Prince of Orange's aide-de-camp. The Prince had himself been actively engaged that day in helping the Prince of Saxe-Weimar (whose brigade of Netherlanders had been driven in on Quatre Bras) to defend the farm-house there. He had then ridden on to Brussels to see the Duke, and to attend the ball; but, before doing so, he told me to remain where I was (whether it was at the farm of Quatre Bras, or somewhere near, I forget) and bring him certain dispatches which he expected, the instant they arrived. At ten o'clock ———, the minister, came to me, telling me that the advanced guard of the Prussians had been driven in at Ligny; and ordering me, without a moment's delay, to convey the dispatch he put into my hand to the Prince of Orange. 'A horse ready-saddled awaits you at the door,' he said, 'and another has been sent on, half an hour ago, to a half-way house, to help you on the faster. Gallop every yard! You will find your chief at the Duchess of Richmond's ball. Stand on no ceremony; but insist on seeing the Prince at once.' I was in my saddle without a second's delay; and, thanks to a fine moon and two capital horses, had covered the ten miles I had to go within the hour! The Place at Brussels was all ablaze with light; and such was the crowd of carriages, that I could not well make way through them on horseback; so I abandoned my steed to the first man I could get hold of, and made my way to the porter's lodge. On my telling the Suisse I had dispatches of moment for the Prince, he civilly asked me if I would wait five minutes; 'for,' said he, 'the Duchess has just given orders for the band to go up-stairs, and the party are now about to rise. If you were to burst in suddenly, it might alarm the ladies.' On that consideration I consented to wait. I peeped in between the folding doors and saw the Duchess of Richmond taking the Prince of Orange's arm, and Lady Charlotte Greville the Duke's, on their way to the ball-room. The moment they reached the foot of the stairs, I hastened to the Prince's side and gave him the dispatch. Without looking at it, he handed it behind him to the Duke, who quietly deposited it in his coat-pocket. The Prince made me a sign to remain in the hall. I did so. All the company passed by me, but I hid myself in a recess from observation for fear of being asked awkward questions. As soon as the last couple had mounted the *première étage*, the Duke of Wellington descended, and espying me beckoned me to him, and said, in a low voice, 'Webster! Four horses instantly to the Prince of Orange's carriage for Waterloo!'"

The very day after hearing this account, I went to lunch with Mr. and the late Lady Jane Peel, who, as the Duchess of Richmond's daughter, I knew to have been present; and I asked her if she could recall distinctly the circumstances of that historic night. "Do you think," she asked, "that any one who was there ever *could* forget the events of that night? Well I remember what Sir Henry Webster has told you—namely, the rising from that supper-table, and all that followed immediately after it. I know I was in a state of wild delight—the scene itself was so stirring, and the company so brilliant. I recollect, on reaching the ball-room after supper, I was scanning over my tablets, which were filled from top to bottom with the names of the partners to whom I was engaged; when, on raising my eyes, I became aware of a great preponderance of ladies in the room. White muslins and tarlatans abounded;

but the gallant uniforms had sensibly diminished. The enigma was soon solved. Without fuss or parade, or tender adieux, the officers, anxious not to alarm the ladies, had quietly stolen out; and before they had time to guess the nature of the news which had robbed them of their partners, and changed the festive aspect of the scene, they found themselves, instead of asking questions, holding their breath, while the musicians ceased to play; for the dub-a-dub of the drum, and the rolling of artillery-wagons, and the blast of the bugle, and the tramp of large masses of infantry, and the neighing of cavalry horses, told them how near they were to the seat of war, and how imminently a great battle was impending."

"Ah! then and there was hurrying to and fro,
And gathering tears, and tremblings of distress,
And cheeks all pale, which, but an hour ago,
Blushed at the praise of their own loveliness;
And there were sudden partings, such as press
The life from out young hearts, and choking sighs,
Which ne'er might be repeated: who could guess
If ever more should meet those mutual eyes,
Since upon night so sweet such awful morn could rise!"

The Three Parishioners.

The following sketch of three old "lean and slippered pantaloons," parishioners of mine, is not in the least exaggerated. The conversation, which I am about to describe as having taken place between one of them and myself, is given verbatim. I wrote it down instantly, in Charles Mathews's presence, and at his request. It requires not only imitation, but ventriloquism, to give a just idea of the ludicrous degrees of feebleness of voice displayed in the "childish treble" of the youngest, and his mimicry of the still weaker voice of the eldest.

James Baker was a moping old malcontent — sour, selfish, and stricken in years. I think he was seventy-eight. His outer man was distinguished by a dirty and dilapidated smock-frock, a battered straw hat, and brown gaiters, "a world too wide for his shrunk shanks."

Solomon Cox was eighty-three, nearly bent double by infirmity and age, and tottered and trembled as he walked: he leaned heavily on his crab stick, wore a hideous fur cap of Norwegian extraction, and looked every inch what he really was, the very incarnation of "hatred, malice, and all uncharitableness."

Thomas Nash was but seventy-five, and was looked down upon by his two veteran companions; not more on the score of his comparative youth, than of his manners, which they deemed volatile and puerile. He was blessed by nature with a genial and mercurial temperament. He was the cricket on their hearth. It was impossible to see him, with his quaint three-cornered Uncle Toby hat, his snuff-brown coat, with its broad skirts and plated buttons, each larger than a crown-piece, without discerning in these vanities the expiring embers of a slowly-smouldering dandyism. His step had a rickety jauntiness about it, ill-suited to a man with one foot in the grave; and in his eye there lurked a latent waggery, which told of buoyancy of spirit "in the old dog yet."

These three lived together on the outskirts of a breezy spot called Hay-down, in a wretched mud-wall hut, allotted to them by "the parish." Reader, if you have ever known in the circle of your miscellaneous acquaintance three sisters, one of whom has been beautiful, another comely, and the third positively plain, but who, classed together, have been spoken of as "the three beautiful Misses ——," you will be able to understand how two members of this antiquated trio, crooning over their scanty bit of fuel, and mumbling and moaning over their hard lot, and looking as if they had just stepped out of one of Teniers' pictures, owed the little interest they inspired in their squire or minister, rather to their association with their amiable and attractive chum, than to any attraction of their own. The following dialogue between Thomas Nash and myself is characteristic.

J. C. Y. "Well, Thomas, how d'ye find yourself to-day?"

Nash. "Very well, I thank your reverence. A fine day it is for drying the clots." (In that part of the world they dry the droppings from cows and use them as firing.)

J. C. Y. "How is Baker?"

Nash. "Much of a muchness, please your reverence; a grumbling in coorse. He's always at that fun. One time 'tis bowl's,[1] then 'tis the rheumatics, and now, he says, 'tis the prelatics (paralysis) or summut. But he's one as 'ull always have summut the matter. He'd be miserable, if he had not!"

J. C. Y. "And is Solomon Cox all right?"

(His answer reminded me of Dogberry to Leonato in "Much Ado about Nothing." "Goodman Verges, sir, speaks a little off the matter: an old man, sir, and his wits are not so blunt as, God help, I would desire they were; but, in faith, honest as the skin between his brows.")

Nash. "Lor' bless you, sir, he's but an old crittur at the best. He's a'most weared out."

J. C. Y. "Well, well, no wonder. Think of his years!"

Nash. "Lor', sir, 'taint age as does it; 'tis envy! I'll tell you summut, master. You mun know, we three old coves have a lug [2] o' ground atween us; and I've gotten a main-few [3] 'taters, and a sight o' nice young peas besides; and he've got none. He were fretting about this amazing t'other day, saying it warn't fair, and one thing or another, for that I could get about a sight better nor he; that he'd got no 'nure [4] for his'n; and that I was always a-scraping and scraping every mossel o' cow-dung I could clap my eyes on: so he'd no chance. Well, I rather pitied the old gennelman; so I says, says I, 'I'll tell you what it is, Master Solomon, — you wants pre-se-verance. Now, I don't want to take no revantage [5] on you; so I'll tell you what I'll do: — I'll gie you a day on't; I'll show you my beat; I'll rig you out wi' my dung-bag and scraper; and if that ain't fair I don't know what is!' Well, sir, I put him in the way o' what I calls my 'preserves,' and started him hand-sum. We seed nothing on him till tea-time; and as soon as he cum in I slapped him on the back, and said, cheery-like,

[1] Bowels.

[2] A lug is a quarter of an acre.

[3] "A main-few" in Hants, Wilts, and many other counties, signifies "a good many.

[4] Manure

[5] Advantage.

'Well, mate, what sport? — what sport, I say?' Blessed if the old gennelman, instead o' saying summut pleasant, did not sink down in his chair, seem faint-like, and then fall to a-crying, like a good 'un. When I could get him to speak at last, he broke out in these werry words: 'Arter the 'ansum manner in which you've cum forward, Thomas Nash, I won't say nothing. But *this* I must say, if I were to die for it next minute, you've that scoured the country up and down, there ain't nothing worth a rush to be got. Here have I been a matter of five hours a-beating and a-beating about, and I've never seed but one poor clot, and I would not have he; there were no walley[1] in it.'"

Charles Mathews, senior, when this dilaogue took place, was indoors at the time; and when I went in and told him of it, he roared with laughter. I never saw him afterwards that he did not make me repeat it — though I think I can chronicle still droller things of him.

Charles Mathews.

"E'en from my boyhood up" I knew old Charles Mathews, the comedian, intimately. The present generation has too often heard of him, and therefore naturally thinks of him as a great *mimic.* I claim for him higher pretensions — namely, that of being the most wonderful *imitator* of his age.

A man may be the most amusing "mimic" that ever "set the table in a roar," and yet be gifted with no great powers of intellect. The mind has very little to do with the matter; for the mimic's success depends principally on liveliness of perception, and the possession of certain physical and corporeal qualifications, neither rare in their manifestations, nor indicative of any mental superiority in their possessor.

The chief requisites in the mimic are quickness of observation, sensibility of ear, flexibility of voice, mobility of feature, and suppleness of muscle. His sphere is a very limited one; for it is generally confined to the mere adventitious accidents of singularity of elocution or oddity of demeanor. The mental

[1] Value.

and the moral of the inner man are beyond his province. That Mathews had no rival as a mimic I am not prepared to assert; for, in "taking off" his brethren of the sock and buskin, I think Frederick Yates was his superior; but as an imitator he was unapproachable.

The old Duke of Richmond, the grandfather of the present, was very partial to Mathews, and so thoroughly appreciated this *specialité* of his, that during his Lord-Lieutenancy of Ireland, whenever he had him to dinner and wished to treat his guests to a specimen of his talent, as soon as the cloth was removed, he would propose his health, not in his own name, but now as Lord Erskine, now as Lord Ellenborough — at one time as Sheridan, at another as Curran; and under whichever metamorphosis it might be, he would make a speech so closely after the manner of each as to electrify his hearers. It was not so much the alacrity with which he would spring to his feet and assume the countenance, voice, and gesticulation of the person he was expected to impersonate, as the individuality of thought and style of speech which reminded his audience of Erskine and Ellenborough, and the felicity of language and profusion of trope and metaphor, which made them fancy they were listening to the voice of Sheridan or Curran.

In Lady Blessington's "Conversations with Byron," she mentions that Walter Scott once asked Byron if he had ever heard Mathews imitate Curran; and, on his regretting that he never had Scott added: "It was not an imitation, it was a continuation of the man." So highly, too, did Coleridge estimate his powers, that on somebody, in his presence, calling him a mere mimic, he said, "You call him a mimic: I define him as a comic poet acting his own poems."

He certainly was unique in his way, and full of incongruities. I never knew any man so alive to the eccentricities of others, who was so dead to his own. I never knew a man who made the world laugh so much, who laughed so seldom himself. I never knew a man who, when *in* society, could make the dullest merry, so melancholy *out* of it. On the other hand, I never knew a man so prompt to resent calumnious imputations on others, or so ready to forgive those who had done himself wrong. In his imitation of others, he was never actuated by malevolence ; but no man was more hasty in attributing unamiable motives to any who made *him* the subject of mimicry. He was very fond of imitating Dignum the singer, and used to tell how, when he took him off to his face, he would say, "Oh, Mathews! you are a wonderful person ; but it is wicked, it really is, to mock natur—you should not do it, 'pon my life." And yet he himself was furious with Yates for taking the like liberty with him.

The intrinsic worth of his character, the purity of his life, his liberality to the necessitous, his simplicty, his untarnished integrity, his love for his wife and son, his fidelity to his friends, his loyalty to his patrons, his chivalrous defense of those he thought unjustly defamed, could not fail to win for him the thorough respect of all who knew him. On the other hand, genius and gentleman as he was, his nervous whimsicality, his irritability about trifles, his antipathies to particular people, places, and objects, rendered him justly vulnerable to ridicule and censure. I have seen him scratch his head, and grind his teeth, and assume a look of anguish, when a haunch of venison has been carved unskillfully in his presence. I have seen him, though in high feather and high talk when in a sunny chamber, if transferred to a badly-lighted room, withdraw into a corner and sit by himself in moody silence. He was strangely impressionable by externals. I have known him refuse permission to a royal Duke to see over his picture-gallery on Highgate Hill, because the day of his call was cloudy. He was such a passionate lover of sunshine, that I have seen him "put out," for a whole day by the lady of a house at which he was calling pulling down the Venetian blinds. "There are not many days in the year," he would say, "when the sun shines at all in this country ; and when he *is* disposed to be kindly and to pay us a visit, down goes every blind in his face, to show him, I suppose, how little we value his presence." Whenever he went out to dinner, in the good old days when moderator and sinumbra lamps were unknown, and wax-candles were in fashion he was wont to carry in his breast-pocket a pair of small silver snuffers, so that, when the wicks were long and dull, he might be able to snuff them, and thus brighten up the gloom that was gathering round the table. I have known him, without the slightest cause, appropriate remarks to himself which were intended for others, and fret his heart-strings over imaginary wrongs for hours. I have known him frenzied with rage, on discovering that a tidy housemaid had picked up from the floor of his bedroom a dirty pair of stockings which he had left there "as a memorandum," on the same principle on which people tie knots in their hankerchiefs. And yet, with all these unhappy infirmities, I never knew a man more formed to inspire, and who succeeded more in inspiring personal affection, or who, though exposed to many temptations, was so unsoiled by them.

I have already implied, if I have not asserted, that he was liable to alternate fits of elation and depression. At one time he was so alarmed about himself, that he begged his razors might be always kept by his man, and never left in his room, lest, under some malign impulse, he might destroy himself. When the black cloud was on his spirit, he was taciturn; and if addressed, laconic and sour in his replies. At such times he would speak as if he were a fatalist; he would vow that nothing ever went right with him; that he was the most ill-starred of men; and then, in confirmation of his assertion, would say — "I never, in my life, put on a new hat, that it did not rain and ruin it. I never went out in a shabby coat because it was raining, and thought all, who had the choice, would keep indoors, that the sun did not burst forth in its strength, and bring out with it all the butterflies of fashion whom I knew, or who knew me. I never consented to accept a part I hated, out of kindness to an author, that I did not get hissed by the public and cut by the writer. I could not take a drive of a few minutes with Terry, without being overturned, and having my hip-bone broke, though my friend got off unharmed. I could not make a covenant with Arnold, which I thought was to make my fortune, without making his instead. In an incredible space of time (I think thirteen months) I earned for him twenty thousand pounds, and for myself one. I am persuaded, if I were to set up as a baker, every one in my neighborhood would leave off eating bread!"

I mentioned how easily his equanimity was disturbed by trifles, such as bad carving, ill-lighted rooms, etc. The same feeling extended to other things. If he were paying a call, for the first time, on a new acquaintance, and saw a picture hanging out of the perpendicular, he would spring up to put it straight; if a lady, in her dress, showed a deficient sense of harmony in color, it irritated him greatly, etc., etc. The following anecdote will further illustrate his morbid sensibility to things which most people would deem insignificant.

He had an appointment with a solicitor. They were to meet at a particular hour at a small inn in the city, where they might hope to be quiet and undisturbed. Mathews arrived at the trysting-place a few minutes too soon. On entering the coffee-room, he found its sole tenant a commercial gentleman earnestly engaged on a round of boiled beef. Mathews sat himself down by the fire, and took up a newspaper, meaning to wile away the time till his friend arrived. Occasionally he glanced from the paper to the beef, and from the beef to the man, till he began to fidget and look about from the top of the right-hand page to the bottom of the left in a querulous manner Then he turned the paper inside out, and, pretending to stop from reading, addressed the gentleman in a tone of ill-disguised indignation, and with a ghastly smile — "I beg your pardon, sir, but I don't think you are aware that you have no mustard." The person thus addressed looked up at him with evident surprise, mentally resenting his gratuitous interference with his tastes, and coldly bowed. Mathews resumed his paper, and, curious to see if his well-meant hint would be acted on, furtively looked round the edge of his paper, and finding the plate to be still void of mustard, concluded the man was deaf. So, raising his voice to a higher key, and accosting him with sarcastic acerbity, he bawled out, with syllabic precision — "Are — you — a-ware — sir — that — you — have

— been — eat-ing — boiled — beef — with-out — mus-tard ?" Again a stiff bow and no reply. Once more Mathews affected to read, while he was really "nursing his wrath to keep it warm." At last, seeing the man's obstinate violation of conventionality and good taste, he jumped up, and in the most arbitary and defiant manner, snatched the mustard-pot out of the cruet-stand, banged it on the table, under the defaulter's nose, and shouted out: "Confound it, sir, you SHALL take mustard!" He then slapped his hat on his head, and ordered the waiter to show him into a private room, vowing that he had never before been under the roof with such a savage; and that he had been made quite sick by the revolting sight which he had seen in the coffee-room.

Another of the plagues by which he deemed himself to be peculiarly beset, was the pestering offers of attention, from mercenary motives, of urchins in the streets.

I met him one day in Regent Street, mounted on his pretty milk-white pony. Although I was a favorite, I saw that my stopping him was not altogether acceptable. It was soon explained. The young Arabs of the street were round him, and at each side of his bridle, with their "Please, want your 'orse 'olded;" and, with the sort of expression on his face, which one would have expected, perhaps, to see, if he had been on the plains of Egypt, with a swarm of Bedouins swooping down upon him, he shook himself off from me, with the and words, "The plague's begun," uttered in a tone of despair, galloped off as fast as intervening cabs and carriages would allow him.

During the entire period of his stay with us he was delightful: always ready to fall in with our quiet and monotonous mode of life, and appearing pleased with everything and everybody with whom he was thrown in contact. At the termination of his night's performance at Andover, I was made aware of one of his whims, of which I had, till then, been quite unconscious I mean his singular and inexplicable aversion to the touch of money. A certain man, who, for prudential reasons, I will not name, always travelled with him, as his secretary and check-taker. He received all the money taken at the doors. On leaving the Town Hall with Mathews, I asked him if he were content with the receipts. "Oh," said he, "I don't know what they are: I leave it all to B——. I am quite at his mercy. I never know what really is taken at the doors. I only know what I receive. I hope and believe B—— is honest; but, even if he is not, I could not wrangle about money. I do so hate the very touch of it." "What!" I exclaimed, with genuine incredulity, "hate money!" "I did not say I hated money, but that I hated *the touch* of money — I mean coin. It makes my skin goosey."

One more of his oddities I must mention. He used often to declare, that he never could understand why it was that, when other people so frequently had cause to complain that they could not find things they lost, he never could lose anything he wished to get rid of. I must plead guilty to having twice ministered, with malice prepense, to this superstition of his.

On leaving any house where I may have been staying, I have a confirmed habit of looking into every drawer, wash-stand, table, etc., so as to insure myself against leaving anything behind me. Mathews once left me at a country inn, where we had been together. When I was about to take my departure, with my usual precaution, I took care to ransack every possible and impossible nook or cranny, behind which any article of mine might have fallen; and, in doing so, observed, secreted behind a huge old mahogany dining-table, with deep flaps, which was placed against the wall of our sitting-room, a dress shoe, so dapper in shape, and so diminutive in size, that I had no difficulty in recognizing it as one of my friend's. Rejoiced at the opportunity of having a bit of fun, I inclosed it in a brown paper parcel, and dispatched it after him. Instead of thanking me for my trouble, he wrote to me, and told me that I was "his evil genius; that, having worn out the companion pump, which was that of the foot of his lame leg, the one I had forwarded to him was of no earthly use to him; that in the faint hope of getting rid of it, he had placed it where I had found it; and that in consequence of my inquisitive and officious disposition, he had been compelled to pay for the recovery of this useless article as much as would have purchased an entirely new pair."

About a month after he had left us, at Amport, I happened to go to my wardrobe in search of an old pair of trowsers which I reserved for gardening purposes. As I was putting them on, I felt that there was something in them. My first impression was, that, when I had last worn them, I had left my purse in them. But, on inserting my hand into the pocket, I drew out an oddly-shaped object, neatly wrapped up in Bath note paper, with these words inscribed on the outside, in the quaint but vigorous handwriting I knew so well, "To be lost, if possible." On opening the little packet, I found inside it a circular nail-brush, worn to the bone. It would seem that, on looking over the articles in my wardrobe, he thought the trowsers he had selected were too shabby for me ever to put on again, and therefore chose them for a hiding-place. But he was deceived. I made up another neat parcel for him, and directed it to his house in London. Unfortunately he was on a professional tour in the provinces, where it followed him; till by the time it reached him, the "carriage" had amounted to some shillings. I was not long in receiving a letter of ironical thanks "for my kind and *dear* attention." I was penitent for having put him to such expense, and I confessed my sin to him.

Many years after, I was telling his son Charles of these amusing incidents, when he said, "I can cap your story." He then told me, that once he and his father had an engagement with one of the East India Directors at the India Office. As they were approaching Blackfriar's Bridge, the father said to the son, "We must stop a minute at the first draper's shop we come to, as I want to buy myself a new pair of gloves; for I have mislaid the fellow to the one I have on my right hand." As soon as he had effected his purchase, they proceeded on their way; and, on reaching the bridge, the son observed his father looking before him and behind him, as if, having some felonious purpose in his mind, he wished to see that the coast was clear before he executed it. At last, when the traffic seemed for a moment to diminish, he leaned over the parapet of the bridge — as if to notice the wherries and steamers on the river — hurled over the odious glove, which was disturbing his serenity, and then limped off in an agitated and guilty manner, as though he were trying to evade the emissaries of justice. So eager was he to get off the bridge, and thread his way unobserved through the crowd, that he outstripped his son; and just as he was waiting for him, and was congratulating himself on having, for once, got rid of an obnoxious article, a breathless waterman ran up to him, tapped him on the shoulder, and said, "I beg your honor's pardon, but I think you dropped this here glove in the river." "How — how, sir, do you know it to be my glove?" "Why, sir, I was a sculling, and was just giving my boat a spurt under the arch of the bridge, when this here glove fell; and on looking up I see'd that the gentleman from whose hand it dropped had a white hat on with a black crape round it; so I pulled with all my might and main after you, and ran up the steps from the river-side, and I thought I never should have catched you," — wiping his forehead with his sleeve as he spoke. Of course such disinterested civility had to be rewarded with a shilling, and the impoverished donor, like Lord Ullin's daughter, was "left lamenting!"

Again. During Mathews's visit to us at the end of October, 1833, one of the sons of the nobleman (at whose gate, almost, we lived) dined with us; and having an acute sense of fun, and thoroughly appreciating our guest's wit and humor, and learning from us that the star of his genius always began to rise when that of ordinary mortals set (namely, at bed-time), he used to drop in about eleven o'clock P. M., for the pleasure of enjoying our visitor's incomparable society. These *Noctes Amportianæ*, delightful as they were, and temperately as they were conducted (for potations were not required by way of stimulus), were very trying to me; for, about a week after our little party had broken up, the late hours to which I had been exposed, and the excess of laughter in which I had indulged, told upon me and I fell ill. The night before Mathews left Amport, he told us that he was going to Oxford the next day to give two or three entertainments; and he implored my wife and myself so urgently to accompany him, that, in compassion to his anticipated dejection, we consented. As we were only some twenty-five miles from Oxford, I undertook to drive him there in my phaeton. When the noble lord already alluded to found that my wife and myself were going to Oxford with Mathews, he begged permission to accompany us. As I had one vacant seat, I was only too glad to have so agreeable an addition to our party; and on the following morning we set off. From nine in the morning till six in the evening it poured with rain incessantly. Mathews sat in front with me; Mrs. Young and her noble companion behind. We started about twelve o'clock, and baited two hours on the road Mathews besought me to get him into Oxford by six P. M., as he was engaged to meet a large party at the Rev. Mr. Rose's, of Lincoln College, at seven. It was a curious fact, and one, so far, justifying Mathews's theory of his invariable ill-luck, that, though Lord F. P—— had merely a dreadnought on, my wife her ordinary cloak, and I a common great-coat, Mathews, who was enveloped in waterproof wraps, in addition to a great-coat and cloak, was the only one of the party who was soaked through and through. Fearing that, on his arrival, he might be hurried, and, in order to save himself the trouble of unpacking his portmanteau in undue haste, he had taken the precaution of wrapping up the clothes he would require for dinner in two towels. Boundless, therefore, was his disgust on unpinning his packet, which had lain at our feet protected, as we thought, alike from wind and rain by the thick leathern apron over our knees, to discover that his dress coat and kerseymere pantaloons were saturated with wet, and that the pattern of his sprigged velvet vest had been transferred to his shirt-front. When, therefore, he entered our sitting-room at the Star Hotel, and observed the table laid for dinner, the clean cloth, the neatly-folded napkins, the glittering glass, and the blazing fire, he could not help contrasting our cosy condition with his own draggled plight, and began to reflect gloomily on the length of time his clothes would take to dry, and on the several disadvantges under which he would have to make his rapid toilet; till, at last he vowed that "Mr. Rose might go to Jericho, and all the heads of houses be drowned in the Red Sea, before he would desert us." It was in vain that we expostulated with him on the indecency of such behavior; in vain we depicted the cruel disappointment he would inflict on a gentleman who had paid him the compliment of asking the Vice-Chancellor and other men of University distinction to meet him. In vain we appealed to his self-interest, telling him that he would, by his rudeness, estrange his friend, and convert a patron into an enemy. The more we urged him to consider what he owed to others, the more obstinately he vowed he would not victimize himself for the sake of acquiring a reputation for good manners. Dine with us he would.

As we were enjoying, with keen relish, our salmon and cucumber, the waiter entered, and thus addressed the culprit: — "Please, sir, here's a messenger from Mr. Rose of Lincoln, to say that his dinner is waiting for you." "My kind compliments to Mr. Rose of Lincoln," was his rejoinder; "I am sorry I cannot dine with him, as I am obliged to share the fortunes of three friends who have been nearly drowned. I dine with them. Tell him I have not a dry rag to cover my nakedness with, and that we are all four now steaming before the fire preparatory to going to bed to nurse."

Every instant I sat in fear and trembling that we should either see the much-wronged gentleman *in propriâ personâ*, or have to receive a deputation from him, or else an angry note; but fortunately our threatening evening passed off without a storm; and as, after our meal, we drew together round the fire, and Mathews sipped his negus, and lolled back in his arm-chair, his spirits rose, and "Richard was himself again."

He had an inveterate propensity to keep late hours; and he was given to lie in bed till midday in consequence. If he were disturbed earlier, he would say he had been woke in the middle of the night. It was as good as a servant's place was worth if she called him before twelve o'clock. Knowing all this, it was greatly to the diversion of Lord F. P——, Mrs. Young, and myself, that, the morning after our arrival, one of the waiters told us there was a messenger from Mr. Rose of Lincoln waiting in the hall to see Mathews. We desired him to be shown up, and then, pointing to Mathews's bedroom, which was on the same floor with our sitting-room, and well within our view, we advised him to rap at his door and give him the note with which he was intrusted. In the spirit of mischief, and longing for a scene, we three ensconced ourselves behind our own door, impatient to witness the result. The messenger at first tapped humbly and hesitatingly. No answer. A second rap, and then a third, waxing louder each time. As the patience of the messenger was giving way, a strange figure, clad in a long night-shirt, with an extinguisher cotton night-cap on his head, and irrepressible fury in his visage, emerged from the room, and, with clenched fist, asked his visitor—"If he was weary of life?—if he desired to be ruthlessly murdered?" etc., etc. "No, sir." "Then how dare you disturb me at this unearthly hour?" (N. B. 9.30 A. M.) He then slammed the door violently to, in a state of wrath implacable, and bolted himself in. Once more the poor "scout," in undisguised trepidation, appealed to us for advice, as to what he should do next, adding that his master had enjoined him strictly, on no consideration, to return without an answer. Greedy of more fun still, we insisted on his attending, above everything, to his own master's instructions; and, disregarding Mathews's bluster, again to try his door, and not to leave it without receiving the answer required.

With evident misgiving, he again crept up to the dreaded bedroom, and, after a free and frequent application of his knuckles to the panels of the door, finding he received no reply, he took heart, and halloed through the key-hole: "I 'umbly ax your pardon, sir, but Mr. Rose of Lincoln says he *must* have an answer." The hero of my tale, exasperated beyond all bounds by this persecution, once more appeared, in the same questionable attire as before, and, indifferent to the observation of the waiters and chambermaids who were flitting up and down the corridor, and unconscious that his friends were watching him, screamed out: "Confound Mr. Rose of Lincoln, and all Mr. Rose of Lincoln's friends, and all Mr. Rose of Lincoln's messengers! Mr. Rose of Lincoln *must* have an answer, eh? Then let him get it by law. Does Mr. Rose of Lincoln think that I go to bed with a pen in my mouth, and ink in my ear, that I may be ready to answer, instantly, any note Mr. Rose of Lincoln may choose to write to me?"

I forget whether we remained at Oxford more than two nights; but, having first ascertained that he had made matters straight with Mr. Rose, we left with easy conscience. He did not return to Amport with us, but followed afterwards, in a day or two. After sleeping a night with us, he asked me if I would go with him to Salisbury, where he was due for one night's entertainment. It was on our road across Salisbury Plain that the accident befell us which is told in Mrs. Mathews's memoirs of her husband. I never was more surprised than at reading, in the "Morning Chronicle," two or three days afterwards, the particulars of our adventure. It seems that Mr. Hill, the original from whom John Poole took his "Paul Pry," was sitting with Mrs. Mathews in Great Russell Street, when a letter from her husband was put into her hand. She begged permission to read it, and as, in doing so, she could not suppress a few ejaculations of surprise, he begged he might hear it. She was quite willing to gratify him, and, at his request, gave him permission to take it home and show it to his wife. On that understanding he was allowed to take it; but, instead of taking it home, he took it to the printer of the paper with which he was connected, and inserted it in its columns. As many may never have read it, I shall presume to give my own version of the accident, which is much fuller in its details than the one given in Mrs. Mathews's Life of her husband.

Before he left our house, I had promised Mathews, who could not bear being alone, to drive him to Salisbury, and keep him company while there. The distance from Amport to Andover was five miles ; from Andover to Salisbury, by the road, eighteen ; but across the intervening Plain, fully three miles shorter. Now, although, under the pilotage of Lord W. and Lord George P——, I had ridden that way two or three times, I had never driven it. To the rider nothing could be more delightful than the long unbroken surface of untrodden turf ; though the tameness of the surrounding scenery, and the absence of landmarks to steer by, made the route rather a difficult one to find. Before starting, I had serious misgivings that the frequent intersection of deep wagon-ruts, of the existence of which I was quite aware, might put my charioteering powers to a severe test ; but the prospect of a "short cut" was a temptation not to be withstood. For the first two or three miles we got on capitally ; but afterwards we encountered such a succession of formidable inequalities in the ground, that Mathews got nervous, and my horses became excited. Out of consideration for his hip-joint, I advised him to alight, and walk a few yards till we had passed over the roughest part. This he was only too glad to do ; while I, throwing the reins over the splashboard, went to the horses' heads, and, by voice and gesture, endeavored to coax them gently over the uneven ground. However, in descending a sharp dip in the ground, which was succeeded by a rise as sudden, the pole sprang up, hit me a violent blow under the chin, and sent me spinning to the ground. On recovering my footing, I saw my carriage jolting and bumping along at the rate of twenty miles an hour, rendering any hope of my overtaking it, for a long time to come, an apparent impossibility. In utter dismay, I appealed to my friend for advice, but found him all but paralyzed, and incapable of giving it. "Good heavens, Julian !" he cried out, "in that bag of mine, are, not merely all my clothes, but three hundred sovereigns in gold, the fruit of four 'At Home's,' and all that I have written of my autobiography. Run ! Run !"

It was easy for him to say "Run," but not so easy for me to do so ; for, owing to the extraordinary velocity with which the panic-stricken animals had darted off, and the undulation of the land over which they had passed, they were lost to sight in no time.

The foremost difficulty which suggested itself to me was how, even if I recovered my carriage and horses, I was to find my disconsolate companion again; for, in consequence of the complete circumnavigation of the hill which the runaways had probably made, I knew I should find myself, before long, in a *terra incognita*. As Mathews could not walk, I pointed to some miserable furze bushes, and told him to lie down under them, and not to stir until he saw me again. He squatted down most submissively; while, in attestation of my good faith, and, at the same time, that I might run the easier, I disencumbered myself of my great-coat, flung it to him, and left it in pawn till I should return and redeem it. Away I darted, and ran and ran — till I could run no more: and I was about to fling myself on the grass to regain my wind, and rest awhile, when I beheld in the distance, four carriage wheels in the air, and a pair of grays, detached from the vehicle, standing side by side, as if in one stall, trembling in every limb, sweating from every pore, and yet making no attempt to stir. I felt re-nerved at this sight, pursued my object, went up to my truant steeds, and captured them without any show of resistance on their part. They were thoroughly blown. They had been seen by a band of gypsies, encamped hard by, to charge a precipitous embankment which separated the Plain from the high-road; but unable, from exhaustion, to surmount it, they thought better of it, turned round, and, dashing down again into the valley, ran with such headlong fury against the stump of a blighted old pollard oak as to upset the phaeton, break the traces, snap the pole in twain, and scatter Mathews's precious treasures far and wide over the ground. My first anxiety was to rejoin their owner as quickly as possible; for it was then half-past three o'clock, and I knew that he had to reach Salisbury, dress, order and eat his dinner, and be on the stage by seven P. M. I went, therefore, up to the gypsies, described how the accident had occurred, told them of the dilemma in which I had left a lame gentleman a mile off, assured them that it was of the greatest importance that he should arrive in Salisbury by five o'clock, and begged them to spare somebody to lead one of the horses, while I rode the other in search of my friend.

Seeing that they had a tent pitched in sight, I told them, with a frankness that most people would have deemed imprudent, that the contents of the carpet-bag confided to their care was very precious to the proprietor, and that, if they would be kind enough to set up the carriage on its wheels, and protect my property, the instant I reached Salisbury I would return in a post-chaise with ropes to take the fractured phaeton in tow, and reward them handsomely for their trouble.

They undertook to carry out my wishes, while I, jumping on one of the horses (with all its traces and trappings, and breeching, and collar, and pad upon him), and followed by my esquire on foot with the other, galloped off to look for him who, I was certain, was for once anything but "at home" where he was.

In my feverish impatience to overtake my horses, I had forgotten to take notice of the ground I passed over, though it was in a totally different direction from that I had been used to. Whichever way I went, my gypsy aide-de-camp had orders to keep me well in sight. For some twenty minutes, which appeared an hour, I whooped and halloed at the top of my voice, directing it north, south, east, and west; but neither received answer nor beheld sign of living creature. Turn which way I might, there was nothing before me but a wide expanse of dreary plain. The bray of a jackass, the bark of a watch-dog, the bleating of a stray sheep, even the quack of a duck, would have been as music to my ears. To contribute to my perplexity, the skies began to assume a leaden and lowering hue, and sleet and flakes of snow to fall. Our stipulated trysting-place, the furze-bushes, could nowhere be seen, for the projecting brow of table-land on which I was. They were at the base of the hill, and I was on the summit. As I sat bewildered, on my horse, with my esquire behind me, I fancied I saw something stirring below me which resembled the fluttering of a corn-crake's wings, though they certainly seemed unusually long and unsteady, and the wind appeared to have extraordinary power over them. I made towards the object, and, as I did so, I found to my ineffable relief, that it was no bird I had seen, but a white silk handkerchief tied to a stick, doing duty as a signal of distress. As I drew nearer to it, I saw my lost companion drop on his knees, and raise his hands to heaven in token of thanksgiving. No wonder. Had I not found him, he must have passed the livelong night in utter helplessness and solitude, and perhaps have fallen victim to hunger, cold, and mental perturbation.

When we met, I found Mathews almost speechless from agitation. He threw his arms around me, and was so extravagantly and comically demonstrative, that, in spite of all my sympathy for him, I could not refrain from laughter. I feared he would be offended with me; but was delighted to ascertain from his published letter that my ill-timed mirth was attributed to an "hysterical affection." As soon as I could persuade him to hearken to me, I told him there was not a moment to be lost, that we had three or four miles to go before we could reach the high-road, and that manage we must, somehow or other, by hook or by crook, to get there in time to catch "The Light Salisbury" coach, and reach his quarters at the White Hart, by five P. M.

On my further telling him that he must get on the horse from which I had dismounted, and that I would lead it for him, he said, "My dear fellow, I never, in the prime of life, bestrode a bare-backed horse; how then can I do so now, old and crippled as I am?" I said no more; but, making my gypsy follower stand at the horse's head, I went on all-fours by its side, and insisted on his stepping on my back, and holding by the horse's mane, while I gradually raised myself up, so as to enable him to fling his leg over the animal. It was a weary and an anxious walk for both of us. However, as luck would have it, we had no sooner sighted the chalky road, than I saw my old acquaintance Matcham, driving "The Light Salisbury" towards us. I gave both my horses to the gypsy to lead leisurely to Salisbury, while I mounted on the outside the coach with my sorely harassed friend. He was in a most devout frame of mind, thanking God loudly and earnestly for his merciful deliv erance from a miserable death, when a Dissenting minister behind him, learning from the coachman who he was, thought it a good opportunity for "improving the occasion," and preached to him in such bad taste, and with such utter want of consideration for his feelings, that Mathews, humbled as he was, could not brook it, and told him his mind. "Until you opened upon me, I never felt more piously disposed in my life; but your harsh and ill-timed diatribe has made me feel quite wickedly. Hold your canting tongue, or you'll find me dangerous, Mr. Mawworm!"

To finish my tale: — As soon as I had seen Mathews comfortably seated at his dinner, I called for a post-chaise, drove to the scene of action, and was rather mortified to find that the gypsy family had not touched the carriage, though I had begged them to set it up again upon its wheels. On remonstrating with them, they very civilly said, "Why, you see, sir, if, in moving it, anything had gone wrong with the carriage, owing to some injury you had not detected, or if anything were missing, you'd ha' been sure to suspect the poor gypsies; so, on second thoughts, we considered 'twould be better to leave it — as they leaves a dead body before a hinquest — without moving or touching anything."

They then turned to with a will, in my presence, — put the carriage on its legs again, helped me to cord it on to the hinder part of the post-chaise, and thrust inside Mathews's carpet-bag and portmanteau, and a few articles for the night, which I had put up for myself. I sprang into the chaise, wishing to get back and relieve Mathews's mind about his goods. I drew out my purse, and was going to take out money to give the gypsies, when one of them came up to me and said, "Are you sure, sir, that you have got everything belonging to you?" "Yes, yes; thank you." The man smiled, and, by way of answer, thrust into my hand my oil-skin sponge-bag, which had fallen out of my hat-box, and which I had overlooked. "Now, my good fellows," said I, "what shall I give you? You deserve something handsome, and you shall have it. Will a couple of sovereigns satisfy you?" "No, sir, no!" they all cried out. "We won't have nothing. You've paid us enough! You've trusted us, gypsies as we are! You've left your property in our keeping, and never cast a suspicious glance at it, when you came back, to see if we had been tampering with it."

I pressed them over and over again to reconsider their determination, and consider my feelings. "Well, sir, we will ask one favor of you. Tell your friends that, whatever your glass and crockery and brush-selling tramps may be, a *real* gypsy *can* be honest."

On the first night of one of his "At Homes," when the theatre was packed to the very ceiling, and all his best friends and supporters were there to support him, I witnessed a singular instance of his sensibility to the opinion of others. At the end of the first part of the entertainment, Manners Sutton, the Speaker (afterwards Lord Canterbury), Theodore Hook, Gen. Phipps, and others, went behind the scenes to congratulate him, and assure him that, as far as the piece had proceeded, it was an indubitable success. He accepted their compliments rather ungraciously. All they said, to buoy him up, only seemed the more to depress him. At first they could not make him out, till he explained himself by blurting forth the truth. "It is all very well, and very kind of you, who wish me well, to tell me the piece is going well; *I* know better. It ain't 'going well,' and it can't be 'going well' — it must be hanging fire, or that man with the bald head in the pit, in the front row, could not have been asleep the whole time I have been trying to amuse him!" "Oh," said the Speaker, "perhaps he is drunk." "No, no! he ain't; I've tried hard to 'lay that flattering unction to my soul,' but it won't do. I've watched the fellow, and when he opens his eyes, which he does now and then, he looks as sober as a judge, and as severe as one; and then he deliberately closes them, as if he disliked the very sight of me. I tell you, all the laughter and applause of the whole house — boxes, pit, and gallery put together — weigh not a feather with me while that 'pump' remains dead to my efforts to arouse him." The call bell rang; all his friends returned to their seats in front, and he to the stage. The second part opened with one of the rapid songs, in the composition of which James Smith, the author, excelled so much, and in the delivery of which no one ever equaled Mathews, except his son, who, in that respect, surpasses him. All the time he was singing it, as he paced from the right wing to the left, one saw his head jerking from side to side, as he moved either way, his eyes always directed to one spot, till, at the end of one of the stanzas, forgetful of the audience, and transported out of himself by the obstinate insensibility of the bald-pate, he fixed his eyes on him, as if he were mesmerizing him, and, leaning over the lamps, in the very loudest key, shouted at him "Bo!" The man, startled, woke up, and observing that the singer looked *at* him, sang *to* him, and never took his eyes off him, he became flattered by the personal notice, began to listen, and then to laugh — and laugh, at last, most heartily. From that instant, the actor's spirits rose, for he felt he had converted a stolid country bumpkin into an appreciative listener. After such a triumph, he went home, satisfied that his entertainment had been a complete success.

This excessive sensibility to public opinion is not uncommon. The late Sir William Knighton told my uncle, George Young, that if George the Fourth went to the play, which he rarely did, and heard *one* hiss, though it were drowned in general and tumultuous applause, he went home miserable, and would lay awake all night, thinking only of that one note of disapprobation.

Curran, again, was so notoriously susceptible to inattention or weariness on the part of his hearers, that, on more than one occasion, advocates engaged against him, perceiving his powerful invectives were damaging their client's cause, would pay some man in the court to go into a conspicuous part of it, and yawn visibly and audibly. The prescription always succeeded. The eloquent spirit would droop its wing and forsake him; he would falter, forget the thread of his argument, and bring his peroration to an abrupt and unsatisfactory conclusion.

Mathews was, one day, riding down Highgate Hill from his

cottage, to rehearsal, when he met a post-chariot crawling up, with my father and another gentleman in it, who happened to be the late Lord Dacre. Mathews, not knowing him by sight, or even by name, asked my father, as he saw he was going into the country, if he was going down to Cassiobury, to Lord Essex's (where, at that time, he was a constant visitor). "No," replied my father, "I am on my way to 'The *Hoo*.'" "*Who?*" asked Mathews. "I am going to stay a few days at Lord Dacre's," was the answer. Mathews, imagining Young to be poking fun at him, by ennobling Bob Acres, laughingly exclaimed, "I have half a mind to go with you. Mind you give my kind regards to Sir Lucius O'Trigger, who is sure to be staying with him." No man could have enjoyed the mistake more than the noble lord himself.

Mathews had such an inordinate love of drollery in every form, that he would often engage very indifferent servants, if they had but originality to recommend them. I remember a gardener he had, a Lancashire man, who was a never-failing fund of amusement. I was on the lawn at the cottage at Milfield Lane one day, when I overheard the following dialogue.

"I say," said the master, patting a huge Newfoundland by his side, "we shall have to put a muzzle on this brute. I am having so many complaints made about him from the neighbors, that I shall have to get rid of him. He worried Mrs. ——'s dog, I hear, the other day, and frightened two little children nearly to death."

"Well, I doan't know aboot that; but if you wants to get rid on't, I know one as 'ud like to have un; for t'other day, as I was a-going by Muster Morris' labyratoury (laboratory), Duke St. Aubon's cam louping over t' edge, and he says, says he, 'Who's dog be that?' So I says, says I, ''tis master's, Muster Mathews.' 'Would you sell un?' says he. 'No.' says I; 'but I dussay master would let you have a poop.' 'Oh, no,' says he; 'Doochess has poops enough of her own!'"

"How," asked Mathews, "did you know it to be the Duke of St. Alban's?'

"How did I know it? How did I know it? Lor bless ye; any one might ha' knowed it was a duke. He had gotten a great gowd chain, wi lots o' thingumbobs hanging to it, round his neck, and it run all the way into his waistcoat pocket."

At one time he had a footman, whose boundless credulity recommended him to his notice. A title inspired him with awe, and having seen a nobleman, now and then, at his master's table, he took it for granted that he was familiar with half the peerage. The Duke of Sussex called one day to see the picture-gallery. On announcing his Royal Highness, Mathews fully expected he would have gone off by spontaneous combustion: for he retreated backwards, puffed out his cheeks to their fullest powers of expansion, and then poised himself on one leg, like a bird, awaiting to see the effect produced on his master by the appearance of such a visitor. Knowing his weakness, Mathews used to tell all his intimates, whenever they called, to be sure to present themselves under some assumed title. Thus Charles Kemble always announced himself as the Persian Ambassador; Fawcett called himself Sir Francis Burdett; my father, the Duke of Wellington.

This habit of jocular imposition once involved Mathews in an awkward scrape. He had no idea that there existed such a title in the peerage as that of "Ranelagh." So that when the veritable nobleman of that name called one day on horseback at the door, and sent up a message by the manservant to say that "Lord Ranelagh would be much obliged if Mr. Mathews would step down to him, as he could not dismount," Mathews, convinced it was one of his chums under a feigned title, sent down word to say that Lord Ranelagh must be kind enough to put up his horse in the stables, and walk up, as he could not go out of doors, having a cold, and being particularly engaged with Lord Vauxhall.

Lord Ranelagh could hardly believe his ears when he received this familiar, flippant, and impertinent message. He rode off in a state of boiling indignation, and forthwith dispatched a note to the offender, commenting severely on his impudence in daring to play upon his name. Of course, as soon as Mathews discovered his mistake, he wrote and explained it, and apologized for it amply.

Mathews had often told Charles Kemble of the great amusement his manservant's peculiarities afforded him, but Kemble said he had never been able to discover anything in him but crass stupidity. "Ah," said Mathews, "you can't conceive what a luxury it is have a man under the same roof with you who will believe anything you tell him, however impossible it may be."

One warm summer's day, Mathews had a dinner party at Highgate. There were present, among others, Broderip, Theodore Hook, General Phipps, Manners Sutton (then Speaker of the House of Commons), and Charles Kemble. The servant had learned by this time the name of the Persian ambassador. Dessert was laid out on the lawn. Mathews, without hinting his intention, rang the bell in the dining-room, and on its being answered, told the man to follow him to the stables while he gave the coachman certain directions in his presence. The instant Mathews reached the stable door, he called to the coachman (who he knew was not there). looked in, and, before the manservant could come up, started back, and, in a voice of horror, cried out, "Good heavens! go back, go back — and tell Mr. Kemble that his horse has cut his throat!"

The simple goose, infected by his master's well-feigned panic, and never pausing to reflect on the absurdity of the thing, burst on to the lawn, and, with cheeks blanched with terror, roared out, "Mr. Kemble, sir, you're wanted directly." Seeing Mr. Kemble in no hurry to move, he repeated his appeal with increased emphasis, "For heaven's sake, sir, come; your poor horse has cut his throat!"

From that time the Persian ambassador admitted fully that if his friend's servant was not funny himself, he could be the fruitful cause of fun to others.

Whenever Mathews brought out a new "At Home," he was sure to receive a summons to Windsor to produce it before George the Fourth. On one such occasion, after having given imitations of Lords Thurlow, Loughborough, Mansfield, and of Sheridan, he concluded with the most celebrated one of all, that of John Philpot Curran. The felicity of his impersonations of the first four, the King readily admitted, nodding his head in recognition of their resemblance to their originals, and now and then laughing so heartily as to cause the actor to pronounce him the most intelligent auditor he had ever had. He was, therefore, the more mortified after giving his *chef-d'œuvre.* to notice the King throw himself back in his chair, and overhear him say to Lady Coningham, "Very odd, I can't trace any resemblance to Curran at all." He had scarcely uttered his criticism before he regretted it; for he perceived by the heightened complexion and depressed manner of the performer that his unfavorable stricture had been heard. As soon, therefore, as the entertainment was concluded, the King, with generous sympathy, went up to Mathews, shook him warmly by the hand, and, after presenting him with a watch, with his own portrait set in brilliants on the case, took him familiarly by the button, and thus addressed him: — "My dear Mathews, I fear you overheard a hasty remark I made to Lady Coningham. I say, advisedly, 'a hasty remark,' because the version you give of Curran, all those who know him best declare to be quite perfect; and I ought, in justice to you, to confess that I never saw him but once, and therefore am hardly a fair judge of the merits of your impersonation. You see, I think it very possible that, never having been in my presence before, his manner under the circumstances may have been unnaturally constrained. You will, perhaps, think it odd that I, who in my earlier days lived much and intimately with the Whigs, should never have seen him but once. Yet so it was.

"I always had had a great curiosity to know a man so *renommé* for his wit and other social qualities; and, therefore, I asked my brother Frederick, 'How I could best see Curran?' He smiled and said, 'Not much difficulty about it. Your Majetsy has but to send him a summons to dinner through your Chamberlain, and the thing is done.' He came; but on the whole he was taciturn, and *mal à son aise.*"

"Oh, sir," replied Mathews, "the imitation I gave you of Curran was of Curran in his forensic manner, not in private. Would your Majesty permit me to give you another imitation of him as he would appear at a dinner-table?" On receiving the King's sanction to do so, he threw himself with such *abandon* into the mind, manner, wit, and waggery, of his original, that the King was in ecstacies.

He then went up to Mathews, and resumed his chat. "I was about to tell you that, after my brother's suggestion, I said to him, 'You shall make up the party for me; only let the ingredients mix well together.' I don't think, between ourselves, that he executed his commission very well; for he asked too many men of the same profession — each more or less jealous of the other. The consequence was, that the dinner was heavy. However, after the cloth was removed, I was determined to draw out the little ugly silent man I saw at the bottom of the table; and, with that object in view, I proposed the health of 'The Bar.' To my unspeakable annoyance, up sprang, in reply, Councillor Ego.[1] He certainly made a very able speech, though rather too redolent of self. He wound it up with some such words as these: — 'In concluding, he could only say that, descended as he was from a long and illustrious line of ancestry, he felt himself additionally ennobled on the day he was admitted to the rank of Barrister.' I was not going to be thwarted of my purpose; and, therefore, the next toast I proposed was 'Success to the Irish Bar.' Then up sprang our little sallow-faced friend, and by his wit and humor, and grace of speech, made me laugh one minute and cry the next. He annihilated Erskine by the humility of his bearing; and closed his speech, I recollect, as follows: — 'The noble Lord who has just sat down, distinguished as he is by his own personal merits, has told you, sir, that, though ennobled by birth, he feels additionally so by his profession. Judge then, sir, what must be my pride in a profession which has raised me, the son of a peasant, to the table of my Prince.'"

[1] Namely, Lord Erskine, a brilliant advocate in the Law Courts, but a dead failure in the House of Commons.

William Lisle Bowles.

When we resided in Wiltshire, in the year 1836, the Rev William Lisle Bowles, the parson poet, was my neighbor. It was to the reading of his sonnets, when a youth, that Coleridge attributed his earliest poetic inspiration. He resided at the pretty village of Bremhill, which was within an easy walk both of Calne and of Bowood. He was a clever, well-read, humorous, single-hearted, but eccentric person — morally as brave as a lion, physically as timid as a hare. It was a matter of equal indifference to him whether he had to measure swords with Lord Byron, the merits of Pope the battle-field; or to wrestle with deans and chapters, church patronage the bone of contention between them. But to confront a situation involving the slightest personal risk was beyond his powers of nerve. For instance, he never entered my doors without first sending his footman forward on a reconnoitring expedition, to ascertain that there was no stray dog or cat prowling about for his special discomfiture.

One day, Lord Lansdowne, hearing that Bowles was going to Bath to attend a particular meeting, at which he himself meant to be present, offered him a seat in his barouche. Always happy in his lordship's company, he gladly accepted the accommodation: but as the carriage drove up, and he entered it, he was observed to become ghastly pale. He had seen that there were four horses to the carriage. He had hardly seated himself when one of them shied. He instantly exhibited disquietude, first looked out of one window, then out of the other, and never spoke a word until they reached Chippenham, when, calling out to the postilions to stop, he burst open the carriage-door, and insisted on being let out. It was in vain Lord Lansdowne attempted to pacify him. Out he got, and followed in a one horse fly, having first bribed the coachman to drive very slowly.

On another occasion, I had an opportunity of witnessing a ludicrous display of his infirmity. Bowood was full of guests, and Moore, Rogers, and Milman being among the number,

Mr. and Mrs. Bowles were invited to meet them. Bowles was no sooner dressed, than, on entering the drawing-room, he walked up to Lady Lansdowne, and made some complaint or other to her, which caused her at once to leave the room. He forthwith followed her. In a few minutes they both returned. As Lady Lansdowne passed me, she said, "Bless the dear man, there is no pleasing him." I did not know to what she alluded, until Bowles came up to me with a face of blank dismay, and asked me if I were going to sleep there. On my telling him that I was not, he exclaimed, "I wish I were going home too. I sha'n't sleep a wink here. I was shown into a bedroom to dress in, in which I was intended to pass the night; but it was on the ground-floor, where there was nothing whatever to prevent thieves from getting in and cutting my throat! I have remonstrated with Lady Lansdowne, and the dear lady by way of rendering me easier in my mind, has transferred me to a room so high, that, in case of fire, I shall be burned to a cinder before I can be rescued!"

He was so cowed by the prospect of the imaginary perils of the coming night, that his usual flow of conversation was reduced to the lowest ebb, and he hardly ate a mouthful. It had been understood from the first between Lady Lansdowne and Mrs. Bowles, that, in consequence of the crowded state of the house, she should return to Bremhill at night, and leave her husband to the enjoyment of his bachelor's bed and the congenial society of his friends. His nervous apprehensions, however, got the better of his social propensities; and, as the ladies were leaving the dining-room, he whispered to his wife, "I won't stay. Go home with you I must, and will." An hour or two after, as Mrs. Bowles's carriage was coming round from the stable yard, dark sulphurous clouds darkened the sky, a terrific thunder-clap, succeeded by a blinding flash of forked lightning, shook the nerves of the ladies, and at once determined the terror-stricken husband again to change his mind. He told his wife that, as she was not afraid of the angry elements and he was, she had better start at once, and leave him to his fate. This she did; and, after giving infinite trouble to his noble host and hostess by his childish fears and vacillation of purpose, it was at last arranged that he should sleep in a room adjoining Rogers's, with the door between the rooms left open, so that he might have the protection of his more valiant brother poet.

Again. He was invited by the late excellent Dr. Law, Bishop of Bath and Wells, to stay at Banwell. As usual, the first thing he did, when he went to his room to dress for dinner, was to inspect his quarters, and see if he could detect any assailable point from which danger might be expected. He crept about suspiciously, looked to the fastenings of the windows, tested the working of the door-locks, peeped into the closets, and then into a small adjoining dressing-room, in which there was a tent-bed, unmade. From that fact, and the absence of washstand, towel-horse, etc., etc., he concluded it was to be unoccupied. Out of this dressing-room (if I remember rightly what I was told by one of the Bishop's sons) there was a door of outlet on to a back stair. The idea of sleeping alone in a room so exposed to nocturnal assault on two sides so appalled poor Bowles, that, when a maidservant brought him up his hot water, he took her by the hand, and told her that, if she would consent to occupy the vacant bed in the adjoining room, he would give her a sovereign. Conceiving that he meant to insult her, she bounced out of the room, and told the Bishop that he must get some one else to wait on the nasty old clergyman who had just come, as he had made improper advances to her. The Bishop insisted on knowing what he had said: and on hearing his *ipsissima verba*, told her that she had quite misconceived him, for all that he wanted was the protection of some one within ready call. "I wish," he added, "that you and the underhousemaid, would oblige me by taking up your quarters together in the room next to my timid friend. You can place the bed against the door; and, as it opens in on your side, you will be safe from any intrusion on his part, if you are silly enough to fear it; and I shall have the satisfaction of knowing that if my friend should be taken ill in the night he will have some one near him." It so happened that the Bishop forgot to tell his guest of the considerate arrangement he had made for him; so that on retiring at night to his chamber, still believing the dressing-room to be empty, he locked, not only the door by which he entered his own room, but that of the smaller room. In the middle of the night he fancied he heard footsteps in the direction of the back stairs. It then occurred to him that he had neglected to lock the outer door of the little room, which communicated with them. He jumped out of bed to rectify his oversight, and unlocked the door which communicated with the dressing-room. On trying to push it open, he felt a powerful resisting body opposed to him (namely, the maid's bed), and as he pushed he distinctly heard whisperings. This at once confirmed him in his conviction that there were thieves in the house. He ran back to the other door, bawling out "Murder! Thieves!" with such stentorian energy, that the Bishop and all his family were roused out of their beds, though not frightened (for the Laws are all remarkably fearless); and it was long before their guest could be reconciled to his position, and induced to go again to bed. I should surmise it would be long before he was invited again to Banwell.

These instances which I have given of his constitutional infirmity are not more diverting than others which display his remarkable absence of mind.

My wife, Tom Moore, and I, and two or three others, were dining with him one day. He was holding forth on the wit of many epilogues — Garrick's among the number; and telling us of his having heard Mrs. Siddons once deliver the prologue to a play which had been got up in behalf of the volunteers, in which there occurred these two absurd lines,

> "The volunteers, rewarded by no pay,
> Except their feelings on some future day,"

when his servant presented to him my plate for some hare. At first he did not heed the man's presence, until, becoming dimly conscious of some one hanging over him, he turned round, and angrily asked him why he kept standing there. "I'm waiting, sir, for some hare for Mr. Young." "I have helped Mr. Young to some hare already." "No, please, sir, you have not: you've only helped him to gravy." Which was the fact.

Dessert ended and coffee introduced, we adjourned to the drawing-room, where Moore's singing kept us in a state of enchantment until the hour for breaking up. Our carriage had been ordered at ten P. M.; but it did not come round till a quarter past. During the interval between Moore's departure and ours, Bowles, who was longing to get to bed, came up to us, and said, "Your carriage is very late: I can't make it out;" and then, walking up and down, and muttering to himself, we heard him say, "Niceish people; but why did not they order their coachman to be more punctual? It's a horrid bore. Never mind; it will be a good long time before we have to ask them again."

He went once to dine and sleep at the Rev. William Money's, at Whetham. Mrs. Bowles's toilet was soon made: she was in the drawing-room as soon as Mrs. Money herself. But Mr. Bowles, not having come down when the dinner-bell rang, his wife requested they would not wait for her husband, but go at once in to dinner. Soup and fish had been served, when a servant tapped at the door with a message, desiring Mrs. Bowles to step up to her husband, as she was wanted. On going to him she found him in a state of boiling indignation, with no trowsers on, with one leg in a black silk stocking, and the other bare. "Here, Madam," he cried out, "that idiot of a maid of yours has put me up only one silk stocking for my two legs: the consequence is, I can't go down-stairs to dinner, or have any dinner at all, unless some is sent up to me here." "Oh, my dear," said his amiable wife, "you need not stand on much ceremony with such old friends as the Moneys. Put on again the stockings which you have taken off, and come down in them. I will explain matters to the company." He took the hint, and was in the act of peeling off the black silk stocking from his leg, when he discovered that he had put the two stockings on the same leg, utterly unconscious of what he had done.

I do not ask any of my readers to give credence to the following additional illustration of his absence of mind; and yet there are many in his old neighborhood who believe it implicitly; and the man who told it me, the late Rev. Anthony Austin, Rector of Compton Bassett, told it me as a fact.

A little distance out of Calne, on the road to Derry Hill, there used to be, and may be still, for aught I know to the contrary, a turnpike. One very hot day in summer, Bowles, astride of his favorite old pony, with the reins dropped on its neck, was seen by three or four stone-breakers by the roadside, absorbed in the perusal of a book. Although the rider and his pony thoroughly understood each other, each ministering to the other's infirmities, yet on this occasion, the former finding himself, it is presumed, inconvenienced by the occasional stumbling of his veteran ally, and frequently interrupted by his straying to the roadside to graze, he dismounted, tied him to a gate, walked on a few yards, seated himself on a verdant bank, and surrendered at discretion to the captivating influence of the book in hand.

When he had half digested the chapter he had been devouring, he arose, pondered further on it, argued it out aloud with himself, opened the book again where he had left off, and, forgetting the pony altogether, sauntered leisurely up the hill, reading as he went, till he arrived at the turnpike-gate. On reaching this familiar spot, which he had been almost in the daily habit of passing through for years, with his eyes still riveted on his volume, he shouted out, with a lusty voice, "Gate," — then inserted his hand into his breeches pocket, took from it the toll, which he had already paid in going to Calne, and offered it to the gatekeeper. "What is this for, sir?" said he. "Why, for my pony, you goose," was the answer. "But you have no pony; and if you had, you paid me already in the morning." On hearing the man say he had no pony, Bowles cast down his eyes as if he had expected to see it between his legs; then became strangely confused, and only through the suggestion of the man, was enabled to remember where he had left the animal.

I am bound in justice to admit, that I remember the subject of this story being twitted with it in a large company, and positively denying that there was a word of truth in it. But it is only fair to add, *per contra*, that the turnpike-keeper and the stone-breakers adhered stoutly to their assertions; and the general impression was, that their evidence was more to be relied on than that of one so exceptionally oblivious and dreamy as the hero of the tale himself.

One more anecdote of Bowles, and I have done with him.

When very old, and when his mental faculties were painfully on the wane, he was seated in his arm-chair at the window, in his prebendal house at Salisbury, when he perceived an unusual crowd of people of all sorts, tag, rag, and bobtail, hurrying with eager steps in one direction.

He inquired of his attendant the cause of all this ferment, and was told it was the first day of the great assizes. On hearing this, he hung his head and betrayed symptoms of profound depression. Presently, with an abruptness that might have startled men of less sensibility, the loud blast of a trumpet was heard. "Good heavens!" he cried out, "what is that?" His servant informed him that "the Judges were come." He had no sooner heard this, than he fell to the ground, crying out in accents of piteous alarm, "Guilty! Guilty!" Then turning his silvery head to the person nearest him, he said, "If my doom is sealed, and I am to go to prison, I implore you not to allow that solemn coxcomb F—— to attend me." N. B. A clergyman against whom he had conceived an unaccountable antipathy.

William Beckford.

Soon after attaining his majority, he started on what was then called the grand tour. His suite consisted of a musician to play to him, of a doctor to watch over his health, of an artist to paint and copy for him, and of Dr. Lettice to aid him in literary research. He was followed by six or seven carriages, a proportionate number of fourgons for the luggage of such a retinue, and a stud of first-class horses. He first made for

Venice, by way of the Tyrol, and reached it by moonlight in a gondola. On setting foot on the piazetta, his sense of enjoyment was so intense that he could only give vent to it in tears. Abruptly breaking away from his party, and without giving any of them a hint of his purpose, he jumped into the first gondola he came near, and, captivated, yet enervated by his sensations, told the boatmen to convey him to one of the least frequented of the islands in the Adriatic, where he might remain a while, safe from intrusion, and give the reins to his overwrought imagination. As soon as he had left the boat, he told the gondoliers to go to sleep if they liked, but to remain where they were till he returned. It was near midnight before he was traced by Dr. Lettice, and then only through the help of some sailors, who had watched the course Beckford's gondola had taken. He found him alone, wrapped in visionary speculations, which he did not thank him for disturbing. He afterwards confessed to him that the combined effects of the climate, the scenery, and association, classical, poetical, historical, pictorial, and theatrical, had wrought so powerfully on his brain, that he believed that he should have gone mad, but for the timely relief of tears. The same effect was subsequently produced upon him by his first evening in Rome, and his first sight of Cintra and Vallombrosa. He used to say, in after years, that in those few nights he had lived through years of feeling.

Venice was a place so entirely after his own fancy, that he lingered there long: never so happy as when, at full length, with closed eyes, he was floating lazily across the lagunes in his gondola, and yielding to the balmy influences of the atmosphere till evening, when he would go home and dress and dine, and hurry to the opera to listen to the notes of Paccharetti. He found himself soon so beset with invitations from the leaders of *ton* in the place, that, society becoming irksome to him, he tore himself away from its exactions, and hurried on to Rome. On first reaching the heights of Monterosi, and beholding the dome of St. Peter's, he flung himself prostrate on the ground in speechless rapture. It was late in the evening when he entered the town itself; and on reaching the Piazza del Popolo, leaving all concern about luggage and passports to his followers, and calling up one of his grooms with a led horse, he flung himself into his saddle, and attended by his courier, galloped off to the object of his longing. He reached St. Peter's as the great doors were being closed. Extending a well-filled purse to the sacristan, he told him that every farthing in it should be his if he would but suffer him to remain in the mighty temple alone for a couple of hours. The man stared, scrupled — but consented. Beckford begged to be locked in, taking the precaution, *ad interim*, of returning his purse to his pocket. As he entered the vast building and heard the doors close behind him, and found the twilight deepening round him, his teeming brain ran riot. The odor of incense still clung to the walls, light still twinkled round the high altar. With stealthy steps and breath suspended he wandered *slowly* from chapel to chapel. Much which he wished to see was hidden from his view by the intervening shadows of the lofty pillars; when — joy beyond his fondest hopes! — the clear full moon arose and shed her silvery beams athwart great part of the interior. He could scarcely believe that two hours had passed, when he was reminded of it by the entrance of the door-keeper, to whom he gladly tendered the promised guerdon, and who was so well satisfied with his bargain that he gave his patron *carte blanche* to repeat his visits whenever he was so disposed — a privilege of which he was not slow to avail himself. He would often remain there from midnight till dawn of day with no other seat to rest on than the steps of the high altar.

After devoting considerable time to the careful exploration of the antiquities of Rome, he went on to Naples. He was enchanted with it, of course, but still, amid all the attractions of that lovely city, he pined for his first love — Venice. Thither he returned; and while thinking seriously of a prolonged stay there, an urgent summons to enter public life compelled him once more to return to England; though, at that time, the solicitations of his friends and relatives did not shake him in his resolution to decline the proffered representation of the borough of Hendon. Having no ambition to enter on the stormy arena of politics, which were at that time agitating the senate, he retired to Bath, where he met with Lady Margaret Gordon, his own cousin. He quickly became intimate with her — loved, and married her. After presenting her at Court, and paying the necessary round of complimentary visits to his friends, he turned his back on London, and repaired, with his bride, to the favorite haunts of his early youth, and pitching his tent at Melhabeau de la Tour, at Evian, there lived in blissful retirement. It was there his first daughter was born; and there fifteen months later, after giving birth to another girl, that his wife died.

Shortly after, in quest of new scenes, in the hope of alleviating his grief for his irreparable loss, and accompanied by Dr. Lettice, his "guide, philosopher, and friend," he betook himself to Portugal, having sent his two children to Fonthill to be under his mother's care. He soon found wholesome distraction in building his well-known house at Cintra, Ra Mathao. There he had ample scope for the indulgence of his extravagant passion for Eastern architecture: with which the exquisite climate, and the almost tropical vegetation, were thoroughly in keeping. The recollection of his sumptuous manner of life was still green, when Byron made his pilgrimage there.

"On sloping mounds, or in the vale beneath,
Are domes, where, whilom, kings did make repair;
But now, the wild flowers round them only breathe:
Yet ruined splendor still is lingering there,
And yonder towers the prince's palace fair.
There thou, too, Vathek! England's wealthiest son,
Once formed thy Paradise, as not aware
When wanton wealth her mightiest deeds hath done,
Meek peace voluptuous lures was ever wont to shun."

The scale of his establishment, and of his general expenditure, surpassed anything that had ever been witnessed in that country. The consequence was, that he was overwhelmed with applications from the proudest magnates in the land for permission to visit him. With the Marquis di Marialva, the prime minister, and also with the Grand Inquisitor, he cemented a cordial friendship. One day Marialva called him aside, and told him that he was anxious to take him to some curious old Moorish remains, which stood in a singularly picturesque and sequestered situation. Having readily consented to go, early the next morning they started together on their expedition. When they drew near to the spot, Marialva desired his companion to order his numerous attendants to remain where they were, while they withdrew by themselves. In a few minutes they came upon the buildings, which were sufficiently striking to excite Beckford's admiration; but while he was examining them, Marialva, without any perceptible motive, whispered to him, "Seem to be drawing. Pretend to be drawing."

Fortunately, Beckford had his sketch-book in his hand, and was in the act of taking a view (which, by the by, long after hung in the Duchess of Hamilton's boudoir at Easton Park), when a door in the building opened, and a tall thin young man, with a fine intelligent countenance, and an undefinable grace of movement, came forward and stood before the presumed artist. He was so full of majesty that Beckford, convinced he was no ordinary personage, and concluding that he wished to maintain his incognito, merely returned his salutation, and offered him a seat, while he went on with his drawing. It was not long before he found himself drawn into conversation with him. One topic followed another in rapid succession, until the political condition of England, France, Italy, Spain, and, finally, Portugal itself, was freely discussed. Home questions were put, and counsel sought of Beckford, on subjects of such delicacy that it required both courage and presence of mind to answer them to one entirely unknown. His enthusiastic disposition was however piqued by the singularity of the interview; and, being partial to the people of the country, from whom he had received much respect, he uttered the honest sentiments of his heart about them without reserve.

The stranger was so captivated with the liberality of his opinions that he threw off all further disguise, and made himself known as the Prince of the Brazils. He had heard so much about the Englishman that he had hit upon this expedient as a means of knowing him without himself being known. From that hour they became fast friends.

After visiting every place in Portugal and Spain possessing objects in art or nature worth seeing, he returned to England, more bent than ever on building the abbey at Fonthill. His original idea was not to reside in it, but to erect for himself a more modest retreat hard by.

While the new building was in course of erection he went to Paris, where he remained during more than twelve months of the Revolution. He remained equally undismayed by Jacobins or Girondists, taking no part in the political feuds which disturbed other men's minds, and maintaining a dignified attitude of reserve. Strange to say, at a time when the worst passions of human nature were let loose and anarchy usurped the place of law, he lived on terms of equal good-will with the Duke of Orleans and with Mirabeau.

It was in the year 1793, when men of peace could once more move about without fear, that Beckford was induced to go and see a very remarkable lion, which no man could tame; and which, from his exceeding ferocity, was a terror even to beholders. The instant Beckford entered the place in which he was confined, his angry roars ceased; he approached the bars of the cage where Beckford stood, and rubbed himself caressingly against the spot. Every one present was struck with the strange sight, and watched the actors narrowly. The keeper went up to Beckford, and said that he was sure that if he would enter the den with him the lion would not harm him. Although curious to make the experiment, he had no idea of making an exhibition of himself: so he told the keeper if he would wait till the hour of closing, he would not hesitate to enter the cage in his company. When the general public were dismissed, and Beckford walked towards the cage, the lion stood still, narrowly scrutinizing his movements. Beckford fixed his eyes steadily on him; the lion returned an equally steadfast gaze After mutual investigation, the lion having taken his visitor's measure, and seeing that he did not quail before him, went up to him, lay on his back, fondled him, and putting forth his tongue, licked his hands till the skin was nearly rubbed off. Luckily no blood was drawn. From that day, go when he might, Beckford was sure of an affectionate welcome from the king of beasts. The good understanding existing between the lion and the Englishman became a subject of court gossip; and many years after, when Charles the Tenth was residing at Holyrood, he asked the Duchess of Hamilton whether her father still possessed the same power of eye over wild beasts which he had displayed in the case of ferocious lions.

He continued in the French capital till after the death of Louis XVIII., making acquaintance with all the most conspicuous persons of that day: among the number, with Madame de Staël, whose talents he appreciated more than her morals. On his return to Fonthill, he dedicated himself in earnest to the realization of the projects he had long ago conceived — which had grown with his growth and strengthened with his strength.

When he was residing at Naples, he received much civility from Sir William Hamilton; and it so happened that he, his lady, and the illustrious Nelson, volunteered him a visit in the course of the ensuing winter. He resolved to commemorate it by a grand *fête*. Nearly seven hundred workmen were employed in carrying out his plans. Torches were burning all night to enable successive gangs of workmen to continue their labors. The consequence was that in little more than two months the abbey had so far advanced as to be a model of architectural beauty. From one point in the grounds it was visible in all its grandeur — the turrets, gurgoyles, pediments, and pinnacles imparting to it the more salient features of an enormous monastery. The hall was spacious and lofty; the tower, which was in the centre of the building, was visible at a distance of forty miles. Three wings stretched from it, eastward, northward, and southward — each totally unlike the other, yet each constituting in itself an elegant and commodious residence. The splendor of its furniture and decora tions, with its inexhaustible treasures of art, earned for it the designation of "The Wonder of the West."

The illustrious naval hero was received in the town of Hendon with an ovation worthy of him: the anxiety of the townspeople to get a glimpse of him beggaring description.

When the company invited took their seats in the old hall, the scene must have been singularly imposing. Every one was kept in profound ignorance of what awaited them, the work having been carried on behind an immense screen of timber, so that no one might know of the progress of the works.

To his guests, who begged that they might be allowed to visit the abbey, the erection of which had already created general curiosity, Mr. Beckford replied that "they should certainly see whatever there was to see before their departure." The next day he was busy superintending operations, for he meant to give them a *fête champêtre*, which they should not forget. When the day arrived, and twilight deepened, numerous carriages drove up to the door, followed by a cavalcade of horsemen, in procession, in conformity with the directions of a printed programme. The visitors, not at all prepared for the coming event, chatted gayly as they drove or rode down the road towards one of the grand avenues already mentioned. At a particular turn, every carriage stopped, and one long, loud, ringing shout of amazement and delight burst from every throat. The enormous body of visitors found themselves, in an instant, transported as by magic to a fairy scene. Through the far-stretching woods of pine glittered myriads on myriads of variegated lamps, forming vast vistas of light, and defining the distant perspective as clearly as in sunshine. Flambeaux in profusion were carried about by bearers stationed wherever they were most needed. The Wiltshire Volunteers, handsomely accoutred, were drawn up on either side. Bands of music, studiously kept out of sight, were placed at intervals along the route, playing inspiring marches; the whole effect being heightened by the deep roll of numerous drums, so placed in the hollows of the hills as to insure their reverberation being heard on every side.

The profound darkness of the night, the many-tinted lamps, some in motion, others stationary, here reflected on the bayonets and helmets of the soldiery, there seen through colored glass, and so arranged as to shed rainbow hues on every surrounding object — the music, now with a dying fall, now waking the dormant echoes into life with martial clangor, riveted to the spot the lover of striking contrasts.

Gradually the procession drew near to the abbey itself, the tracery of its splendid architecture relieved by strong shadow, the inequalities of the building marked out by myriads of lights, and revealing to the wondering eyes of the spectators battlement and turret and flying buttress. No grander feature was there in the whole edifice than the tower, shooting up three hundred feet, the upper part lost in total eclipse. Reared above the main entrance fluttered the national banner, and by its side the Admiral's flag, catching light enough as they flapped in the night breezes, to display their massive folds to advantage. All present stood entranced. The moment the abbey was fully disclosed, every one, animated by a common impulse, sprang from their carriages and walked towards it. And when the "conquering hero," attended by his host, entered the walls, the organ thundered forth a pealing sound of welcome, which shook the edifice to its foundations; while notes of triumph resounded through the galleries and corridors around.

From the abbey they adjourned to the grand hall, which had been arranged for the banquet. An entire service of silver and agate of mediæval pattern was laden with the fare of other days. On the beaufet were piled heavy masses of gold and silver plate. On the board, and against the walls of the room, stood wax candles six feet high, in silver sconces; while huge blazing logs of cedar, dried and prepared for the occasion, and constantly renewed, contributed to the material comfort.

The banquet ended, and the guests well-nigh surfeited with the fanciful and gorgeous display they had witnessed, they were desired to pass up the grand staircase. On each side of it stood, at intervals, men dressed as monks, carrying waxen flambeaux in their hands. The company were first ushered into a suite of sumptuous apartments, hung with gold-colored satin damask, in which were ebony cabinets of inestimable value, inlaid with precious stones, and filled with treasures collected from many lands — then through a gallery two hundred and eighty-five feet long, into the library, which was filled with choice books and rare manuscripts, and fitted up with consummate taste. The hangings of crimson velvet, embroidered with arabesques of gold, the carpets of the same color — the windows of old stained glass, bordered with the most graceful designs.

At last the guests reached the oratory, where a lamp of gold was burning by itself, shedding just light enough to display to advantage, in a niche studded with mosaics and jewels of great price, a statue of St. Anthony by Rossi. Here, again, the illusion of the monastery was well maintained. Large candelabras, in stands of ebony inlaid with gold, and multiplied by huge pier-glasses, formed an exquisite perspective, and enhanced the surpassing brilliancy of the scene. When the entire company was collected in this marvellous gallery, a stream of solemn music came floating through the air, none knowing from whence it issued. Beckford always thought the effect of music heard under such circumstances irresistible. Only eighteen months before his death, when he was eighty-seven years of age, he was wont to speak with ecstacy of a scene at which he had been present in one of his juvenile explorations. He had accidentally strayed into a grand but very sombre cathedral: the choir was chanting a solemn requiem for the dead; priests, motionless as statues, were grouped around a catafalque; lofty candles, lighted, surrounded the altar. There was a long pause for meditation, and then, from an unseen quarter, voices of inconceivable sweetness wailed forth a funeral hymn. The priests themselves grew pale, as they sang their parts, in response. "As for me," he would say, "my heart's blood curdled in my veins; and, to my dying hour, the mere mention of that cathedral, and the hymn I heard there, will thrill to my inmost soul."

After gazing their fill on the multiplicity of sights that met them at every turn, the guests were directed to retire in a direction opposite to that from which they had come. But, before they were allowed to depart, spiced wine, sherbet, lemonade, and iced water, in flagons of ruby-colored glass, and caraffes of rose-water, and little cases of ottar of roses freshly imported from Shiraz, the choicest fruit in baskets of gold filagree, were handed round. It was long after midnight before the visitors could tear themselves away. But their host would not permit them to linger, lest they should retire with their impressions impaired by familiarity. So that, before the lamps began to wane, the several bands accompanied by the mighty organ, struck up their most exhilarating airs; and, as these yet hung upon the ear of the departing guests, the night breeze wafting their melody through the air till distance drowned it, they left the abbey grounds scarce able to believe that they had not been enjoying an Arabian Night's Entertainment, instead of an English one.

INDEX.

www.ingramcontent.com/pod-product-compliance
Lightning Source LLC
LaVergne TN
LVHW020229110826
845151LV00003B/869

* 9 7 8 1 4 2 5 5 3 1 6 1 4 *